ENERGY EFFICIENT HOMES FOR DUMMIES®

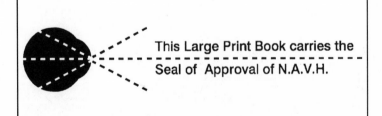

This Large Print Book carries the Seal of Approval of N.A.V.H.

ENERGY EFFICIENT HOMES FOR DUMMIES®

RIK DEGUNTHER

THORNDIKE PRESS

A part of Gale, Cengage Learning

GALE
CENGAGE Learning™

Detroit • New York • San Francisco • New Haven, Conn • Waterville, Maine • London

Thorndike Press® Large Print Health, Home & Learning.

The text of this Large Print edition is unabridged.

Other aspects of the book may vary from the original edition.

Set in 16 pt. Plantin.

Printed on permanent paper.

LIBRARY OF CONGRESS CATALOGING-IN-PUBLICATION DATA

DeGunther, Rik, 1956–
    Energy efficient homes for dummies / by Rik DeGunther.
        p. cm.
    ISBN-13: 978-1-4104-2295-8 (hardcover : alk. paper : large print)
    ISBN-10: 1-4104-2295-X (hardcover : alk. paper : large print)
    1. Dwellings — Energy conservation. 2. Ecological homes. I. Title.
TJ163.5.D86D44 2010
696—dc22
                                                                    2009039682

Published in 2010 in arrangement with John Wiley & Sons, Inc.

Printed in the United States of America
1 2 3 4 5 6 7 14 13 12 11 10

Dedication

Of course this book is dedicated to Katie, Erik, and Ally. Without them, the world would wobble inefficiently on its axis, and this work of art wouldn't exist.

About the Author

● ●

Rik DeGunther attended the University of Illinois as an undergraduate and Stanford University as a graduate student, studying both applied physics and engineering economics (some of this education actually stuck). He holds several United States Patents and has designed a wide range of technical equipment including solar energy platforms, military grade radar jammers, weather measurement equipment, high-powered radar vacuum tubes, computerized production hardware, golf practice devices, digital and analog electronic circuits, unmanned aerial vehicles, guitars and amplifiers, microwave filters and mixers, automatic cabinet openers, strobe light communications systems, explosive devices (strictly on accident), cloud height sensors, fog sensors, furniture, houses, barns, rocket ships, dart throwers, flame throwers, eavesdropping devices, escape routes, and you name it. He's one of those nerdy guys who likes to take things apart to see how they work and then put them back together and try to figure out what the left over parts are for.

Rik is CEO of Efficient Homes, an energy efficiency auditing firm in Northern California. He is actively engaged in designing and developing new solar equipment, including off-grid lighting systems and off-grid swimming pool heaters. He writes weekly op-ed columns for the *Mountain Democrat,* California's oldest and most venerable newspaper. He has also written a highly acclaimed golf book (on putting) and spends most of his free time attempting to improve his relatively impressive but objectively droll golf handicap, usually to no avail. Sometimes the urge strikes him to play a very loud guitar, of which he owns a collection with far more intrinsic quality than the playing they receive. His hearing has been faltering the last few years, so he rebuilt his amplifier to go up to eleven.

Author's Acknowledgments

Many thanks to all those who have contributed to the material in this book, whether wittingly or not. Dick and Betty DeGunther, Professor Mitchell Weissbluth, Professor AJ Fedro, John Lennon, Paul McCartney, Leland Stanford, Mike Pearcy, Jordan Cobb, Eric Micko, Vikki Berenz, Connie Cowan, Betsy Sanders, Jim DeGunther, Sarah Nephew, Freddie Mercury, Dave and Perla DeGunther, Brad, Melinda, Samantha and Emily Schauer, Chuck Albertson, Tilly and Evonne Baldwin, Joe and Marcia Schauer, Kim and Gary Romano of Sierra Valley Farms. Thanks to Dr. Keith Kennedy and Watkins-Johnson Company for showing restraint above and beyond the call of duty. Thanks to John Steinbeck for making me understand what's important and what's not, and in the same vein, Derek Madsen.

Thanks to the excellent crew at Wiley: Mike Baker, Tracy Barr, and Christy Pingleton, as well as the Technical Reviewer, Greg Raffio. Readers of this book will be amazed at how well it's written; it's not really my fault — I have the editors to thank for that. And thanks to Stephany Evans at FinePrint Agency for getting all the ducks in a row.

Thanks to all the *For Dummies* fans out there who have made the series what it is today.

Publisher's Acknowledgments

We're proud of this book; please send us your comments through our Dummies online registration form located at www.dummies.com/register/.

Some of the people who helped bring this book to market include the following:

Acquisitions, Editorial, and Media Development

Project Editor: Tracy L. Barr
Acquisitions Editor: Mike Baker
Copy Editor: Christy Pingleton
Assistant Editor: Erin Calligan Mooney
Technical Editor: Gregory Raffio
Senior Editorial Manager: Jennifer Ehrlich
Editorial Supervisor and Reprint Editor: Carmen Krikorian
Editorial Assistants: Joe Niesen, Jennette ElNaggar
Cover Photos: Somos©
Cartoons: Rich Tennant (www.the5thwave.com)

Composition Services for Original Edition

Project Coordinator: Katie Key
Layout and Graphics: Stacie Brooks, Reuben W. Davis,

Melissa K. Jester, Christin Swinford, Christine Williams
Proofreaders: John Greenough, Caitie Kelly, Nancy L. Reinhardt
Indexer: Christine Spina Karpeles

Special Help

Alicia South

Publishing and Editorial for Consumer Dummies

Diane Graves Steele, Vice President and Publisher, Consumer Dummies
Joyce Pepple, Acquisitions Director, Consumer Dummies
Kristin Ferguson-Wagstaffe, Product Development Director, Consumer Dummies
Ensley Eikenburg, Associate Publisher, Travel
Kelly Regan, Editorial Director, Travel

Publishing for Technology Dummies

Andy Cummings, Vice President and Publisher, Dummies Technology/General User

Composition Services

Gerry Fahey, Vice President of Production Services
Debbie Stailey, Director of Composition Services

Energy Efficient Homes For Dummies®

Useful Contacts

For information on energy-efficient technology, guidelines, and resources for energy efficient products and services, check out these organizations:

Energy Star (www.energystar.gov): For basic information on appliance performance

Energy Federation Incorporated (www.energy federation.org): For a variety of energy efficient lighting options

Rechargeable Battery Recycling Corporation (www.rbrc.org): For a list of battery recycling centers and rules on how to dispose of old batteries

The Family Handyman (www.thefamilyhandyman.com): For information on do-it-yourself projects and how to fix almost anything in your home

Alliance to Save Energy (www.ase.org): For a variety of ways to save energy with children's things

Database of State Incentives for Renewables & Efficiency (www.dsireusa.org): For the latest information on state rebates and other money saving programs

Consumer Energy Center (www.consumerenergycenter.org/renewables/estimator): To calculate cost savings for a variety of different energy efficiency investments

PV Watts (rredc.nrel.gov/solar/codes_algs/PVWATTS) and The PV Watts Solar Calculator (www.pvwatts.org): To calculate cost savings for various energy efficiency investments

Find Solar (www.findsolar.com): For a list of solar contractors and resources in your area

Tax Incentives Assistance Project (www.energytaxincentives.org): For the latest government rules and regulations concerning solar tax subsidies

National Association of Energy Service Companies (NAESCO) (www.naesco.org): For a list of companies in your area that offer energy efficiency products and services

Ask an Energy Expert (e-mail doe.erec@nciinc.com): To ask specific questions about your energy consumption problems (requires patience, but is worth a try)

Energy Efficiency and Renewable Energy Clearinghouse (EREC) (e-mail doe.erec@nciinc.com): For a list of government published documents pertaining to energy efficiency and renewable energy

Real Goods (www.realgoodscatalog.com): For a wide range of consumer products, particularly solar, that have been time tested and proven

Solar Components Corporation (www.solar-components.com): For an *Energy Savers Catalog*, listing a range of proven consumer products, particularly solar

Solar Depot (www.solardepot.com): For a listing of contractors and local solar resources in your area

AAA Solar Supply Inc. (www.aaasolar.com): For design guides and useful literature pertaining to solar power

Determining Power and Energy Usage

Power, specified in watts, is the rate at which energy is being consumed. *Energy,* specified in watt-hours (or more commonly in kWh for kilowatt-hours), is the amount of work required to get a job done. Use the following as guides to determining how much power your appliances or systems use:

✔ **To find out how much power an appliance uses:**

- Look on its label for a watts rating.

- Look up the device on power consumption charts.

- Purchase a meter, such as Kill-A-Watt, from a hardware store or online.

✔ **To find energy consumption:**

- Multiply wattage by hours used per day. A 100-watt light bulb on for six hours draws 600 watt-hours, or 0.6 kWh (k stands for 1,000).

- Your HVAC system's power draw, noted in horsepower (HP), should be labeled clearly. 1HP (horsepower) = 750 watts. 1 kW = 3,400 Btu. (Most HVAC units are labeled with Btu.)

Typical Appliance Power Draws

Refrigerators	1,100 watts per day for new, energy-efficient models; 3,000 watts per day for older models
Microwave	1,500 watts
Pool pump	1,000 watts or more (typically 6 kWh per day)
27" TV	170 watts
Home entertainment center	1,000 watts
Really loud electric guitar	6,000 watts
Electric blanket	400 watts
Dryer	5,000 watts and up (Use a clothesline!)
Air conditioner	2,000 watts
Computer/monitor	200 watts (combined)

Contents at a Glance

Table of Contents

29

Introduction

● ●

A well-maintained home is integral to a comfortable, secure lifestyle. As long as you maintain your home's integrity and promote its efficiency and harmony, it will nurture and comfort you in return.

Energy Efficient Homes For Dummies can help you make changes in your household lifestyle to save money and energy and reduce pollution. Every single home can use this book. It doesn't matter what kind of dwelling you live in (apartment, house, condo, geodesic dome, tent, you name it); nor does it matter whether you're a renter or an owner. It doesn't matter where you live or what your climate is. Everybody can benefit from seeking better efficiency. Regardless of whether you want to make small, incremental improvements, or grandiose, world-shaking changes, this book points you in the right direction.

You don't need to sacrifice your quality of life. Many of the tips and projects I show you in this book are easy and inexpensive. Many projects even make your lifestyle more comfortable and enjoyable.

A theme you see running through this book is the idea of *payback* — how long it takes for an efficiency investment to begin saving you money. Well, here's good news about the payback of this book: You can easily save ten times more money in your annual operating costs than the price you paid for this book (unless you stole it, which is about as efficient as you can get, although not recommended by either me or law enforcement).

About This Book

A number of energy-efficiency books are on the market, as you undoubtedly know already. So a lot of information is available: some of it scientific, some anecdotal, and some of it just plain wrong. In this book, I offer my years of experience in the subject of energy efficiency, but perhaps even more important, I condense all the myriad ideas, beliefs, and notions about energy efficiency into that which is the best and most helpful. You can find a lot more ways to make your home energy-efficient than what's in this book, but in keeping with the *For Dummies* modus operandi, I give you the best ones.

This book provides you with ample knowledge of energy- and cost-efficiency concepts to turn your home into a marvel of efficiency. You can do most of the projects and improvements I describe yourself. And when you need to hire a contractor, I tell you how best to go about the process.

People have their own fundamental reasons for wanting to achieve efficiency. Some people simply want to lower their operating costs, particularly with regard to energy consumption. Some people want to minimize their pollution footprint on the environment and will pay extra money to do so. Others just want to simplify their complicated lifestyles. In this book, I present you with the tradeoffs. I make no judgments about how you should order your priorities. I simply tell you how best to proceed, given the various alternatives. In other words, in this book I present the pros and cons of every issue and let you decide what's best for you. I leave the nagging to somebody else.

In this book, you find information like

- ✔ What efficiency means and how you can put together your own efficiency plan

- ✔ What a home energy audit reveals about your household energy use and how you can perform an audit yourself

- ✔ How to seal your home against the weather, get better performance from your heating and air-conditioning systems for less cost, and other helpful suggestions and advice

- ✔ How to take advantage of Mother Nature and a few key tricks to maintain comfortable temperatures in your home

- ✔ How to reduce your waste by reusing and recycling

- ✔ The advantages and disadvantages of different energy alternatives — such as wood stoves, gas stoves, solar power, geothermal systems, and so on — which are becoming more common as the price of energy rises

- ✔ Your options for financing efficiency improvements

Some readers look at the table of contents and skip straight to a particular section that addresses an immediate need. Others start in Chapter 1 and work their way diligently to Chapter 25. And either approach is just fine and dandy because all *For Dummies* books are structured so that you can jump in and out or read them straight through to get the information you need.

Conventions Used in This Book

For simplicity's sake, this book follows a few conventions:

- ✔ *Italicized* terms are immediately followed by definitions.

- ✔ **Bold** indicates the action parts in numbered steps. It also emphasizes the keywords in a bulleted list.

- ✔ Web site addresses show up in monofont.

- ✔ When this book was printed, some Web addresses may have needed to break across two lines of text. Rest assured that I haven't put in any extra characters (such as hyphens) to indicate the break. Just type in exactly what you see in this book, pretending as though the line break didn't exist.

What You're Not to Read

I don't flatter myself into thinking that you are interested in reading this entire book, although I do have to admit that it's excellent reading, full of wit and humor which nicely complements the robust, energy-saving information. In the name of efficiency — in this regard, saving you time — let me tell you what you can safely skip:

- ✔ **Material in sidebars:** Sure, these are interesting. Some are fun. I like to think that all are helpful. But they contain info that you don't absolutely, positively, without-a-doubt need to have to become more energy-efficient.

✔ **Paragraphs marked with the Technical Stuff icon:** Some people like details: the nuts and bolts of why or how things work; the statistics that back up a point; the nitty-gritty, down-and-dirty esoterica that every topic — especially one like this — has. If you're not one of these people, you can safely skip these paragraphs without missing any need-to-know info.

Foolish Assumptions

In writing this book, I made a few assumptions about you:

✔ **You want to make your home more efficient, in a number of different ways.** You have already decided to move forward, but aren't sure which direction is the right one, or what speed to move at. You want to make the best decisions, and understand that those decisions are entirely yours to make.

✔ **You have some handiwork skills.** You can handle a screwdriver and perhaps a power drill, although this isn't strictly necessary. You know a few basics about how to get things done, and you understand that with every project there are safety rules (I'll help you out here, when appropriate).

✔ **You want to get to the end product as sensibly and efficiently as possible.** (Note I didn't say quickly, because that inevitably leads to errors in both judgment and facilitation.) You don't have an engineering degree, and you don't want to know every technical detail concerning the various technologies. You simply want to get the job done, once you've made up your mind which job you want to do.

✔ **You need working knowledge of a project so that you can hire professionals and discuss matters with them.** You don't plan on handling a major project yourself, but you want enough information to make informed decisions sensibly and efficiently.

How This Book Is Organized

This book is divided into parts, each one dealing with a particular topic related to energy efficiency. Each part contains chapters relating to the part topic. The following sections give you an overview of the content within each part.

Part I: Solving the World's Problems from Your Front Porch

The place to start when you want to become more energy efficient is to understand the very basics about energy — namely, where it comes from and where and how it's used. The next step is to take a look at your own energy consumption so that you can decide where best to invest your time and efforts to improve the efficiency of your home. In addition to covering this information, Part I also reviews some financial options to make your investments more affordable and provides practical information on how to make the decisions that are best for you from a financial point of view.

Part II: Reducing Inefficiencies throughout Your Home

You'll probably find this part one of the most productive because it deals with the biggest energy consumers in your home. Here you can find details on how to change your consumption habits as well as how to invest in new equipment to achieve better efficiency. If you're interested only in getting moving, right now, go to this part first.

Part III: Putting Alternative Energy Sources to Work for You

As energy costs rise, the need for alternatives to the standard oil/utility energy sources grows. You can cut yourself loose from the utilities by employing stoves or geothermal, solar, and other alternative sources in your home. This part lists the alternative energy options that are available and tells you about both their advantages and disadvantages.

Part IV: Considering Efficiency When You Buy, Build, or Sell a Home

If you're in the market for a house or selling one, you can make energy efficiency one of the key features to look for or promote. If you're a buyer, what do you look for? And if you're a seller, what do you emphasize? This part has the answers. And because many folks have their homes built, this part also explains how to build your own energy-efficient home from the ground up. Finally, because your environment dictates your options to a large degree, I tell you what to keep in mind as you pick a community to live in.

Part V: The Part of Tens

Like every *For Dummies* book, this part includes quick resources that provide plenty of information and sage advice compacted into few words. Want a list of the best efficiency investments? How about efficiency projects you can do in an hour or less? This part offers this information and more.

Icons Used in This Book

This book uses several icons that make it easy for you to identify particular types of information:

 This icon highlights important information to store in your brain for quick recall at a later time.

 This icon indicates a nifty little shortcut or time-saver.

 Look out! Quicksand is afoot. You don't want to skip over the warnings. They point out dangers to your health and well-being, your property, or your bank account.

 The Technical Stuff icon lets you know that some particularly nerdy information is coming up so that you can skip it if you want. (On the other hand, you may want to read it, and you don't actually have to be a nerd. You only have to be able to read.)

Where to Go from Here

On your mark, get set, GO! "Where?" you ask. Anywhere you want. If you're not sure where to begin, I suggest starting in Chapter 1 or glancing through the Table of Contents for a topic that interests you. Or you can go to the index to find a specific topic that you want to know more about.

After that, get your tools out, tear open the boxes of stuff you delightedly bought, don your coveralls and safety glasses, and get to work. And have fun while you're at it.

 Attitude is the one and only thing you have complete control over in your life. Projects rarely, if ever, go the way you envisioned as you were drawing up the plans. As a lifelong practitioner of projects big and small, I have learned to be patient and enjoy the road every bit as much as the destination. When you run into problems — which you will — smile, take a step back, and come up with a witty joke. The one thing I have learned over and over again (I always have to learn things more than once before they sink in) is that the harder a project is, the more rewarding it will be when it's finished. I can pretty much guarantee that you're going to find out precisely what I'm talking about. Above all else, remember this: Measure twice, cut once.

Part I

Solving the World's Problems from Your Front Porch

The 5th Wave   By Rich Tennant

One of the things we do to conserve energy in the house is to make sure all the lights are turned off before we go to bed.

In this part . . .

Energy usage is becoming an increasingly important aspect of our personal lives. Energy costs are rising, a trend that will surely continue. Because of the political ramifications of obtaining the energy we need, we all can help mitigate the huge problems that our energy consumption creates. The easiest, and often the cheapest, way for each and every one of us to reduce energy consumption is by being more efficient with the energy that we use.

In this part I explain general concepts about energy so that you can make the decisions that let you reach your own energy efficiency goals. I show you how to accurately assess and measure how you use energy in your home so that you can decide how to invest your own personal energy and time in making improvements. I also give you a simple way to analyze financial investments so that you can get the most bang for your hard earned bucks.

Chapter 1

Defining Efficiency

Efficiency is the production of a desired effect with a minimum amount of effort or waste. That's the official definition, but you probably already have an intuitive sense of what *energy efficiency* means. Maybe to you it means using less. Maybe it means saving more. Believe it or not, those two goals don't always mean the same thing. That's because there are different kinds of efficiencies — energy, financial, pollution, and labor. (Yes, I know that the title of this book is *Energy Efficient Homes For Dummies,* and that angle takes front and center, but it's not the whole picture. I think it's important to understand some of the tradeoffs that are inherent in most of your decisions.)

To set and achieve your own efficiency goals, you need to be familiar with the different kinds of efficiencies, understand how these can be at cross-purposes, and get an idea of how you can begin to pursue your energy-efficiency goals. This chapter gives you the lowdown.

Examining the Four Main Spokes of the Efficiency Wheel

There are four different aspects of efficiency:

- ✔ **Energy efficiency:** Getting the most useful output from energy sources

- ✔ **Financial efficiency:** Getting the most for the least amount of money

- ✔ **Pollution efficiency:** Polluting as little as possible

- ✔ **Labor efficiency:** Spending the most time relaxing on the couch

To find the right balance among these different types of efficiencies, you need to ask yourself what you value the most. If you're only interested in lowering your costs, financial efficiency is your sole criterion. If you're interested in *going green,* living an efficient, energy-conserving lifestyle, you want to consider pollution and energy efficiency. An ultra-green lifestyle implies pollution efficiency more than energy efficiency or financial efficiency. And going green also requires more labor than a conventional lifestyle. But perhaps your only goal in life is to maximize the amount of time you spend at leisure (believe me, I'm empathetic). In this case, labor efficiency is your most important goal.

In this section, I present some detailed examples of these different types of efficiencies, and in the process, set up the basic premise of this book: Making investment decisions for efficiency improvements in your home always involves tradeoffs. To determine where the energy inefficiencies are in your home, head to Chapter 3. Chapter 5 gives you advice on how to decide which tradeoffs are best for you.

Energy efficiency

The energy efficiency of a device is a comparison, or ratio, of the useful energy output to the total energy input. This ratio is *always* related to the particular situation (the season, timing, desired end result, and so on).

For example, we want a light bulb to produce light. But we all know that a light bulb also produces heat — sometimes a great deal. In the summertime we don't want the heat, so the process is inefficient. A typical incandescent bulb converts only 10 percent of input electrical energy into light energy; the rest goes into heat. Therefore, the efficiency is 10 percent, or very poor. If enough light bulbs are turned on at the same time, the air conditioner may have to be turned on, which means even more inefficiency.

However, in the wintertime you can readily use that "inefficient" heat because it essentially decreases the load on your heating system. In this case, the efficiency may be close to 100 percent. You don't have to turn on your inefficient heating system nearly as much, so using incandescent light bulbs in the winter is a highly energy-efficient process.

Of course, outdoor incandescent light bulbs are just as inefficient in the winter as in the summer. And light bulbs in an unoccupied room are inefficient as well.

 As you evaluate where inefficiencies exist in your own home, consider all the factors that the come into play: the season, the desired outcome, and so on.

Conservation versus efficiency

Conserving energy simply means using less. Turning all the lights off in your house is conservation. Efficiency, on the other hand, is using less energy to achieve the same result. Plugging in fluorescents is practicing energy efficiency. Turning off the light and stumbling around in the dark is conservation. The meanings overlap, but the distinction is useful. For instance, if you use a programmable thermostat to turn your heater off during the day while you're at work and then turn it back on right before you get home, you're achieving better efficiency by conserving.

Financial efficiency

The financial efficiency of an appliance is the comparison, or ratio, of cost savings to the cost of the appliance (which includes the original equipment cost plus installation costs and maintenance costs, including energy). The better the ratio of cost savings to price, the more financially efficient an investment is. Another term for "financially efficient" is "cost effective." I use these terms interchangeably.

Solar photovoltaic (PV) panels, for example, are capable of saving costs on a power bill, and they have a well-defined initial price. Similarly, the cost of a new, more efficient appliance can, over a relatively short time period, be earned back by the energy savings.

Pollution efficiency

The pollution efficiency of an appliance is a comparison, or ratio, of the useful *output work* (the job that is being done) to the amount of pollution that is generated in the process. Solar PV panels create impressive output power while generating essentially zero pollution. Coal stoves create a lot of output power but also generate a lot of pollution. In evaluating pollution efficiency, you need to consider more than just how much pollution the appliance or system outputs. Solar panels, for example, create no pollution while they are operating, but pollution is created in the process of manufacturing a solar panel.

As you weigh the costs and benefits of pollution efficiency, keep in mind that there are usually no easy answers because the values being compared aren't always mathematically measurable. How much value, for example, do you attribute to helping the environment? Acceptable costs differ depending on your viewpoint. Some people, for example, want only to go green, in which case they will accept poor financial efficiency in favor of good pollution efficiency. Others try to balance financial and pollution efficiencies.

Labor efficiency

Labor efficiency is a comparison, or ratio, of how much work an appliance does to the amount of personal labor required to run and maintain it. A wood stove, for example, is labor inefficient because you have to stack wood, haul it inside, set it in the burn chamber, watch and stoke the fire as necessary, and then clean ashes. A gas stove, on the other hand, is very labor efficient — you only need to turn it off and on. Labor also includes pre-buy research, purchase hassles (like financing or delivery truck rental), installation (including cost of tools and hourly labor), and the maintenance and operational burdens over time.

Analyzing efficiencies

When analyzing efficiencies, be sure to consider the life expectancy of a particular investment. Answer these questions for every option you're considering:

- ✔ How long will an appliance last?

- ✔ How does the pollution output vary over time?

- ✔ Will the energy efficiency decrease over time (the answer is almost always yes because parts wear out, friction increases, and so on) and if so by how much?

- ✔ How much maintenance will be required over time, and will you be able to do the labor and maintenance, in years hence?

- ✔ How long is the warranty, and how much will unwarranted repairs cost?

- ✔ Who will be doing the service and where do parts come from?

- ✔ How will the future costs of energy affect the financial efficiencies?

- ✔ What are the financing costs and are there tax advantages now? Will there be tax advantages in the future that aren't available now?

To find out how to determine the payback of energy-efficient improvements you're thinking about, go to Chapter 5.

Opening Your Eyes to Inefficiency

Most people don't understand just how inefficient energy-consuming processes are. If you're only interested in cost

Looking at energy storage and efficiency

Some forms of energy are easy to store. Gasoline is a liquid that pours easily and can be transported readily. It can sit in a sealed container for years. Wood pellets can be stored for years with little loss in potential. Corn, on the other hand, attracts rodents and can very quickly go from being fuel in your storage bin to "food" that attracts large, furry assaults in the middle of the night. The heat from a fire can be stored in the materials in a room, but it doesn't last very long after the fire goes out. It's beneficial to consider energy not as a go/no-go proposition, but as a continuum.

Solar energy, on the other hand, can't be stored, so it must be converted into a different form in order to be stored. Solar power can be stored as heat, which is how a solar domestic hot water heater works. Or it can be converted into electricity and fed into a battery, which then converts the electrical energy into chemical energy. When the energy is to be used, later that night or the next morning, the chemical energy is then converted back into electrical energy, which is fed into an appliance. This whole chain process is extremely inefficient because each step in the process is inefficient and the inefficiencies only multiply.

effectiveness, you don't really need to know how inefficient processes are because, for you, saving money is the bottom line. But if you're interested in energy efficiency, and particularly pollution efficiency, you should understand just how utterly inefficient most energy consuming processes are. It would be impossible to define all the ways energy consumption processes are inefficient in a single book, much less a short introductory chapter, but it is important that you get a feel for the scope of the problem. The following sections offer two examples to illustrate.

Electrical grid inefficiencies

Most household appliances are powered by electricity, which is the least efficient method of consuming energy (more on this in Chapter 2). In many cases, it's also the most polluting alternative, because a majority of electrical energy comes from coal-fired furnaces. In addition, electrical energy is transmitted via the power grid, which uses power lines and transformers to deliver the AC voltages to your home. There are *line losses* (lines heat up and lose energy in the process) in the power wires, sometimes as much as 50 percent if the distances are great. Every transformer and substation is inefficient as well.

As a general rule, electrical systems are only around 30 percent efficient. This means that the electricity that comes into your home is mostly wasted before you use it. And when you use it — even if you use it wisely — you're wasting a good deal of it as well.

Consider a vacuum cleaner. How much energy does it take to move a small pile of dust from your floor to the vacuum bag? Very little. But by the time you get done plugging your vacuum cleaner into the wall socket and turning on a big, noisy electrical motor and swishing the wand across the floor, you've used hordes of energy. So vacuuming is maybe around 5 percent efficient. Compound this with the electrical inefficiencies from the utility grid and you come up with a net efficiency of less than 2 percent! This means that you've used 50 times more energy than you really needed to clean that dust up off your floor. At the same time, you've released 50 times more carbon dioxide into the atmosphere. An alternative? Get out the broom and dustpan.

Transportation inefficiencies

Autos take a lot of energy to produce. Factories consume copious amounts of electrical power, and most factories have their own power substations with transformers and high-voltage lines. So before you even drive your new car off the lot, you've consumed nearly as much energy as your car will consume to transport you the first 30,000 miles. This is true for even the most fuel-efficient autos and trucks. And it's certainly true for a hybrid auto, which consumes even more energy to produce than a conventional auto.

Your car weighs around 30 times more than you, so the vast majority of energy it expends to transport you to work and back is actually dedicated to transporting itself back and forth. You represent just a small fraction of the total work expended. Now that's inefficient!

The big oil companies burn around two gallons of gasoline to get you a gallon at the pump. Energy is required for drilling the crude from the ground, and then transporting the raw crude to a refinery some distance away. The process of *cracking* (breaking down raw components so as to output refined products such as gasoline, heating oil, and so on) requires a great deal of energy. Then the refined products need to be transported, first to the regional hubs and from there to the local gas stations. Gas stations consume energy and resources so that they can operate and sell you the gas.

All in all, your auto represents about 1 percent efficiency compared to a bicycle.

Becoming More Efficient

Efficiency is the cheapest and easiest way to save the world from the runaway effects of human consumption. A wide number of new technologies are coming onto the market with the express goal of reducing the amount of energy it takes to perform a particular task. A myriad of new devices purport to reduce pollution while doing the same essential work. But it's a simple fact that the easiest, fastest, and cheapest way to reduce pollution and energy usage is simply by using less energy with the equipment you already have.

When you recycle, you are saving resources, energy, and landfill space. Go to Chapter 14 to find out how simply using less, reusing more, and recycling what's left over can yield big efficiency benefits.

Getting greater efficiency from your current systems

You don't need to invest in new equipment to achieve impressive results. For example, when you drive less, you use less gas. Two people in a large SUV use less gas per person than two people each in their own separate hybrids, so carpooling is much more effective than fuel-efficient autos.

Similarly, when you turn your thermostat down in the winter and put on a sweater, you are immediately using less energy, and this is just one simple example.

There are myriad other ways to reduce inefficiencies in nearly every aspect of your home: sealing leaks and beefing up your insulation, taking advantage of natural air movement, using your appliance more efficiently, and so on. Head to Part II for system-by-system solutions.

Supplementing or replacing existing systems

Sometimes the way to greater efficiency is to replace or supplement your existing systems with more-energy-efficient systems. When you replace an open fireplace with a high-efficiency wood or gas stove, for example, you not only eliminate the unbelievable amount of energy waste associated with open hearths, but you supplement your existing HVAC system, meaning you can use it less. Part III explains how these alternative energy sources and others — solar power, radiant heat, geothermal heating systems and so on — can enhance efficiency.

Every contribution you make adds up. There are no "little" contributions. The U.S. Department of Energy has estimated that if everybody were to pitch in, energy consumption could be reduced by up to 20 percent. That's a major and immediate change in not only our dependence on foreign oil, but our contribution to greenhouse gases. If everybody were willing to pitch in not only by being more energy-efficient, but also by investing a few hundred dollars for improvements, energy consumption could be reduced by up to 30 percent. This would drop the cost of energy because demand would decrease, and the net effect would be more like a 40 percent reduction in cost for all of us.

Chapter 2

Energy Sources and Sinks

• •

In This Chapter

▶ Understanding where energy comes from
▶ Looking into where energy goes in a typical household
▶ Sustaining the environment through wise choices

• •

Richard Feynman, one of the most famous physics lecturers of all time, began his courses on energy by stating that nobody really understands what energy is. That being said, we all have an intuitive idea of what energy does, namely perform work. It takes energy to make something happen. This book is interested in making do with less energy consumption. If you are interested in jumping right in and saving energy, you may want to skip this chapter. But if you truly want to do the best you can, you need to understand a few basic ideas. When it comes to energy, it's important to know the currency as much as how to spend it.

In this chapter, I present data on where energy comes from, and how and where it's used on both a national and household level. Understanding the course that energy follows puts you in a better position to make good decisions on how to increase your own efficiencies. I present data on the typical household energy use in North America so that you can compare your own usage to see how it stacks up. (In Chapter 3, I get into a lot of detail on this subject, but I give you a rough idea here). I also discuss a number of ways that your own energy usage varies depending on where you live and what kind of home you occupy.

Energizing North America

A variety of energy sources are used in North America. You've probably already heard of many of them; others may be unfamiliar. The most common energy sources are

- **Petroleum products:** Petroleum products, which account for 39 percent of all the energy used in North America, are gasoline, propane and heating oil.

- **Natural gas:** Natural gas is drilled from beneath the surface of the earth, just like petroleum, but it comes in gaseous form instead of liquid or solid, and it makes up 24 percent of total energy consumption. It burns cleaner than petroleum products and coal, and is generally favored by environmentalists. Transport is problematic; so is storage.

- **Coal:** Coal is mined from the ground and comes in a solid, blackish, oily form that's easy to burn but very difficult to burn cleanly. Coal is the most common form of energy in North America because there's so much of it, and compared to petroleum, it's easy to extract from the ground. Around 23 percent of residential and commercial energy consumption is provided by coal.

- **Nuclear:** The same atom-splitting physics that provides us those wonderful nuclear weapons is used to heat water, which is then used to turn large electrical generating turbines. Nuclear energy is controversial, as the waste products are very difficult to deal with. But nuclear is coming back into favor because it doesn't generate the carbon pollution blamed for global warming and other problems. Nuclear only comprises 8 percent of North American energy consumption. Look for this percentage to increase dramatically in the next couple decades.

- **Hydropower (dams):** Tremendous water pressure is built up at the bottom of large dams built on riverways, and this pressure is harnessed to turn turbines that generate electricity. The power is very clean, but the problem is that the river's ecosystem is affected. Salmon runs are obliterated, and the natural beauty of the river is permanently altered, almost always for the worst (unless you like to water ski). Hydropower accounts for 3 percent of North American energy consumption, particularly in the American Pacific Northwest.

- **Biomass (firewood and other stuff):** Leaves falling from the trees in autumn are biomass, so are cow manure, horse manure, hay, weeds, corn husks, and so on. Firewood is the most common form of biomass used for energy. Total biomass energy production accounts for only 3 percent of North American energy usage. Because of its wide availability, biomass is seen as an excellent sustainable energy source.

- **Geothermal:** The air you breathe and the ground beneath your feet provide the source for geothermal

energy. The physics is complicated, but suffice
to say that you can generate heating and cooling
by using heat exchange mechanisms that move
temperature differences from one place to another.
If you want heat in your home, you take some from
the air or the ground. Geothermal energy provides
0.3 percent of North American energy needs.

- **Wind:** Traditionally windmills have been used
  to pump water from the ground (you see them
  on old western movies at nearly every ranch and
  nearly every poster from Holland), but modern
  embodiments produce electrical power as well. Wind
  power is a form of solar power because wind is
  caused by thermal temperature differences between
  regions of the globe. Wind power only provides 0.11
  percent of energy needs, but this is changing fast
  since wind is a very clean source. The problems are
  that windmills are unsightly, and they make noise.
  They also may kill wildlife, particularly birds.

- **Import electricity:** Our electrical grid is an
  extensive matrix of interconnected power wires that
  span borders. North America imports from nearby
  countries around 0.1 percent of its energy needs.

- **Solar:** The sun radiates a tremendous amount of
  energy — 37,000 times as much energy as humans
  use — onto the surface of the earth, pollution free.
  Unfortunately, tapping into this energy isn't simple.
  Nevertheless, people have figured out ways to use
  solar energy to heat water and to produce electricity.
  There is a tremendous push to increase solar
  production, and many governments are subsidizing
  solar equipment in both residential and commercial
  settings. Right now solar power accounts for only

A word about global warming

I don't take a position on global warming one way or another in this book. My opinion is that it's not really relevant in encouraging people to conserve and practice efficiency. The fact is, we use too many resources, and in the process we end up altering the planet in material ways that will affect future generations in one manner or another. Global warming is just one way that we might be affecting the planet, and in my view the overwhelming attention placed on this one aspect of our environmental defamation does a disservice to the other aspects, and the overall balance and harmony that we should be striving for. What if it turns out that there is no global warming? Should we then go right back to the old days of unlimited exploitation of resources? Of course not.

0.06 percent of energy production (if you don't include all the natural light and heat the sun produces), but that's changing fast.

The majority of our energy sources produce power through combustion processes (burning) that require a burning chamber, oxygen, and exhaustion capacities. From time immemorial, humans have burned wood for fires, and the process was simple; pile some wood, light it, hang around close to it. Modern combustion processes are engineered to be more efficient (modern wood burning stoves are around 100 times more efficient than open fires, for example), but the combustion processes, regardless of how efficient they are, are notorious pollution sources.

Non-combustion processes, such as solar power and nuclear, don't exhaust pollutants the same way that combustion processes do, but they have their own problems. For instance, solar photovoltaic (PV) panels require a lot of energy to manufacture, and most of this energy comes from electrical power which itself often comes from coal and combustion. So while solar is pollution free in its implementation, it entails a lot of pollution in its manufacture.

The point is there is no such thing as a free lunch. Every energy source has pros and cons, and trying to decide how best to provide the power an economy needs is a complex problem. Many believe that the current energy predicament will be solved when we wean ourselves away from petroleum consumption, but even as people develop new alternative sources, the problems don't go away; they simply change in nature.

Looking at Energy Costs: Raw and Otherwise

Not all energy costs the same. Some types of energy are more expensive than others. How costly an energy source is depends on what it takes to deliver the energy to your home (raw energy costs) and what it takes to convert the raw energy into fuel you can use (conversion costs). By understanding where a particular energy source falls on the cheap-to-dear scale in both of these areas, you can gain a better understanding of how you can plan and control your energy usage to attain better efficiency.

Recognizing raw energy costs

Taking a look at the relative costs of different types of raw energy is illuminating. (By raw, I mean the cost at delivery to your home; this doesn't take into account how you may actually use the energy within your home, or how much the equipment costs to convert the raw energy into usable

To put the energy consumption of the United States in perspective, take a look at how much energy is used (per capita) in different countries around the world:

Country	Btu per person per year
Canada	418
United States	339
Western Europe	149
Japan	172
China	33

Canada is cold, so its citizens require a lot of heat. But their high consumption also reflects the fact that energy is relatively inexpensive in Canada. When this is the case, regardless of where in the world it may be, there is little incentive to conserve or practice efficiency.

What's more interesting is to compare American consumption with that of Western Europe. It would be very difficult to argue, as one can do when comparing the United States to China, that the large difference reflects quality of lifestyle. Western Europeans, in many ways, enjoy better lifestyles than Americans. So why is their per capita consumption so low? Because they've been inculcated by high energy prices for so long that energy conservation and efficiency are ingrained into the very fabric of their societies.

form). Relatively speaking, electricity is the most costly, nuclear energy is the cheapest, and a bunch of other types of energy fall somewhere in between (see Table 2-1).

Table 2-1
Comparing Raw Energy Costs

Type of Energy	Cost (in $) per Million Btu
Electricity	$ 29.3
Liquid propane gas	$ 18.54
Gasoline	$ 15.19
Kerosene	$ 11.11
Heating oil	$ 10.82
Natural gas	$ 10.00
Coal	$ 9.52
Wood	$ 7.50
Uranium (nuclear)	$ 0.00033

Btu stands for *British thermal unit,* a standard unit of energy equal to 754 kWh, or kilowatt hours (one thousand watt hours). To put this into perspective, a typical incandescent light bulb consumes around 75 watts, and so in a ten-hour evening consumes 750 Wh. Typically, large appliances like heaters and air-conditioners are rated in Btu, while smaller devices are rated in watts. No technical abracadabra here, just tradition.

As Table 2-1 shows, electricity is by far the costliest energy source. This is because the *power transmission grid,* the huge matrix of power wires and transformers used to get the power from the utility generators to your home, is so big and unwieldy. Think of it this way: When you generate solar power on your roof, it's created and used within a space of a hundred feet, maybe less. But when you use electricity from the grid, the production chain begins in a coal mine, then the coal must be transported to a power plant, and then power is generated in huge, expensive machines. This electrical power gets transmitted over long lengths of wire until it finally reaches your home. Several companies are involved — a coal mining company, a transport company, and a utility company with linesmen, managers, secretaries, lobbyists, and lawyers — not to mention that a whole host of governmental regulations have to be met, and taxes and tariffs need to be paid.

Even though electricity is the most expensive, it's used almost exclusively in a majority of homes. Why? Because it's the most convenient way to use power. All you have to do is plug in to a wall socket and voilà! You don't need a storage tank (like you do with propane or fuel oil), and you don't have to worry about the danger of explosions or flames (although you can get a shock without even trying too hard). You don't need to go into the woods with a chainsaw and cut it down, and you don't need to stack it on the side of your house and keep the spiders out of it. Best of all, the utility company is responsible for maintaining a continual flow into your home.

Looking at actual energy costs

Raw energy cost, explained in the preceding section, is only part of the picture. Most energy sources need to be burned or combusted on-site in order to extract their potential energy. Some conversion methods are more efficient than others. The list in Table 2-2 shows the same fuels as those

The link between coal and electricity

Due to its high carbon and sulfur content, burning coal is extremely dirty. Coal byproducts are the leading contributor to global warming (nearly 1 billion tons of carbon dioxide are produced each year in the United States alone; China has surpassed this). Mercury is another byproduct; it pollutes air, land, and water. Because about 90 percent of the coal produced in this country is used to produce over 50 percent of our electricity, electrical power is generally a very polluting source of energy. Reducing electrical usage is always a good idea, especially if you're concerned about pollution and global warming.

listed in Table 2-1, but this time with all the various production factors that come into play.

Table 2-2	Comparing Actual Energy Costs
Type of Energy	*Cost (in $) per Million Btu*
Gasoline	$75.96
Electricity	$29.30
Liquid propane	$23.18
Coal	$15.87
Kerosene	$13.89
Heating oil	$13.52
Wood	$12.50
Natural gas	$12.05
Uranium (nuclear)	$0.024

Using It Up: Where Energy Goes

Different sources of energy may be used to provide different functions within a single home — for example, natural gas may be used for heating, electricity provides energy for lighting and the appliances, and fireplace wood provides supplemental heating. So how does a typical North American home use energy? The following table shows you. (**Note:** These percentages are averaged over the course of a year; month-to-month breakdowns vary quite a bit.)

Function	Percentage of total energy used
Space heating	47%
Water heating	21%
Lighting	8%
Space cooling	6%
Refrigeration	5%
Electronics	3%
Cooking	4%
Clothes washing/drying	3%
Computers	1%
Other	2%

Of course this breakdown varies widely from home to home and region to region. For a clearer picture of how your own home uses energy, you can adapt these percentages to your specific scenario. Here are some things to consider:

- ✔ If you're in a hot climate, you spend a lot more on cooling than heating. If you're in a cold climate, you spend a lot more on heating than cooling. In Chapter 3, I show you ways to calculate your heating and cooling costs in detail, and I give you some pointers on how to do something about those costs in Chapter 8.

The most productive way to improve household efficiency usually is to consider your heating and cooling systems first and foremost. If heating is your greatest expense, you can save the most money by reducing your heating bill. Then you want to take a look at how you use hot water, and so on down the line. Another factor to consider is how much equipment costs. In a home, HVAC equipment is usually the most expensive, closely followed by major appliances like washers, dryers, and refrigerators. In making decisions on how to become more efficient, both the cost of the energy being consumed and the cost of the equipment come into play. Head to the section "Turning Your Eye to Improved Energy Efficiency" for advice on how to approach this topic.

✔ If you're in a moderate climate, you may not spend anywhere near as much on heating or cooling as somebody in Illinois, where the weather tends to all extremes. Your month-to-month fluctuations also vary less.

✔ If you have a well for water, you need to include that category in the list and figure the percentage based on how much water you use. Small working ranches with electrically pumped wells may spend up to 20 percent of their utility bill on pumping.

✔ If you use a wood stove and chop the wood yourself, your energy use percentages may be close to those in the preceding chart, but your costs will be skewed because you're not paying for your heat at all.

✔ If you're in an apartment, with common walls, your heating and cooling percentages will be lower because there will be less loss. If your neighbors set their thermostat high and you set yours low, you're essentially using their heat because it migrates into your apartment.

- ✔ If you don't have an air-conditioner, your cooling costs will be zero, or minimal if you use fans.

- ✔ If you take a lot of hot showers, your water heating percentage will be higher; take fewer (or cold) showers, and it will be lower.

- ✔ If you use energy to charge a golf cart, power a motor home sitting in your driveway, or power a workshop with heavy-duty tools, adjust your figures accordingly. These types of things take a lot of energy and may overshadow even the heating component.

- ✔ If you never open a single window in your home and your HVAC is on all the time, even when the weather is nice, heating and cooling will comprise a larger percentage of the total.

- ✔ If you rarely use your HVAC at all, instead favoring thick sweaters in the winter and a lot of sweating in the summer, your heating and cooling will comprise a smaller percentage of the total.

Turning Your Eye to Improved Energy Efficiency

The preceding sections are devoted to background information, but this book is about achieving tangible results. In this section, I present some generalities that you should keep in mind — like how to reduce the amount of electricity you use, how to maximize your sustainable energy sources, and more — regardless of the details of your energy efficiency program.

The big Kahuna: Electrical energy

As stated earlier, a typical household uses more than one energy source. Of all the energy sources folks use in their homes, however, electrical energy is the most widely used, as well as the most convenient. And that's why it's the most important to think about when you think about energy efficiency.

Electrical energy holds the most potential for efficiency improvements because the methods of making improvements are the most easily accessible and understood.

Where electricity comes from

Ben Franklin and his kite experiment aside, electrical energy doesn't just drop from the sky. It's generated through processes powered by other energy sources. For instance, coal is burned and water is boiled and the pressure is used to turn huge turbines that generate electrical power. In North America, electrical energy comes from these sources:

Source	Approximate Percentage of Total Electricity Production
Coal	51%
Nuclear	20%
Natural gas	18%
Hydro	7%
Petroleum	2%
Other renewables	2%
Other gas	0.3%

The problems with electrical energy

Although electricity is typically considered clean and environmentally friendly, it is often generated through processes that rely on "dirty" energy sources. Even those processes that use renewable energy sources have their own problems. Bottom line: Electrical energy is subject to many common inefficiencies and problems. Here are some of the biggest ones:

- Electrical energy, while clean once it reaches your home, has most likely been generated by a combustion process, so don't kid yourself into thinking that electricity is environmentally benign. Many people believe that electrical cars that you charge up at home are the key to a green future, but if you consider just how inefficient the electrical system is, and how most electricity is generated by coal-fired plants, you come to a different conclusion.

- In the process of generating and using electricity, a lot of hot water is discharged — first into the river system and then into the ocean. This affects the ecosystem. For instance, some biological lifeforms require very specific water temperatures for breeding purposes; by warming the average river temperature, these species die out.

- Wind generators cover open hillsides with noisy, ugly windmills. Birds and bats get killed, sometimes in large numbers. Compared to the alternatives, though, windmills are practically pristine.

- Hydroelectric generators dam up rivers and affect such diverse phenomena as salmon runs and the plants and animals that live along the riverside. Dams also create a lot of underwater decay in the upper reservoirs that doesn't exist when water runs naturally; this decay releases carbon dioxide into the atmosphere, and we all know what that means (global warming).

✔ Geothermal wells release arsenic into the environment.

✔ Power lines emit radiation, heat the air, buzz, and catch birds and planes. Their potential for danger is even greater when they're downed.

✔ Nuclear power plants produce horrendous wastes, and people have yet to figure out a good way to get rid of these byproducts.

Renewable and sustainable energy sources

The words renewable and sustainable are being knocked around quite a bit. Both are inherently associated with energy conservation:

✔ **Renewable forms of energy** constantly replenish themselves with little or no human effort. Solar energy is just one example — no matter how much you use, the supply will never end (okay, it may end after billions of years, but your using solar power won't make the sun burn out any faster). Other examples of renewables include firewood, water (via hydroelectric dams), and wind power.

The term *renewable* does not necessarily imply good environmentalism. Firewood, a renewable energy source, is notoriously polluting, and it has another potentially severe drawback: People go out into forests and cut down trees, often without much thought to the overall health of the forest (a good example of not seeing the forest for the trees).

✔ **Sustainable forms of energy** are not only renewable, but they also have the ability to keep the Earth's ecosystem up and running in perpetuity. The basic notion behind sustainable energy sources is that by their use, society is not compromising future generations' health and well-being, or their ability to use their own sustainable resources to the same extent that we do now. Who can argue with this very fundamental version of the Golden Rule?

To make sure that resources last, humans need to focus on renewable and sustainable energy sources. Energy sources that fail to meet these criteria could eventually be depleted and thus cease to exist.

Invested energy and recycling

Invested energy is the energy that's used to manufacture a product (in the literature, you may see this referred to as *embodied energy,* but it means essentially the same thing). Take solar panels, for example. When solar energy was first conceived back in the 1960s as part of the space program, a solar panel took over three times more energy to produce than it would ever generate in its lifetime. Bad economics, but satellites need energy sources, and solar panels are the only practical source. Nowadays panels are far better, and the disparity between the energy invested to make solar panels and the energy that the solar panels generate no longer exists.

If you're truly interested in reducing your energy consumption, you need to consider invested energy when choosing products. Unfortunately, because the concept of invested energy has just begun to take root, the information is not widely available (although an entire industry is dedicated to meeting the burgeoning demand of "green" customers who want this information). In the future it will be more and more common for products to list their total invested energies alongside the current energy efficiency information.

 If you're intent on finding out invested energy levels, contact manufacturers and be prepared to exhibit robust patience. In many cases, manufacturers haven't even considered invested energy and won't even know how to answer your query. The best bet is to patronize manufacturers that publish their numbers, for these will most likely be the ones trying to minimize those numbers.

 The point is, everything takes energy to manufacture, and when considering how much energy is used in your household, you need to consider invested energy as well as the energy you gobble up in your home.

In fact, invested energy is a big force in favor of recycling. From an economic standpoint, recycling may not seem like such a great idea. It takes time on your part and requires you to set up systems and stick with them. But you're not just saving money when you recycle; you're saving invested energy, and all the pollution and environmental costs that go with it.

Green homes are becoming more common, and one of the more important aspects of choosing materials is invested energy. Although recycled products are popular, new materials that may cost a little more but use far less energy to produce and bring to the building site are also a good choice.

Musing over manpower

Some people have asked me about connecting a turbine to their exercise equipment so that they can turn their efforts into usable household energy. It's not worth it — not by a long shot. If you're watching a TV while you're working out, the TV is probably consuming more power than you're generating.

A male human being, in good condition, can generate only 200 watts of power. One horsepower is equal to 746 watts, so it would take around four strong men to equal the power of a single horse. It would take one physically fit man five hours on a treadmill to generate 1 kilowatt-hour, which is the same amount of energy the sun radiates onto a one square meter area in only one hour.

Humans may not be able to generate enough power to produce the amount of energy that U.S. society is accustomed to, but that's not to say that man is powerless to make a difference. Here's some food for thought: Think of how much more energy the average American uses than do those in countries where electricity is common and people make do without it. Our lives here in North America are surely much easier. But is the difference in the quality of our lives equal to the difference in the amount of energy we consume? Personally, I think not.

In fact, one could make a compelling argument in the other direction. Complexity is inefficient, and not just physically. Complexity inhibits aesthetic harmony, which may be the real reason for living. How many of you would like to trade in your hyper-driven lifestyles for something simpler? In this book, I help you simplify.

Chapter 3

Eliminating the Guesswork with Home Energy Audits

. . . .

In This Chapter

▶ Weighing in on what determines your energy usage
▶ Understanding how energy companies structure their fees
▶ Looking into the details of your energy consumption
▶ Considering your carbon contribution
▶ Performing energy audits in your home

. . . .

If you want to improve the energy efficiency of your home in an efficient manner, you need to first understand the economics of your overall consumption. When you make investments in either time or money, they should be focused and deliberate in order to ensure good payback (I get into payback in Chapter 5). Unfortunately, most people don't have a good handle on the specifics of how and where they're using energy and other resources in their homes. As the saying goes, "The devil is in the details." In this chapter, I present a detailed system for analyzing your resource use (I leave the devil out of it, however).

75

Getting a Handle on Your Energy Usage

The ultimate goal is to deduce how much you're paying for different sources of energy and then tackle those costs based on what your main objective is. For example, your primary goal may be cost reduction as you strive for efficiencies, or your main objective may be pollution mitigation or energy conservation. In any case, you need to first consider the total resource consumption in your home.

Energy use in a typical North American home

Looking at nationwide statistics gives you a baseline to which you can compare your energy usage. Does your own usage make sense, or can you make easy changes? Do you need to simply change your habits, or are you going to have to invest time and money in equipment improvements? Table 3-1 shows how a typical North American home uses energy (averaged over the course of a year). For the purposes of this data, a typical home has 1,600 square feet, two baths, three bedrooms, and 2.3 occupants in a region with moderate weather patterns.

Table 3-1   Yearly Energy Use for a Typical Home

Purpose or Use	Percentage of Total Energy Used
Space heating	47%
Water heating	21%
Lighting	8%
Space cooling	6%

Refrigeration	5%
Cooking	4%
Electronics	3%
Clothes washing/drying	3%
Computers	1%
Other	2%

These values represent total energy used, not how much that energy costs. The cost of different energy sources varies widely. For instance, if you heat your home by chopping wood yourself and burning it in a wood stove, your heating costs may be near zero, but that obviously doesn't mean you are consuming zero energy to heat your home. If you have a solar water heater on your roof, your water heating cost may be zero, but 21 percent of your energy consumption can still be attributed to heating water. The cost of equipment also factors into the equation. For instance, you had to buy that solar heater, and that's not cheap. Refer to Chapter 2 for details on the costs associated with different types of energy.

Focusing on your own home-sweet-home

Obviously, if you don't fit the typical profile described in the preceding section, your energy consumption will be different. To a large degree, personal lifestyle dictates energy consumption. If you're gone all day and the home is empty, for example, you can lower your thermostat and save. If you're diligent about turning off unused lights, your lighting component will be less. If you tolerate heat and cold better than most, you can save on heating and cooling. And so on.

As you evaluate how your home varies from the typical energy consumption numbers, spend some time going around your house, looking at all the different ways you consume energy and resources. Just by paying more attention, you can learn a lot.

Where you live and the type of house you live in

Where you live has a big impact on how much energy you use. Folks sweating through summers in the sunny Southwest don't have the same heating and cooling needs as those shivering through winters in the Upper Peninsula of Michigan. If you're in a hot climate, you may need very little heat, but your cooling bill is higher. If you're in Alaska, your heating bill is much higher.

Different home styles — whether you live in an apartment, a house, or a condo, for example — also make a difference. Apartments and many condos have common walls, and the heat and cooling losses are less. Homes with a lot of windows have poorer insulation, while those that are surrounded by trees and natural windbreaks suffer less heat loss. And so on.

The type of HVAC you have

HVAC stands for *heating, ventilation and air conditioning*. Most homes have forced air systems, which means ducts and fans push air through the home. Some homes have radiant heat, and many homes have wood stoves or other combustion appliances. Heating is the biggest single component of the utility budget in most homes, and it's subject to the most variation in energy consumption. Thus, it pays to know as much as you can about your home's heating resources. Ask yourself these questions:

✔ **What kind of heating source(s) do you use?**

A wood-burning stove, gas fireplace, electric heat pump, baseboard heater, free-standing heater, radiator, and so on? Figure out how much you spend on each source of heat.

✔ **How old is your system, and what's its expected lifetime?** In general, the older the system, the less efficient it is — not because old technology is inferior, but because back in the day, people didn't worry about energy efficiency as much as we do now, and paying more for an efficient system just wasn't worth it.

✔ **Do you have a central air conditioner or window units?** Do you use fans, an evaporative cooler, dehumidifiers, and so on? Include them in your assessment of your energy consumption.

 As you think about your own energy consumption, look at your neighbors and see how their consumption differs from yours. What is the most popular HVAC system in your area, for example, and what are new homes in your area being equipped with? The answers to these types of questions can give you valuable information about the kind of technologies that work best in your region. Heat pumps, for example, work well in moderate climates but not in extremely cold climates. If nobody in your area uses a heat pump, there's probably a good reason. And if everybody is burning wood in a stove, it's probably because the availability and cost of wood is advantageous.

The people who live in your home

Heating and cooling don't depend on how large your family is, but on the ways that people in your family use energy. You may have to turn the thermostat lower in the summer and higher in the winter because of personal preference and potential health issues. If a member of your family has special needs, such as air filtration for asthma, you should factor that in. If your family is very sensitive to exposure to contaminants, you're probably paying more for filters and cleaning services.

Your water usage

Where do you get your water from and how much do you use? If a well supplies your water, your electric bill will be larger, but your water bill will be nonexistent. If you take long, hot showers or if your family is large, your water heating component will be higher. If you have a solar water heater, this component may be costing you next to nothing on a monthly basis. And if you have kids, as any parent can tell you, you probably wash a lot of clothes.

The type of amenities you have

Be sure not to leave life's little extras off your radar as you scope out things that consume energy around your home. For example, do you have a swimming pool or spa? Pool pumps consume a lot of electricity, especially in the summer. Spas consume a lot of power, especially in the winter. What about a massive home entertainment center? These can easily consume more energy than an old refrigerator, which is about the most inefficient appliance ever made. And if you're charging a golf cart or powering a motor home in your driveway, keep in mind that they take a lot of power, too. Room full of aquariums? Giant gym? You get the point.

Special situations

If you're running a business in your home, your lighting, heating, and cooling costs will be higher. Your power bill may also be higher if you're running heavy equipment.

Other things to think about

Many people who want to become more energy efficient do it for two reasons: to save money and to save the planet. If you're one of the many people interested in polluting less, add the following to your list of possible areas for improvement:

- ✔ **What kind of garbage service do you have?** Are there alternatives? Does your trash collection agency offer recycling, for example, and if so, what kind of recycling? You can call the customer service number for answers.

- ✔ **Do you have sewer service or are you using a septic tank?** If you're using a septic tank, how old is it and how long has it been since it was serviced? If you don't stay on top of your septic system, you may incur extra costs when problems arise.

- ✔ **How much carbon and other pollutions are you producing in the process of consuming energy in your home?** If you have a cheap wood stove, your cost may be very low (if you cut your own wood), but your carbon footprint astronomical. Is this important to you? (See the section "Calculating Your Own Carbon Footprint," later in this chapter, for details on how to do this.)

Do you have equipment that you know is going to need replacement? Are you paying a lot of repair bills for a particular piece of equipment? Would you like to invest in improvement? Check to see whether government agencies in your area are offering subsidies for certain types of equipment. Your utility may offer subsidies, too. See Chapter 4 for more details.

Paying Up: The Various Rate Structures

To figure out what you spend on energy consumption, you need to know not only how much energy you use, but how you pay. Find out the answers to these questions:

- ✔ **What, if any, utilities are bundled together?** Are you charged separately for your sewer and the water you use, for example, or is your sewage bill part of your water bill?

- ✔ **Do you pay flat rates for your utilities or are they metered?** Municipalities that don't use meters have very high rates of consumption, and some are experiencing political pressure to change to meters. If you're on a flat rate for water or electricity, is your municipality one that's considering the change to meters? If so, try to anticipate how such a change may affect what you pay. If you're frugal (which you probably are because you're reading this book), you could end up paying less with a meter.

- ✔ **When do you pay each of your utility bills?** Most likely you write a monthly check, but you may be on a different program. If you use propane or oil, do you pay each time the tank is filled? How often is this, and what are the annual and seasonal totals? Most trash bills are fixed monthly, but you may have another structure.

- ✔ **Have unit costs changed over the last few years for each of your resources?** What's the trend? (Natural gas fluctuates a lot in price, whereas solar never varies.) Ask yourself what you expect prices to do in the future, and evaluate how this would affect your household economy.

This type of information is important because you can find ways to save money by simply changing a habit or two. For instance, if you're on a TOU (time of use) rate structure, you can take showers in the morning or evening instead of the afternoon, when rates are at their peak.

Utilities charge you in a wide range of ways, particularly for electric service. You should study your utility bills and determine which structures you're operating under. The answer makes a big difference in terms of how you can best invest your money and time to make your home more efficient. The following sections outline the main rate structure options.

 Averaging, or amortizing, is common on power bills and sometimes on water bills. It's a way the utility company allows you to even out the severe ups and downs in your bill. Some utilities average by simply reading your meter every three or four months and then charging you proportionally for those months. Another way is to average over an entire year, say the previous year's consumption, and charge you the same amount for all 12 months. At the end of the year, you're charged for any net surplus or shortage, and that amount gets amortized into the next year's billing.

Simple rate structure

Under a simple rate structure, the same rate applies to every unit of energy you use, regardless of the amount of energy you use, when you use it, or any other factor. This type of rate structure is rare because it doesn't discourage overconsumption. If your bill simply lists a single price for electricity, this is the type of structure you are on.

Tiered structure

A tiered structure is the most common. For example, an electric utility may charge 15 cents each for the first 300 kWh of electric energy you use in a given month. The next 300 kWh may cost 30 cents each. The next 300 kWh cost 45 cents each, and so on. By its progressively penal nature, this structure encourages efficiency and conservation.

Time of use (TOU) structure

A time of use (TOU) structure charges depending on what time of day you use power (it requires a special meter with a clock function). The most difficult time for a utility to provide its customers with all the power they need is in the afternoon, when businesses are using the greatest amount of power. Utilities often have to buy power from other utilities in order to meet this peak demand, and this costs the utilities quite a bit more than the power they generate themselves. So they charge you more for it — usually a lot more. Generally, prices are at their highest between noon and 6 p.m. (referred to as *peak time*), although the hours may vary. This is a difficult rate schedule to work with if you need a lot of air conditioning in the summer, because it's during this peak time that you want your air conditioner on.

You probably won't be able to ascertain whether you're on this schedule by looking at a single power bill because seasonal variations in pricing are very common. You need to look at a power bill from the winter and compare it to one from the summer (summer is almost always more expensive, because of air-conditioning issues). Summer rates generally start in May and go through September or October.

Combination structures

Combination structures are the most common. In Northern California where I live, we have tiered, TOU, seasonal rate structures. Very difficult to understand, and it doesn't help that most utility bills are virtually indecipherable. Your best bet is to take it one piece at a time. Understand the tiered nature on its own merits, then tackle the TOU structure, and so on. You can also call the customer service number and talk to a representative; in my experience, these people are very good, and patient, in explaining the details.

Figuring Out What You Spend

The best way to figure out what you spend — and where you potentially can cut back — is to dissect your utility bills. By doing this, you get good data on specifically where to look for the most rewarding investments in efficiency. This is basically a three-step process: Gather all your data, plot it month by month, and then analyze your results. The following sections give you the details.

Collecting the data

The first thing you need to do is collect a stack of utility bills. If you don't already have them, call your utility companies (customer-service numbers are always listed on the bills) and have them send you copies of your bills for the past few years. Most utilities don't charge for this service, and some even do data analysis for you (they graph the data, which is much nicer than a load of raw numbers; ask when you call). They may even offer other services, like a free home energy audit.

In addition to your utility bills (water, electric, gas, trash, and sewer), you need to compile a list of all the expenses associated with the resources you use. Here's a sampling of what you need, but you may have other items not on this list:

- ✔ **Trash runs to the dump:** If you take trash to the dump yourself, estimate the cost by including everything: gasoline for your truck, other transport expenses, costs at the landfill, and so on.

- ✔ **Manufactured logs:** If you use manufactured logs, you don't need to come up with receipts; just estimate how many you use and how much they cost. Transport and storage may also be significant.

- ✔ **Power generator:** If you bought one, how much did it cost? If you rent one, include the rental cost. Also include the cost of the gasoline you use to run it.

- ✔ **Firewood:** If you use firewood, include costs for the chainsaw, saw blades, transportation for firewood, and rental (or purchase price) of a wood splitter. And if you broke your arm while cutting firewood, include the associated medical expenses, too.

- ✔ **Wood pellets and bio-energy products of any kind:** Include all costs associated with these.

- ✔ **Propane or natural gas:** If you use either of these, include not only the cost of the product, but also rental agreements, maintenance, and so on. A lot of people pay a yearly rental for their propane tank.

- ✔ **Barbecue grill:** Calculate how much you spend for charcoal, the propane, and the tanks. How much did the grill itself cost?

- ✔ **Lawn tools:** Include any gasoline you buy for them,

as well as the gas canister if you bought one. If you buy gas (and/or a gas canister) for a generator, include those costs, too.

✔ **Kerosene:** If you use kerosene for lanterns, cooking, or heating, include those costs.

✔ **Space heaters, portable air conditioners, dehumidifiers, swamp coolers, and so on:** If you bought any of these, include how much they cost and estimate how much they cost to run. Check their labels for power consumption; then estimate how much time they're on, and when.

✔ **Candles and light bulbs:** If you use them, add them to your list.

✔ **Batteries and chargers:** Batteries can be very expensive, and most people don't consider them a part of their power consumption, but they definitely are.

✔ **Maintenance and repair costs:** These apply to energy equipment, such as a woodstove, HVAC filters, appliances, and so on.

✔ **New equipment:** If you bought a new water heater, new HVAC, or anything else along these lines, add the replacement costs to your list, as well as any delivery and installation charges.

✔ **Insulation:** If you insulated your pipes, the cost is directly related to your energy consumption.

✔ **Loans to buy energy-creating equipment:** If you took out a loan to buy something like a generator or woodstove, be sure to include the interest on the loan as you calculate your energy costs.

✔ **Permits, fees, and taxes:** Some additions require permits; some up your taxes. You may have to obtain a county permit for installing a wood or gas stove, for example. Or you may pay higher property taxes because of a sunroom addition.

✔ **Bottled water:** If you drink it, estimate how much and the cost.

As you compile your list, you're likely to find that you're spending a lot more for resources than you thought, and you may be surprised by some of the details. You're already moving forward!

Plotting the details, month by month

Ultimately, you need to do some month-by-month estimations. The power company bill is the easiest, along with water and trash. Here are some rules for allocating other resource costs by month:

✔ If you have a propane tank that's filled periodically by the propane company, you'll have a tough time figuring out the monthly usage. Just get the yearly total and divide that up on a monthly basis. If you only use the propane for heat, allocate the cost to those months when you use heat. If you use some for hot water and some for heat, divvy it up as best you can. Make sure the total is right.

✔ Ditto with firewood and all the associated expenses. Most people buy a big stack once a year. How much did you use each month? Divvy up the costs as best you can and make sure the total is right.

✔ Servicing for equipment should be allocated according to the use of that equipment. If you serviced a heater, allocate the cost only to those months when you use heat.

✔ Even if your water bill is fixed, estimate how much water you used on a monthly basis. If possible, you should try to divide your water usage according to the various functions for which you use it, such as sewer, laundry, dishwasher, and so on. Landscaping may be the biggest water consumer in your household, and this is important to know.

To determine monthly costs of a piece of equipment, follow these steps:

1. **Determine what you paid.**

    Example: A gas fireplace costs $4,000 plus tax, plus another $200 for permits and inspection. The total is $4,480.

2. **Estimate how much that equipment increased the value of your home.**

    A gas fireplace may increase the value by $2,500.

3. **Subtract how much the equipment increased the value of your home from its total cost to get the net cost.**

    Subtract $2,500 from $4,480. The net cost of the fireplace is $1,980.

4. **Estimate the lifetime of the equipment, in months.**

    The fireplace should be usable for ten years, or 120 months.

5. **Calculate the monthly *depreciation* (loss of value) by dividing the net value by the number**

of months in the equipment's lifetime.

Divide $1,980 by 120. The fireplace costs $16.50 per month.

You can get fancy, if you want. Say the cost of the fireplace in the preceding example is better allocated to only the winter months. The cost would then be $33 over the six months from October through March.

You may want to plot several years' worth of graphs to get a comprehensive idea of your energy consumption. Individual years may be subject to strange weather patterns or one-time-only events, like a big wedding or a lot of relatives visiting at Christmas. You also want to watch out for isolated events on your bills. If, for instance, one of your monthly statements includes a one-time deduction as a result of your electric company settling a lawsuit with energy providers who charged too much, you need to factor this sort of thing out because it has no bearing on your habits.

Keeping Up With the Joneses: A Real-Life Scenario

The best way to illustrate how to put all your data together is to use Bill Toomuch as an example. Bill and his small family live on a five-acre ranch in California in a 2,700-square-foot house. With the exception of a small gas fireplace in their great room, all their energy comes from the electric company. They have an above-ground swimming pool and a hot tub. Water is supplied by a well. Analyzing Bill's energy consumption demonstrates by example how to go about systematically analyzing your own situation.

Big reasons for high energy bills

Do you have a really high bill? One that sticks out like a sore thumb? Here are the most likely reasons:

- The addition of occupants in your home
- The addition of appliances, like a freezer in the garage
- Faulty appliances
- High rates of outdoor air infiltration into your home (You may have a faulty weather seal on a door that needs fixing, or you may have a bad attic trap door.)
- The use of too much electrical resistance heating
- Hot water leaks
- Use of appliances with large motors (pumps, compressors, air conditioners)
- Seasonal appliances — electric blankets, a dehumidifier, lots of shop lighting, power tools
- An estimated bill or one that reflects a higher time period
- A wedding or a big party
- Uncle Bill's motor home parked in the driveway

Looking at Bill's resource costs

Bill lists his resource costs as follows:

- Bill called PG&E and got four years' worth of history, broken down by month. Figure 3-1 shows one of Bill's typical electric utility bills. The bill is for the period from 1/12/2007 to 2/12/2007. The total for the bill is $403.30.

- ✔ Because they have a well, Bill doesn't have a water bill, but the cost of his water supply shows up on his electric bill because the well is powered by an electric pump.

- ✔ The household fills a 64-gallon trash container every week. They also fill a 64-gallon container for recyclables every other week. Paper, cardboard, bottles, cans, and plastics are all placed into a single recycling bin. The cost is $32 per month.

- ✔ Bill uses three gallons of gasoline a month in lawn mowers, leaf blowers, and so on. That's around $8 per month.

- ✔ Bill spends $15 per month in propane for a barbecue.

- ✔ The HVAC system broke down and cost $267 to fix, for a monthly total of $22.25.

- ✔ In the colder months, Bill burns liquid propane in the gas fireplace in the great room. His costs by month are

Month	Cost
January	$242
February	$180
March	$65
April	$10
October	$142
November	$265
December (Christmas cheer!)	$342

- Bill's wife loves candles; they cost around $28 per month.

- Bill spends $23 per month in batteries for remotes, flashlights, sprinkler controllers, and so forth.

- The house is on a septic tank, so there is no sewer. Every three years the tank must be pumped out (yuck . . .) at a cost of $300, which is $100 per year, or $8 per month. Last year a repair was made (double yuck!) at a cost of $480, which is amortized over ten years at $48 per year.

Bill Toomuch has a tiered, seasonal rate structure. The baseline usage rate for the first 1,033 kWh is $0.11430. (I didn't even know a thousandth of a penny existed.) For 101 to 130 percent of that baseline, the rate goes up to $0.12989, not much of an increase. For 131 to 200 percent of the baseline, usage costs $0.22944, and for 201 to 300 percent, the cost is $0.32146. This latter rate is nearly three times the base rate — quite a penalty! From a conservation standpoint, this means that if Bill can reduce his energy consumption by a few kWh, he'll save 32 cents per kWh because the upper tiers will be erased from the bill first.

1-800-743-5000
Assistance is available by
telephone 24 hours per day,
7 days per week.

| Local Office Address |

4636 MISSOURI FLAT RD
PLACERVILLE CA 95667

| Account Number |

February 2007

ACCOUNT SUMMARY

Service	Service Dates	Service
Electric	01/12/2007 To 02/12/2007	$402.79
Energy Commission Tax		0.51
TOTAL CURRENT CHARGES		$403.30
Previous Balance		560.58
01/23 Payment - Thank You		560.58 -

TOTAL AMOUNT DUE	$403.30
DUE DATE - 03/05/2007	

Rate Schedule : E1 SH Residential Service
Billing Days : 32 days

Serial	Rotating Outage Blk	Meter #	Prior Meter Read	Current Meter Read	Difference	Meter Constant	Usage
N		J78867	45,435	47,746	2,311	1	2,311 kWh

Charges

01/12/2007 - 02/12/2007
Electric Charges $402.79

Baseline Quantity	1,033.60000 kWh		
Balance Usage	1,033.60000 kWh	@	$0.11430
101-130% of Baseline	310.08000 kWh	@	$0.12989
131-200% of Baseline	723.52000 kWh	@	$0.22944
201-300% of Baseline	843.80000 kWh	@	$0.32146

Net Charges $402.79

The net charges shown above include the following component(s).
Please see definitions on Page 2 of the bill.

Generation	$190.05
Transmission	18.09
Distribution	142.04
Public Purpose Programs	18.38
Nuclear Decommissioning	0.69
Trust Transfer Amount (TTA)	14.60
DWR Bond Charge	10.84
Ongoing CTC	0.32
Energy Cost Recovery Amount	7.78

Taxes

Energy Commission Tax $0.51

TOTAL CHARGES   **$403.30**

Usage Comparison	Days Billed	kWh Billed	kWh per Day
This Year	32	2,311	72.2
Last Year	32	2,449	76.5

Figure 3-1: Sample electric utility bill.

94

To get some meaning out of all this gobbledygook, Bill simply divides the total of his bill by the number of kWh used. The result: 17.5 cents per kWh. (Comparing this to some other parts of the country is instructive. In central Florida, the overall rate is around 11.6 cents per kWh. In Milwaukee it's around 10.4 cents. As usual, California is leading the way into the future, which in this case is higher energy prices.)

Plotting Bill's energy expenditures

Table 3-2 shows an example of annual energy expenditures plotted by month.

Table 3-2   Monthly Energy Expenditures, Plotted by Month

Month	kWh used	Charges	Price/kWh	Total Utility Cost
Jan	2290	$380	$0.166	$762
Feb	2449	$433	$0.177	$753
Mar	2452	$456	$0.186	$602
Apr	2266	$407	$0.18	$547
May	1715	$290	$0.17	$430
June	1676	$325	$0.194	$465
July	1948	$404	$0.21	$544
Aug	1963	$443	$0.226	$583
Sep	1444	$267	$0.185	$407
Oct	1460	$267	$0.183	$549

Nov	1663	$312	$0.188	$717
Dec	2319	$406	$0.175	$888
Total		**$4,390**	$0.186 average	**$7,247**

Do a little calculation, and you see that Bill uses, on average, 1,970 kWh a month. For all his energy needs, he spends about $604 a month, $361 of which is for electric only.

Analyzing Bill's energy costs

If you take a close look at Bill's data, you'll notice a few interesting — and enlightening — details:

- ✔ The heater is on a lot in the winter, and the air-conditioner is on a lot in the summer. The rates are higher in the summer than they are in the winter. Your data should look similar, unless you have unusual climate conditions. If you're in a cold climate, the magnitudes of the data may be different, but the overall shape will be similar.

- ✔ You can establish your baseline usage by looking at the months in which no heating or air-conditioning is used at all. April and October are the usual candidates. In the example, Bill's approximate baseline electric usage is around 1,600 kWh. By subtracting each month's total from the baseline, it's possible to determine approximately how much Bill is spending on heating and air-conditioning:

Month	Cost
Jan	$368
Feb	$345
Mar	$183
Apr	$148

96

May	$37
June	$34
July	$94
Aug	$105
Sep	$0
Oct	$142
Nov	$295
Dec	$485

✔ The average American consumes around 20 kWh per day. Bill uses over three times that amount. His house is bigger, with a lot of extra goodies, but there still seems to be room for a lot of improvement.

✔ You can see how the kWh charge is higher in the summer on the seasonal rate structure.

Calculating Your Own Carbon Footprint

In addition to auditing your personal costs, taking a look at how much pollution you're generating in your home is worthwhile, particularly if your main goal is pollution efficiency. A very common term these days is *carbon footprint,* which just means how much carbon you're emitting into the atmosphere through your various energy consuming activities. Carbon (or more precisely, carbon dioxide) is important because it's the main cause of global warming.

Here's a fact of physics: When you consume energy, it doesn't simply go away; rather, it changes into some other form. Burning gasoline creates carbon dioxide and a thousand other pollutants. The chemical and atomic bonds between the molecules and atoms in the gasoline are broken down, and heat is released in the process. To put things into perspective, consider that a gallon of gasoline weighs

Greenhouse effect and global warming

The best way to understand the phenomenon of global warming is to consider your own car sitting in the hot sun. Window glass transmits sunlight so that it enters the interior of your car. The sunlight then hits the seats, the floor, and so on and is converted into heat. The heat begins to build up inside the car because the same window glass that let the sunlight into the car resists letting the heat back out. Windows are excellent transmitters of light, but very poor transmitters of heat (good insulators, in other words).

The earth's atmosphere operates like a window. It lets in sunlight very nicely, but it also has insulation properties. When increased carbon dioxide is trapped in the atmosphere, sunlight transmission is basically unaffected, but the insulation properties are increased, so more heat is trapped. Hence, our planet is getting warmer for the same reason that your car gets warmer when it's sitting in the sun. The phenomenon is called the *greenhouse effect*; it explains why greenhouses work so well in the wintertime (and may get too hot in the summer).

only 6 pounds, but in the process of burning it in your auto engine, 20 pounds of carbon dioxide is released. This is a higher weight than the original fuel because oxygen from the air is combined with the liquid gasoline in the auto's carburetor. So the pollution that comes from burning gasoline weighs more than the original gasoline, and valuable oxygen is taken from the air and replaced with polluting CO_2.

Table 3-3 lists how much carbon pollution is released into the atmosphere due to the consumption of common energy sources.

Table 3-3   Carbon Pollution of Common Energy Sources

Energy Source	Pounds CO_2 / Unit
Oil	22.4/gallon
Natural gas	12.1/British thermal unit
Liquid propane	12.7/gallon
Kerosene	21.5/gallon
Gasoline	19.6/gallon
Coal	4,166/ton
Electricity	1.75/kilowatt hour
Wood	3,814/ton

As you digest the info from Table 3-3, keep these points in mind:

✔ The amount of carbon pollution generated by the production of electricity varies quite a bit depending on the type of generators being used. States with nuclear power can generate as little as 0.03 lb/kWh, while regions with coal plants may produce as much as 2.24. The national average is 1.75.

✔ Wood that is left on the forest floor emits the same amount of CO_2 as it rots away as it does when it's burned, so whether burning wood is really polluting the atmosphere is an interesting question. The same cannot be said for the other combustion sources, because if they're left alone, there is no pollution at all. (Of course, it should also be mentioned that if you're out in the woods working your tail off, you're a lot healthier than the average couch potato, and that has its advantages.)

Did you know that your home is probably emitting more CO_2 than your car? Just because you can't see it with your naked eye doesn't mean it's not there. Consider these tidbits:

- ✔ A typical midsized automobile that travels 12,000 miles annually emits around 13,000 pounds of CO_2 per year.

- ✔ A typical home that uses 600 gallons of home heating oil emits around 13,500 pounds of CO_2 per year.

- ✔ A typical North American home consumes around 700 kWh per month in electricity, for an emission of 14,700 pounds of CO_2 per year.

- ✔ If you burn a cord of firewood for heat, you're emitting around 3,814 pounds of CO_2.

Auditing Your Home to Find Areas for Improvement

Once you've finished crunching the numbers, you're ready for the next phase of your home audit. Now you need to go around and carefully inspect both the interior and exterior of your home and identify areas where you can make improvements. Most people find that a majority of improvements are simple and can be done by a do-it-yourselfer for less than a hundred dollars. Some projects, however, are big, and in Part II, I help you determine how to handle these.

An audit of your home helps you accomplish five key objectives, listed here in order of importance:

- ✓ **Ensuring safety.** Safety is the most important aspect of any home. If your home is not safe and free of contaminants, it doesn't matter how efficient it is in other regards.

- ✓ **Maximizing your house's longevity and durability.** The biggest detriment to a home's lifetime is moisture problems, which only get worse when ignored.

- ✓ **Enhancing your home's livability.** Air leaks affect both the livability of a home and the amount of energy it takes to heat and cool a home.

- ✓ **Analyzing the costs and benefits of making improvements.** The more you know, the better the decisions you make.

- ✓ **Creating a game plan that enables you to make your home more efficient.** Having a plan can save time and money and help you target the most important areas.

 If you have gas-burning equipment and, like most people, are not well-versed in the technology, hiring a professional auditor to inspect it is usually best. I do not give you instructions in this book on how to inspect or adjust gas-fired machinery because there are too many different kinds, and they're too dangerous to be messing around with.

Grunting it out: The inspection

In this section, I explain how to systematically inspect your home. I get into a lot of detail in the bulk of this book on how to address problems when you find them. In this section, I just tell you where to look for problems. If you find one, look at the chapter that addresses that specific issue. For instance, if you find moisture under your washing machine, go to Chapter 11 on appliances. If you find an air leak, go to Chapter 7, which tells you how to seal your home.

So put on your grungiest clothes, because you're going to be climbing around in your basement and attic. First up: Go around your home and carefully look at everything. You've probably glanced around before, but now you're going to sharpen your focus. The following sections take you through the various areas of your home and explain what to pay attention to.

Foundation and structural elements

The place to begin your inspection is outside and beneath your home. Although you live inside, what happens outside is of critical importance:

- Look up into all your eaves. Are there vents? Are they dirty? Are there bug nests? Moisture damage (look for spots and mildew)? Is wood rotting anywhere? How's the paint job?

- Inspect the foundation. Are there openings or gaps? Why? Are the gaps sealed where pipes feed through? Are there vents? Are they dirty? Are there cracks in concrete or masonry walls? Are pads secure and dry?

- Underneath your house, look for moisture issues. Where is the water coming from? Why? Does it stink?

- If you have a basement, go down there and look for water leaks and air leaks. Check to see if the pipes are insulated. Check for signs of pesky little rodents.

- Check out your roof (be very careful; falling off

the roof is more common than you may think). Is it leaking anywhere that you know of? What's the condition? At what point are you going to have to get a new roof?

✔ On the outside of your house, inspect wherever two different types of building materials come together. Are these joints sealed? Is there leakage?

Attic

Checking for water leaks is your first order of business in the attic. Finding evidence of these may be difficult. If you do find evidence of a leak, you may have trouble tracing it up to the roof where it's coming in, but it pays to try.

You also want to pay attention to the insulation in your attic. Are there gaps in it? Are there voids around ceiling light fixtures? Is there evidence of rodents or pests? Do you see a lot of spider webs? Are there vents to the outside world? Are they dirty so that air has a difficult time passing through?

Also check out your attic vent system (see Chapter 13 for more details).

Plumbing

If you can, make a sketch of your plumbing system, including both hot and cold water pipes. Where do they go? Where are the feed-throughs? After you complete this schematic, look at the following things:

✔ Are there any leaks? Are the hot water pipes covered with insulation? Are the pipes adequately tacked down, or are they flopping around? Is the system old? Rusty?

✔ Are there any dripping faucets? Check both inside

and out. Do the faucets work the way they should?

✔ Check for clogged drains (especially in a basement floor; these are incredible sources of microbes).

✔ Are you aware of any plumbing problems? Toilets that don't work the way they should? Shower drains that are too slow? Unpleasant odors in bathrooms, kitchens, laundry rooms, garages?

✔ Check under all your sinks for leaks. They'll usually stink, and the particleboard will be moldering and warped. Where's the leak coming from? Maybe the disposal is leaking. You may have to turn the water on to find out.

Heating and cooling

Since heating and cooling costs are the biggest factor in most home's energy use, it pays to check out heating and cooling systems on a periodic basis.

✔ Do certain parts of your house always seem too warm or too cold? Find out why; if you poke around, you may be able to unearth the cause. Is there a draft somewhere? If you have a difficult time, consult an HVAC professional.

✔ Is one heater vent always too hot compared to the others? Too cold? Check out the ductwork to find potential problems. In my experience, a majority of homes have gaps in the ductwork and don't know it. These are easy and inexpensive to fix. (See Chapter 7 for instructions and suggestions.)

To find leaks in a forced-air HVAC's ductwork, turn your HVAC system on and get access to the ducts (this may be a real hassle in your attic or basement, requiring you to twist into odd pretzel shapes, but forge on for the good of humanity!). Dip your hand into a bowl of water (a wet hand makes air movement much easier to feel) and move your hand around the ducts, particularly where the joints are, and check for air leaks. Check where the ducts join up to the registers leading into your home.

Insulation

Can you find out what kind of insulation is in the walls and ceilings? How thick is it? You don't need a numerical measurement, but you want to try to see whether it fills the voids. If you're in an old house, you probably don't have very good insulation. Also find out whether there's insulation beneath your floors, particularly below the area where you spend the greatest amount of time (probably the family room).

Windows

Are your windows single-pane or double-pane? Do you have storm windows? Do you use them? Do you have blinds? Do you use them? How about solar screens for the summertime?

If you have a window that gets condensation between the two panes of glass, you have a leak in the seal. It won't affect the window's net insulation very much, but the windows will sooner or later become permanently obscured.

Filters

Check out all the filters in your home. Furnace filters are located at the input vent; you should replace these regularly. If you don't, they'll become extremely dirty. Exhaust fans sometimes have filters that you may not even know about.

Look up inside; take off the cover cowling if you need to. Dryers have lint filters. Faucets have filters that regularly collect crud. If your faucet is squirting around erratically, change the filter.

Other places to investigate

In addition to the obvious places to look, here are some more candidates.

- ✔ Check out your fireplace. Is the damper working properly? (It should move so that it opens and closes easily.) Have you been operating it properly? Are any seals old and frayed?

- ✔ Check out your fuse box. Do you have problems with blown fuses for which you can't seem to identify a reason? Are wires frayed? Is the box covered well? Trace some wires and try to get the gist of the overall layout of your home's electrical system.

- ✔ Check under all appliances and sinks for moisture. Where is it coming from?

- ✔ Go through your home and check out the wattage of each light bulb. Note what type of bulb each is. You can probably get by with a lot less wattage, and in a lot of spots you could change to a fluorescent (see Chapter 9 for more details).

- ✔ Look for air leaks. In Chapter 7, I describe a method for finding air leaks in your home.

Hiring professional auditors

If you're not up to the challenge of auditing your own home, simply don't want to, or have gas-burning equipment, you may decide to go with a professional. Several sources are available.

You can call your power company, which will probably do an audit for you. It may be a mail-in type of deal, in which case you may as well just struggle through it yourself because by the time you're done compiling enough information to make the mail-in audit worthwhile, you basically will have done the job yourself. The same applies to Internet audits. Plus, online resources that offer energy audits will probably try to sell you something you don't need.

Professional audit companies will impress you with all their cool stuff. They have fancy gizmos that use invisible infrared light to measure the temperature of your interior surfaces, and they use them to pinpoint leaks. They'll check out your furnace, which is worthwhile. They'll inspect your ductwork and look for cracks in your foundation. They can tell you in precise mathematical terms just how leaky your house is.

But the fact is, the biggest inefficiencies are usually easy to detect, especially if you've never even tried before. I can tell you from experience doing audits that most houses have glaring problems that can usually be fixed for less than a few hundred dollars. The biggest culprit? Loose joints in the ductwork, which result in untold hundreds of dollars of wasted energy costs per year. And you can fix them up with aluminum or duct tape for less than $10.

If you do decide to hire an auditor, look here:

- Consult NAESCO (National Association of Energy Service Companies) at 202-822-0950 or www. naesco.org.

- In the phone book, look under "energy conservation services and products." Locate utility companies under "electric service," "utility providers," or "gas utility companies."

✔ Check out hes.lbl.gov for a free home energy audit and carbon footprint estimates.

✔ For a sample of an energy audit, look at www.pge.com/energysurvey/.

As you check out different auditors, consider the following:

✔ Do you want to make a change or improvement in your home? Ask how this would fit in with the results of your audit and ask for some advice. Auditors have tons of experience, and they're usually proud to expound.

✔ Ask about financing programs the company has for improvements the auditor suggests.

✔ Ask about guarantees for their work. If they tell you that you can achieve a certain cost reduction, how accurate do they warrant that claim to be?

 Tell the auditors before they come out to your home that you want them to tell you which jobs you can do yourself. If they balk, find somebody else.

After you hire a professional auditor, you still need to do a bit of work yourself, which essentially requires amassing some info:

✔ **Assemble all your electric and utility bills.** Go back two or three years.

✔ **Make a list of occupants' habits regarding energy usage.** Are you home all day every day (is anyone?), or are you home mainly during the evenings, for example?

✔ **Note the thermostat setting in your house.** Do you change it depending on the season or other factors?

✔ **Make a list of questions you have.** If something seems wrong with your house, write that down, too.

Chapter 4

Financing Efficiency Improvements

. . . .

In This Chapter

▶ Looking into the various incentives and assistance programs available

▶ Using loans to finance your energy-efficiency projects

▶ Working with banks and financial institutions

. . . .

A lot of government programs are geared toward helping consumers make efficiency improvements. These range from solar subsidies to Department of Energy programs designed to help you decide which appliances are the most energy-efficient. Not only can you get information, but you can also get free money in the form of subsidies, tax breaks, and rebates. I'd rather have free money, so I focus more on that aspect in this chapter.

Utility companies also offer a range of programs, including free information as well as free money. The programs available are too numerous for me to list in detail, and they're constantly changing, so I tell you how to research the benefits they offer on your own.

Last but not least, you may want to consider financing your energy-efficiency improvements via a loan. I tell you the best way to go about doing so, and I give you some tips on how to work with banks.

Understanding the Different Types of Assistance

Many different types of government assistance are available, and it pays to understand exactly how the various programs differ from each other.

For those skeptics out there who are howling, "There's no such thing as a free lunch," I'm with you 100 percent. But if you take into account how much money you pay in taxes and utility bills, all you're really doing here is getting some of it back, and that's hardly a free lunch. It's more like paying for somebody else's lunch for three days in a row, and then having them pay for part of yours one day.

Rebates

Rebates are money that's given back to a customer after a purchase is made. You're probably familiar with rebates for consumer goods like appliances, and energy-efficiency rebates operate basically the same way. But being born of government, the latter are laden with details generally incomprehensible to the average layperson.

The way solar rebates work in California serves as an example of the complexity involved. For a PV system, you can get up to 25 percent of the system's cost in rebates, but the actual amount depends on the system's productivity. (PV stands for *photovoltaic*, which is a solar electrical generating apparatus.) The state has a very specific computer program that predicts system performance. Inputs are

- ✔ **Your geographical location:** Data banks have been created with the statistical weather patterns in your area.

- ✔ **The size and orientation of your solar collectors:** The greatest solar exposure comes from a specific roof angle (depending on your latitude) and a specific azimuth angle — namely, true south.

- ✔ **Whether your solar collectors are in full sunshine or not:** If a tree or building shades your solar collectors, they collect less sunlight energy, which is a form of inefficiency.

- ✔ **The efficiency of your system:** This is also related to a system's productivity.

For a perfect solar location, the state will rebate 25 percent of the cost of your solar system. Most rebates come in at around 20 to 24 percent. When they come in much lower than that, your solar investment quickly loses allure and cost effectiveness declines.

The rebate is paid directly to the professional solar contractor, so the customer does not need to finance the entire investment and then wait to get the rebate back. This is a good facet because it means you don't have to front the money.

A *buy-down* caveat complicates the matter even further. As time progresses, the rebates are scheduled to decrease, which encourages solar customers to buy now rather than later. Ideally, as the rebates diminish, prices will come down due to market forces so the net cost of a system won't change over time. (Well, okay. But when do government programs ever work the way they're supposed to? On the other hand, just be glad you don't get all the government that you pay for.)

As you can see, free government money comes with some complexity and many strings attached, and it pays to understand the details. But it's free money, so what's the beef?

Tax credits

Tax credits are an increasingly common form of subsidy. You must buy a certain type of system to qualify, and the credit is taken on either your state or federal tax return. This means you must carry the cost until your return is filed, and any refund comes back to you. This can take over a year, depending on when you buy a system. Still, a tax credit is far better than a tax deduction, and here's why: A tax deduction is subtracted from your income so that your tax burden is less. If you're paying a marginal tax rate of 28 percent and you get a deduction for $1,000, you save $280. A tax credit, on the other hand, is subtracted from your taxes. A $1,000 tax credit saves you $1,000! Yee-ha!

For example, the federal government allows a 30 percent tax credit for both hydro turbine systems and solar water-heating systems, up to a maximum of $2,000 per year. If your solar water heater costs $6,000 to install, you get $2,000 off the price. If your hydro turbine costs $30,000, you only get $2,000 off the price. This encourages smaller investments because you save a greater percentage. The way to game this strategy is to spread your investments out over time. Install a solar water heater this year, and a hydro turbine next. And if possible, install two small systems instead of one big one.

113

By understanding the precise details, you can achieve more benefit from the programs.

Protection from property tax increases

Many states have laws that prevent your property taxes from rising due to the increase in value of your home from an efficiency investment. So if you install a $40,000 solar PV system, your county cannot reassess your property and charge you extra taxes for having a home that's worth $40,000 more.

Home-operated business advantages

If you have a home business or office, you may qualify for the higher tax credits and rebates that are offered as incentives for businesses to become more energy efficient. Businesses can also take advantage of accelerated depreciation schedules for most energy-efficiency equipment.

Why do businesses get bigger tax breaks and rebates? One reason is that businesses use most of their energy in the middle of the afternoon when the greatest burden is being shouldered by the utilities. Another is that the green spirit that motivates many energy-efficiency investments does not exist for businesses.

 Taking advantage of these incentives can get complex; ask your tax preparer for the details.

Net metering

Net metering means that you can sell your solar generated power to the utilities by hooking up special equipment to your household electrical system. Utilities are not particularly enthusiastic about offering rebates, nor do they really want residential customers to hook solar equipment up to the grid (not because they're grouchy, but because it diminishes their business base). Recognizing this, the 1978 federal Public Utility Regulatory Policy Act (PURPA) mandates local utilities to pay "avoided" or wholesale costs to entities that wish to sell it. In other words, the utilities must pay you exactly what it costs them to produce the power they would be providing; they can't profit from your being hooked up to the grid. They may not pay you exactly what they sell you the power for, but they have to pay you exactly what it costs them.

This is the basis for net metering, which makes solar PV investment viable (see Chapter 16 for details of the whys and wherefores). Without net metering, solar PV would be no more than a rare novelty (like good pop music).

States often have even more stringent net metering rules. In California, the utilities must pay you the same rate that they charge for power (rather than the "avoided cost"). For instance, if you're on a time of use (TOU) rate schedule, the utility must pay you the same rates it charges customers at different times of the day. This is a very strong incentive for installing solar systems because the highest power rates are always in the middle of the afternoon, which is also the time when solar PV systems are outputting at the maximum rate. So if you have a PV intertie system (*intertie* means you're hooked up to the power grid), you can game your power consumption to leverage the exchange of energy (see Chapter 16 for the technical details).

Manufacturers' rebates

Manufacturers' rebates work the same for energy-efficiency improvements as they do for other products. You buy a system or component, and the manufacturer either gives you an instant rebate or one that you send away for by mailing in proof of your purchase. These rebates are very common these days, especially for products that feature the Energy Star label (see Chapter 11 for more details on Energy Star).

Tax-deductible home-equity loans

Although they may not be a direct subsidy of energy-efficiency improvements, tax-deductible home-equity loans are akin to government subsidies because you can write off the interest on such loans (writing it off means subtracting it from your taxable income, resulting in a smaller net tax burden).

If you take out a second mortgage to pay for your energy-efficiency equipment, the government lets you deduct the interest on that loan. So if you're making a monthly payment of, say, $300 for a second mortgage, your net cost may be only $200. It works exactly like a subsidy.

Researching Your Subsidy Options

Things are changing so fast, keeping up with all the different government programs is impossible. I can only point you in the right direction and give you a nudge. It's up to you to poke around and get all the details for yourself. Here's how to research the subject further:

✔ **Talk to your tax preparer.** This person should be well-versed in the details of tax credits and deductions. If not, he'll be able to access the information sources that will be needed to process your rebates and tax credits. Many of these programs are relatively new; give your preparer a break if he doesn't know the details upfront, but keep at him to find out. Expect to pay more for your tax preparation because more forms will be required (indecipherable to the average layperson, so if you're thinking about preparing your own, be forewarned).

✔ **Talk to energy-efficiency contractors.** These people know all the subsidies because this knowledge helps them sell systems. PV contractors are experts at tax credits and rebates, and they will usually help you process them as well. Most stove stores know the ins and outs of local ordinances and whether utility rebates are available.

✔ **Ask your utility company.** Utilities don't necessarily want to give you information, but they have to. So if you push a little, you can get all kinds of information, and it's almost always free. Call the customer service number on your utility bill and go from there. Ask too many questions, even if they don't seem appropriate. You'll be surprised at how much you can find out this way. And be very nice; they're not used to that, being what they are. If you're nice, they may even go out of their way to be nice right back. Just don't expect it.

✔ **Look online.** The Internet is a great source of information. Use a search engine to look up key words like "solar energy tax incentives," "energy efficiency rebates," and so on. Here are some Web sites to consult for more details:

- www.dsireusa.org

- www.consumerenergycenter.org/renewables/ estimator

- www.energystar.gov/taxcredits

- www.energytaxincentives.org

- www.epa.gov

 When doing research, keep in mind that subsidies may be available for all kinds of systems. For instance, if you install an energy-efficient front door, you may qualify for a 10-percent tax credit. Gas fireplaces may get you a credit. Be expansive in your search, and you can find all sorts of little goodies.

Financing through Loans

Many energy-efficiency investments are large enough that you may need to take out a loan to implement them. There are several different types of loans you can pursue. This section gives you the lowdown. (For advice on securing your loan from a bank, see the section "Working with Banks: Their Way or the Highway" later in this chapter.)

Consumer loans

Consumer loans don't require any collateral, so the risk is high. You can get a credit card with a $30,000 credit limit far easier than should ever be possible. The reason it's so easy? The interest rate is sky high; the bank expects a number of defaults, and lets the customers who don't default cover the losses from the ones who do. Plus, you don't get any sort of tax deduction on the interest, so the net result is that these loans are even costlier. These creditors are the modern version of loan sharks, although they no longer break your fingers when you default. If you're a good credit risk, avoid consumer loans like the plague and get a loan that's more beneficial to you.

Supplier loans

Supplier loans are available from manufacturers and suppliers who provide energy-efficiency equipment. They use the equipment itself as collateral. These loans are somewhat akin to automobile loans that are offered by car dealers to buyers who purchase a vehicle. The car is collateral, so if you don't make your loan payment, they come to your house late at night and take back the car — perfectly legal. If you default on one of these loans for your solar equipment, they may come in the middle of the night and grab the collectors off your roof. You probably won't mistake them for Santa Claus.

Equity loans

Equity loans are the most common option, and they're also the best. In those parts of the country where real estate values are rising, homeowners enjoy equity, which is the difference between what is owed in mortgages on the home and the home's market value (or appraised value, which should be the same but rarely is).

You can use your equity to get a loan at a much lower interest rate because the bank's risk is greatly reduced by using real estate as collateral. They don't need to come after the equipment you have financed (they generally don't care what you do with the money, so they may not even know about your new energy-efficiency equipment) because they can go after the house itself. They know that homeowners are going to pay off their debts long before they let a bank take their home away.

Furthermore, home-equity loans are generally tax deductible (consult your tax preparer blah, blah, blah). If your combined state and federal marginal tax rate is 35 percent,

$100 per month in interest payments only costs you $65.

Government-subsidized, energy-efficiency loans

The government is interested in promoting energy efficiency, so it makes a wide range of loan subsidies available. In essence, the government accepts part of the risk of the loan, and a bank therefore can offer you a lower interest rate. Looking into the various government programs is worth your while because you can often get a loan for better terms.

Home energy ratings

A number of financing programs are available for energy-efficiency improvements (solar, in particular) to homes that qualify. In order to qualify, you need to have your home audited and rated by a licensed expert, who writes a report estimating annual energy use and costs. You can also expect some recommendations for improvements that may have to be implemented as a condition of loan approval. To get the best loan terms, you have to convince the financing institution that the improvements you intend to fund with the loan make sense in the grand scheme of things. That's reasonable.

If things look good, you can take advantage of special energy-efficient financing programs that offer lower interest rates than conventional loans. Keep in mind, however, that with these loans you're required to pay for the energy audit and interface with government agencies.

Energy Efficient Mortgages (EEMs)

There are two types of Energy Efficient Mortgages (EEMs):

one for existing homes and another for new ones. Here's a quick breakdown of who's providing what, but keep in mind that we're talking about the government here, so terms and programs are subject to change at the whim of a congressperson from the boondocks:

- Fannie Mae, the Federal National Mortgage Association, encourages lenders to provide EEMs by establishing guidelines and certain types of incentives. Check out what's available at www.fanniemae.com.

- Freddie Mac, the Federal Home Mortgage Loan Corporation, is basically the same as Fannie Mae, but is generally more interested in long-term loans. Check it out at www.freddiemac.com.

- Farmer Mac (part of the U.S. Department of Agriculture) is for those of you who are down on the farm. Go to www.usda.gov.

Here are some other potentially useful government agencies (I said potentially):

- **Department of Energy (DOE):** www.doe.gov.

- **Department of Housing and Urban Development (HUD):** www.hud.gov.

- **State agencies:** Often providers of subsidized loans in addition to federal agencies. Check out the prospects at www.naseo.org (National Association of State Energy Officials).

- **Residential Energy Services Network (RESNET):** A network of mortgage bankers, builders, and so forth. Check them out at www.natresnet.org.

Other sources of subsidized financing

Utilities may provide subsidized financing as well. Not because they want to, but because they're required to by law. You can find a customer-service number on your utility bill, and there may even be a particular branch dedicated to subsidized loans.

Equipment vendors sometimes provide loans, just like car dealers. However, they generally sign up with an equity loan broker and simply act as a sales outlet for that broker's loans. You could probably find slightly better interest rates by going directly to a bank, but the convenience may offset the cost. Or, a vendor may actually offer better terms because they have a strong incentive to close the sale, and making inexpensive financing available helps considerably.

Leasing Energy-Efficient Equipment

Here's a new financing idea that's taking hold: Companies install solar equipment on your roof, but they retain ownership of the equipment. You basically lease it from them for either a fixed monthly cost or a percentage of the system's production. This works nicely if you save more on your power bill than the monthly cost of the lease. You don't have to maintain the equipment because it's not yours.

Alternatively, you can use these programs to lock in the cost of your energy so that when it rises, you are securely hedged. You don't have to have any cash up front, and this is a very popular way to finance a big purchase, as evidenced by how many autos are leased on the same basic principle. Ultimately, financing the equipment yourself — actually purchasing it rather than leasing it — is almost always a better investment from a return standpoint. But many people simply don't have the cash, prefer to spend their money on something else, or don't want to sign up for a loan because it will appear on a credit application.

Be aware that, just as with cars, there is a residual value at the end of the lease, and if your equipment has decreased in value for some reason, you may have to pay a big chunk to get out of the lease.

Working with Banks: Their Way or the Highway

In my view, banks rank (and rank they are) right up there with governmental institutions for charm and affability. Regardless of which financial institution or bank you decide to work with, you're better prepared if you know how banks work and what rules you need to (or should) follow.

The reason people get so frustrated at bankers is that they have hordes of rules and regulations that come from above. This may seem onerous to you, the consumer, but it makes perfect sense from the bank's standpoint because mistakes cost a lot of money and need to be avoided. When you approach a bank for a loan, keep these things in mind:

 ✔ **Banks have very rigid rules and procedures.** The people you will be talking to have absolutely no power to alter these. If you don't package your programs, proposals, and ideas in the bank's format, you're wasting your time.

 ✔ **You, the borrower, are not the bank's customer.** A bank's customers are the people who give them money, not the people who borrow it. Banks make profits (capitalism's central objective) by lending you money at higher rates than they have to pay their customers for their money.

✔ **Banks are concerned with risk.** They constantly strive to make loans at the lowest risk possible. When somebody defaults on a mortgage, especially a second one, it's very costly for the bank. If you want to do business with a bank, your goal should be to present yourself as a low-risk proposition.

Chapter 5

Making Tradeoffs That Work for You

Not all investments in efficiency improvement take cash. You can do many things around your home that involve simply changing your consumption habits or changing the way you set your thermostat. But almost all investments require you to choose from among several alternatives. Having only a single choice on your hands is rare. Choosing wisely requires a system of balancing energy efficiency, financial efficiency, pollution efficiency, and labor efficiency, and everybody prioritizes these criteria in their own way. In this chapter, I show you how to account for the various factors that come into play in your decision-making process.

125

Setting Efficiency Investment Goals

When you make investments — in time, money, or just sheer effort — to become more energy-efficient, the trick is to put together a strategy that works for you and helps you meet your own goals. Whereas one person's goal may be solely to become more "green," another person's goal may be to reduce consumptions simply to save money. And quite a few people, no doubt, want to make gains in both areas: saving money *and* doing more to help the environment.

Think of investments in energy efficiency as you would financial investments. There are more similarities than you may realize:

✔ **Choosing options that work for you.** Financial investment pros help their clients assemble a portfolio, or mixture, of investments from the many options available. You also have myriad options in investments for energy efficiency. One option is not to invest in energy efficiency at all. You can just leave your house the way it is. When something breaks, you don't have to replace it with a new, improved version; you can just put the same thing back in.

Alternatively, you can make small investments that garner small, but real, rewards. Examples include replacing incandescent light bulbs with energy-efficient bulbs, caulking around your window frames to keep the draft out, or wrapping your furnace ducts in insulation to keep the warmth in. Maybe you're into big changes: replacing the old double-furnace in your basement with a brand new energy-efficient model, or scrapping traditional heating

126

systems altogether and going solar. The point is that you can take big steps or little steps, but all steps lead you in the right direction.

✔ **Dealing with risk.** An important factor to consider in building a financial portfolio is the risk profile. Some investments entail more risk than others and need to offer more of a chance for gain to offset the increased risk. The same is true with energy-efficiency investments: To justify the expense of a big-ticket item, you need to see a big return — whether in cost savings, energy efficiency, or feel-good factor.

✔ **Shielding yourself from future price fluctuations.** Hedging, paying a certain amount now to lock in prices in the future, reduces financial risk. If you invest in energy efficiency, you shield your utility bill from energy price fluctuations because when rates rise, you don't feel the pinch nearly as much. If you put a solar system on your roof that reduces your energy bills to zero, that's exactly where they will stay, even if the cost of energy quadruples. That's a powerful form of hedging.

Analyzing Investments

In this section I present a system for analyzing investments. The goal is to compare different options and choose the best one. The idea is to compare costs to gains, with risk and other non-numerical factors moderating the results.

Basically, you need to look at two things:

✔ **How long it'll take to earn back the money**

invested, or *payback*. In the case of most energy-efficiency improvements, you have to invest cash before you see a single dime of savings. Payback is measured in months, or even years. Here's an example. You invest $2,000 in an on-demand water heater, which saves $30 a month in electric costs. Dividing 2,000 by 30 equals 67 months, or about 5½ years.

As you think about payback, remember that good decisions aren't just predicated on dollars and cents. You also need to consider the intangibles, like aesthetic beauty and pollution mitigation, among others.

✔ **How energy-efficiency investments compare to other investments.** This is a key issue for those who see the money savings as the key reason for becoming more energy efficient.

Considering the costs, financial and otherwise

So how much is any particular energy-efficiency investment going to cost you? You need to know before you can determine whether you can afford to implement it or, for that matter, given the potential savings that such an investment can bring, whether you can afford *not* to. When you think about any energy-efficiency investment, consider these potential costs:

✔ **Equipment:** How much will equipment cost, and when will you pay for it? Sometimes equipment costs are spread out over time. You need to specify the time line. For instance, if you are purchasing a new HVAC system on a credit card, the payments

128

will be monthly until the balance is paid off. Chapter 3 tells you how to determine the annual costs associated with a big purchase.

- ✔ **Installation costs:** If you're hiring a pro, how much will it cost and when are these funds due? If you're going to do it yourself, figure in the cost of any tools or other equipment you need to buy.

- ✔ **Refuse cost:** Will you pay to have project trash hauled away?

- ✔ **Lifetime and warranty:** What is the likelihood that you will have to pay for servicing? How often? How much will it cost? Warranties are very important for big ticket items because they usually have big ticket costs associated with repairs. And some manufacturers are better at taking care of warranty issues than others.

- ✔ **Taxes, permits, and fees:** How much are they and when are they due? Will your property taxes go up as a result of an efficiency investment? This is rare, but you should find out whether it applies to you.

- ✔ **Interest:** Will you finance your equipment? If so, the interest is a cost.

- ✔ **Maintenance:** The type of energy-efficiency equipment that's designed to handle big jobs tends to be pretty complex. You need to understand how it works and perform periodic maintenance tasks to keep it working up to snuff. You won't usually know when something's going to need fixing or how much it's going to cost.

- ✔ **Safety:** When you install complex technical equipment, you're introducing dangers into your home. Electrical shocks. Scalding water. Falling off a roof. Discovering stepladder malfunctions. Smoke and ventilation issues. You get the point.

✓ **Inexperience:** If you design and install a system yourself, it may not perform as well as you thought it would. The experts know all the little tricks that you don't. Savings can suffer, and you may have to pay an expert to come in and set things straight.

Of course, financial costs aren't the only ones you should consider. Most changes require readjustments. As you count costs, determine which of the following apply to the change you want to make and how willing you are to either accept them or make the necessary accommodations:

✓ **Changing habits:** With some energy-efficiency equipment, you have to change your consumption habits to take best advantage of the potential. For instance, if you install a solar hot water heater, taking showers in the late afternoon is better than taking them early in the morning. How willing are you to make the changes? Furthermore, with some energy-efficiency investments, the only requirement is to change habits; no cash is invested at all. An example of this is taking shorter showers.

✓ **Inconvenience:** Is your system going to require more work on your part? Wood stoves take a lot of maintenance and cleaning. Are you going to do it? How much is your time worth? Are some jobs more or less repulsive than others?

✓ **The clutter factor:** Do you sometimes feel as though your life is spinning out of control? There's too much of this, too much of that, and too much clutter (not just physical, but emotional as well). Do you want to bite off even more?

- ✔ **The how-it-looks factor:** Sometimes equipment can be ugly. Do the pipes running up the side of your house look industrial? Do PV panels make your house look unearthly? Conversely, many projects make your home look much nicer. Given two projects with equal numbers, you're more apt to choose the one that offers aesthetic beauty or pride in ownership. In fact, you may favor these types of projects enough to choose them even when the payback isn't all that terrific.

- ✔ **The how-it-smells factor:** Yes, some energy-efficiency devices tend to stink, like biomass generators or compost toilets.

Estimating gains

After you think about all the costs — financial, aesthetic, and otherwise — of your potential efficiency investment, you need to think about the ways the investment pays you back. So how can you make money from your investments? Let me count the ways.

Lower monthly utility bills

With most energy-efficiency investments, saving money is the ultimate goal. You need to take a look at how much you're paying now versus how much you'll be paying after the investment. This may be very difficult to estimate, but it's worth a try.

When estimating cost reductions, always use the rate structures that apply both before and after you finish the project. For instance, when you install a solar PV system, you'll likely be getting a new power meter and a new rate structure. You may be going from a tiered structure to a time-of-day structure, in which case you should estimate the new cost savings by the time-of-day structure. (See Chapter 3 for more details on rate structures.)

Sometimes you can save money by doing nothing more than changing rate structures. For instance, if you're away from home all afternoon and you change your electric rate structure from simple (which just charges you the same rate regardless of when you use the power) to TOU (time of use, which charges different rates at different times of day, you will probably save money without doing anything else. Talk to your utility company to see whether this is an option for you.

Appreciation

The value of your home goes up when you make most improvements. The amount of the appreciation depends on the following factors:

- **How much it would cost a buyer to put in new equipment himself.** Don't expect to get much more than that. But if the cost of new equipment increases, the value of your equipment can also go up. For the most part, your home only increases in value by a percentage of what you put into investments. A kitchen remodel, for instance, nominally increases the value of your home by about 70 percent of what you spend (if you contract out the entire job). Installing a gas fireplace insert returns around 65 percent.

- **How much documentation you can provide to verify the energy savings that are achieved with the equipment.** If you can show (with documentation) that you've saved a certain amount of money, you're in a stronger position to recoup your investment when you sell your home.

✔ **How much the cost of energy goes up.** The more energy costs rise, the more your equipment is worth. This should be intuitive. The higher energy costs are, the more money you save from your efficiency investments. Plus, people get warier about future increases and will pay more to hedge against them.

✔ **How trendy the improvement is in your neck of the woods.** Some things sell because they're a fad. This is very true of green products these days (the term for hyped environmental products is *greenwashing*), and in some parts of the country, an energy-efficient home is worth a lot more than the same model with conventional energy. Look for this trend to expand, especially if energy costs spike upward.

Other plusses

Appreciation and cheaper utility bills aren't the only ways to recoup the cost of your investment. Following are other ways that efficiency changes can bolster your bottom line and/or your feel-good factor:

✔ **Deductions:** If you're installing equipment for your business or office, you may be able to depreciate certain items and gain some tax deductions.

✔ **Rebates and subsidies:** These come from utilities, state and federal governments, manufacturers, and so on. See Chapter 4 for details.

✔ **Aesthetics:** If you invest in a maple tree, you'll get shade performance, but the greater pleasure is having a nice tree near your house. When you invest in window coverings, you enjoy better insulation, but the greater gain is probably in the increased enjoyment you get from the improved appearance of your home.

- ✔ **Footprints:** When you invest in efficiency improvements, you're saving a lot of carbon dioxide. In Chapter 3, I give a brief outline for calculating how much this might be.

- ✔ **Money made from salvage:** You may be able to sell some of the old equipment you will be taking out.

Setting a baseline for comparison: Bank accounts and stock market yields

You can always put your hard-earned cash into a bank account and draw simple interest. It's the safest bet, one the Federal Government guarantees. Whenever you consider an investment, the proper starting point is always to consider how it compares to a bank account, so this is where I begin.

Say you put $1,000 in a savings account that earns 6 percent compounded interest. Twelve years after you make your original investment, you'll have $1,000 in interest, so this is the payback period. At any point in time you can pull your money out of the bank with zero risk. So you've done nothing but make money, right? Not exactly.

You pay income tax on interest income, so your net gain is going to be less than 6 percent. If you make $100 in interest and you're paying a 35 percent marginal tax rate (combined state and fed), you'll only net $65.

When you save money by investing in energy efficiency, you rarely, if ever, will be called upon to pay taxes on the

Value today versus value tomorrow

Strictly speaking, when doing payback calculations, changes in the value of money over time must be taken into account, which basically means that you should discount the value today of a dollar you expect to receive in the future.

Suppose you have a choice between two alternatives: $1 today or $1 a year from now. You take the $1 today, of course. But how much would you take today for a dollar in the future? To determine its future worth, you need to factor in the current interest rate or, even more precisely, what the interest rate is going to be over the course of the next year. Say the interest rate is 6 percent. You would then be trading $1.06 a year from now for $1 today.

In calculating payback, it works the other way around. For example, if you're going to save $100 a year from today, at 6 percent interest that $100 is worth only $94 right now. Saving $100 in ten years is worth only $54 today.

For the most part, I ignore this effect in the calculations, and there will be technical purists out there who cry out in indignation. But I'm trying to keep things simple. A good way to factor in the value of money over time without getting into weird math is simply to be liberally conservative (not conservatively liberal) in your estimates. The net effect will be the same.

money you save. This could make a significant difference in your investment decision, so you must always take taxes into account.

If you invest your money in the stock market and get a return of 12 percent, the payback period is only six years. Sounds good, but once again, you'll probably be paying income taxes on the gains. In addition, depending on the type of stocks you buy, the value of your stock could go down rather than up, maybe all the way to zero.

Looking at Real-World Investment Scenarios

The following examples give you a good idea of how to analyze your own investments. In some cases, you can just substitute your own numbers for the ones given. Other times, you may have to adjust the model to fit your exact situation. But the approach to each situation should be the same because the ultimate goal is to compare different investment scenarios; in order to do this, you have to analyze them under the same rules.

Supplementing an existing water heater with a solar system

Suppose you use 1,000 kWh of electricity per month. At 15 cents per kWh, your monthly cost is $150. An energy audit determines that water heating comprises 18 percent of your total electric bill, at a cost of $27 per month. Interested in saving money and reducing your carbon footprint, you look into a solar water heating system (one that works with your existing equipment).

You do your research and discover that the solar water heating system costs $2,000, including parts and installation. A federal government tax credit of 30 percent is available, for a total of $600, making the net cost of the system $1,400. The system comes with a five-year warranty.

Is this a good investment? The following sections take you through various scenarios that are tied to different goals so you can see how to determine the value of the investment in each instance.

Goal: To lower your utility payment and save money

In considering the solar water heating system, you do the calculations and realize that, using the data presented in the earlier example, it will take 52 months (the $1,400 net cost of the system divided by $27 in monthly savings) to recover your initial investment. The 60-month warranty ensures no maintenance costs in this time frame. However, say you live in the north, where there isn't as much sunshine and the winters are colder. You might find that your cost savings in this case would be $13.50 per month, or half as much as those of your counterpart in the sunnier, warmer region, and the payback period would be twice as long — 104 months. This isn't much different than what you'd get if you invested the money with a bank, where the risk would be nil. If you were making your decision solely on cost effectiveness, you'd decide this is a bad investment, and you'd look elsewhere (like maybe at a new gas fireplace).

Goal: To reduce your carbon footprint

How much is reducing pollution worth to you? Ten dollars a month? Twenty? How much would you pay to completely eliminate your carbon footprint altogether? $1,000 a year? This is difficult to estimate, but it gets to the very core of the issue. It's a fact that reducing pollution is going to cost everybody money; who will pay for it is subject to politics, and beyond the scope of this book. But in making everyday decisions, you must answer the question for yourself.

Here's how to proceed. The typical carbon footprint (for a 3-bedroom, 2-bath home with 2.3 occupants — and don't

137

ask me how you get 2.3 occupants) is around 40,000 pounds per year. The typical footprint from a water heater is 3,000 pounds per year, or 7.5 percent of the total footprint. If you are willing to spend $1,000 a year on erasing your carbon footprint, you'll spend 7.5 percent of this on heating water. That's $75 per year, or $6.25 per month. Add this to the savings column in the calculations and instead of only $13.50 per month, you're really saving $19.75. This makes the payback 70 months, which is a better proposition. If you're willing to spend $2,000 a year eliminating pollution, your total cost savings will be $26 per month, which leaves you with a payback of 53 months, almost identical to that in the original example. Now this is a good investment.

Note that if you're willing to spend $2,000 per year mitigating pollution, you don't actually end up spending this amount when you put the solar water heater in. You only spend 7.5 percent of it. But the rationale remains useful in comparing alternatives, some of which will save more pollution than others.

Goal: To offset the higher charges in a tiered rate billing system

In a tiered rate structure, not all watts are created equal. Your energy usage in kWh is structured into tiers (not unlike income tax brackets), and the rate charged per kWh increases from one tier to the next. So the more energy you use, the more you pay. Energy efficiency savings come from the highest tier first, and therefore offer the greatest cost savings. Some tiered rate structures are very punitive, with the highest rates three or four times the base rate. This strongly encourages efficiency investments.

If your energy utility uses a tiered rate structure and you put in the solar water heater, your cost savings can easily be twice as much. Payback is therefore half as long. The solar water heater example offsets 18 percent of the household energy use, but in a typical tiered rate system, this accounts for closer to 35 percent of the total dollar cost in the utility bill.

In a tiered rate structure, small- and medium-sized energy efficiency investments are more worthwhile — that's the entire point. As the size of your investment grows, the payback gets worse because you get less and less return on your investment. You may still want to make a large investment, if your main goal is pollution mitigation.

Goal: To hedge against rising energy costs

Suppose that energy costs rise 12 percent per year instead of staying flat. If you put in the solar water heater, each year your savings grow. If you save $26 per month the first year, as in the earlier example, the next year your savings will grow to $30.24 per month ($27 × 1.12). Then $33.87 ($30.24 × 1.12), then $37.93, then $42.48, and so on. In this case, the payback is 44 months, down from 52 months.

Regardless of how high energy costs go, the amount that you'll spend on heating water is locked in at zero. This is a form of hedging. Here's another form, not quite as tangible but still very real: You won't have to take shorter showers or skimp on that bath, no matter how high energy costs may go. This may be translated into peace of mind.

Goal: To increase your home's value

Suppose you're planning to sell your house five years down the road. If you put in a solar water heating system, at that point in time the savings from the new system will be $48 per month, or $600 per year. A home buyer will pay more for the home when you sell it because of this built-in cost reduction. How much more? The following factors come into play:

- A lot of work is involved in installing a new system, and most buyers don't want to do it themselves.

- Most home buyers take out a mortgage, and balancing monthly payments with a fixed income is the game. Energy cost savings of $48 per month translate into $48 that can be spent elsewhere. A buyer could get a larger mortgage, for instance. For $50 a month, after taxes, he may be able to borrow an additional $14,000. Look at it this way: A potential buyer looks at your energy-efficient home and the same home, minus the energy-efficient system, next door. Your home costs them $48 per month less. If you charge $5,000 more for your home, the buyer is still ahead of the game if he is using a mortgage.

Giving a ballpark figure for how much appreciation you can expect is impossible. In the best case, you may double your original investment after five years. In the worst case, you may not get anything at all if the equipment is old and obsolete. The most likely case is you'll get around the same as new equipment costs.

Replacing broken equipment

Doing nothing is not an option because now you have a broken washing machine, dryer, gas fireplace, you name it. Now you must spend money, and probably a good chunk of it. How much more do you have to spend for a new energy-efficient system? Probably not much. Now is really the time to go for it.

Financing investments with a home equity loan

If you play your cards right, saving more on energy costs than the payment on a mortgage equity loan used to purchase energy-efficiency equipment is common. You have no upfront cost when you finance an investment because you pay for the investment with the loan proceeds. From day one, you can often save more than you pay. Your cash flow is in the black.

Suppose you borrow for the solar water heating system that promises $27 per month in savings. An interest-only home-equity line of credit at 6 percent tax-deductible interest for $1,400 is only $8 per month. That's a net gain of $19 per month, making the payback period for this scenario 74 months (1,400 / 19 = 74).

At some point the loan must be repaid; most likely this will happen when the house is sold or refinanced.

Blowing hot air: A whole-house fan

The investment: a whole-house fan. Equipment costs $350; installation takes three hours and requires brains, ladders, and decent tools.

An energy audit determines that the fan will save $25 per month in air-conditioning (AC) costs over a four-month summer period, while costing only $10 per month to run. At $60 per year, the payback is around six years.

A whole-house fan offers other benefits, too: The house is a lot more comfortable on the days when it isn't hot enough to turn the AC on. And there are more of these days, so the home is more comfortable most of the summer. Plus the house smells better because whole-house fans ventilate so well.

Investing in a full-scale solar PV system

Say you live in a 3-bedroom, 2-bath house with good roof exposure for solar equipment. Your home is all electric and your average monthly electric bill is $260. Energy consumption is 1,600 kWh per month. You had your home audited and, through making smaller changes, you decreased the bill 15 percent to 1,360 kWh per month, or $221.

Now you decide to completely eliminate your electric utility bill and, in the process, reduce your home's carbon footprint to nearly zero. You find a 5kW system that will do the job and costs $40,000 — a lot of money, for sure, but you take into account the following:

- Once the system is in place, a TOU (time of use) rate structure will apply. Plus, you believe you can use 90 percent of your electricity in off-peak, lower-rate hours, and will therefore be selling most of your solar production back to the utility at the top rate.

- The warranty on the panels is 20 years, less for some of the other equipment. Reliability is good on the brand chosen, which was not the cheapest.

- The state will give a rebate of $10,000 directly to the PV system contractor so it's not even billed to you, the homeowner.

All this brings your total out-of-pocket cost to $30,000. But you also qualify for these credits and deductions:

- The feds will give a $2,000 tax credit for the system, bringing the cost down further to only $28,000.

- You finance this with a tax-deductible equity loan at $140 per month. This means that you're immediately saving the difference between the power bill you eliminated ($221) and the cost for the loan.

In this case, that's $141 per month after taxes.

From day one, this deal is in the black.

Using 7 percent as the energy inflation rate, the payback is 11 years, but this does not account for the fact that the value of the equipment is also rising. With this factor included in the equation, the payback goes down to 7 years.

The potential savings in carbon footprint are 13,000 pounds per year.

Part II

Reducing Inefficiencies throughout Your Home

The 5th Wave   By Rich Tennant

"Here's an energy efficient number I think you'll like: double insulated turrets, radiant heated dungeon, polyurethane foam core drawbridge, low flow moat..."

In this part . . .

This part is the bread and butter of the book. Get your grungy clothes on, get out your tool box, and get to work. I show you how to go through your home and make a wide range of efficiency improvements guaranteed to pay off in terms of lower utility bills. I show you how to use less water, less electricity, less gas, and less labor. I also show you how to make your home more comfortable and save money at the same time. Finally, I tell you the best ways to recycle.

You may want to skip directly to a chapter that most affects your own personal situation. Check the table of contents or the particular area you want to tackle, and then go for it. Dummies books are all designed so that you can read from beginning to end, or skip around as you see fit.

Chapter 6

Keeping Your Home Free from Contaminants

. . . .

In This Chapter

▶ Steering clear of manmade contaminants
▶ Detecting carbon monoxide in your home
▶ Honing in on the hazards of Mother Nature

. . . .

Of course you want to keep your environment clean as efficiently as possible, and the best way to do that is to avoid pollution and toxins in the first place. You can control toxins and contaminants in your home by keeping them out whenever possible and by preventing them from multiplying when they do manage to invade. Fortunately, you can do this easily and effectively, but you must be armed with the necessary know-how.

In this chapter, I review a number of the most common sources of home problems. I tell you how to detect them and what to do when trouble strikes.

Know your enemy and it shall be vanquished.

Getting Started with General Guidelines

As the other sections in this chapter explain, maintaining a healthy environment encompasses a lot of details, but some general rules are worth knowing for starters, and most of them are easy enough to follow:

- ✔ **Get wise.** Find out what kinds of things to avoid. Understand where nasty little critters like to live and breed (carpets, anyone?). Pay attention to things you can't see with the naked eye. In particular, read the warnings on labels that spell out precisely what the dangers are.

- ✔ **Ensure proper ventilation.** Ventilation is essential to health. Getting it can be tough sometimes, especially in the winter. But you don't necessarily need to open windows to ventilate your home. Chapter 13 gives you the details.

- ✔ **Store toxic materials away from the living quarters in your home.** The best place to keep them is in your garage. Many people store toxins underneath the kitchen sink, but this is asking for trouble. Of course, the best bet is not to store toxic materials at all. Buy small containers and toss the empties out. This may be a little more expensive, but it makes sense, especially if you have kids.

- ✔ **Pay attention to your cleaning products.** A surprising number of household cleaners are unhealthy. When possible, use environmentally friendly cleaning supplies. Check out the following sources of green cleaning information and products:

  - Eco-Source: www.eco-source.com

  - Household Products Database:

www.householdproducts.nlm.nih.gov

- Natural Choices, Home Safe Products, LLC: www.oxyboost.com

- Seventh Generation: www.seventhgen.com

- Sun and Earth, Inc.: www.sunandearth.com

Avoiding Some of the Worst Offenders

We are surrounded by manmade chemicals, and most of them are quite benign. Pesticides and food additives have helped people tremendously (although insects and molds have a different opinion about this). Humans live longer than ever before, and it's largely because of the profusion of modern chemicals in our diets and our medications.

 If you want to know just how prevalent chemicals are, read some food labels. They list things like butylated hydroxyanisole (BHA) or butylated hydroxytoluene (BHT). The thought of consuming both of these chemicals every single day may make you a little leery, but they're actually making you healthier.

On the other hand, a myriad of hazardous chemicals and contaminants can cause diseases, rashes, coughs, colds, and a long list of other maladies. The trick is to be efficient at sorting out the good from the bad. In this section, I review some of the worst home contaminants, and what to do about them.

Fighting off formaldehyde

Around 10 to 20 percent of the population is highly sensitive to formaldehyde gas, which evaporates (technically referred to as *outgassing*) from a wide range of common household materials, such as

- ✔ Particleboard used as subflooring and in shelving, cabinetry, and furniture

- ✔ Hardwood plywood paneling and decorative wall coverings

- ✔ Carpets, draperies, furniture fabrics, and permanent press clothes treated to resist mold and fire

- ✔ Paints, shellacs, waxes, polishes, oils, and other coating materials

- ✔ Glues and adhesives

- ✔ Molded plastics

- ✔ Insecticides, fumigants, disinfectants, deodorants, germicidal soaps, and embalming fluids

- ✔ Cosmetics, shampoos, nail hardeners, mouthwashes, and antiperspirants

- ✔ Household cleaning products

- ✔ Water heaters and gas ranges

- ✔ Old mobile homes and prefab-style houses

 Exposure to formaldehyde results in cold-like symptoms: coughing, runny nose, sore throat, fatigue, vomiting, and nosebleeds. It can also cause menstrual disorders, chronic headaches, and periodic memory lapses. To test for formaldehyde, obtain a simple testing monitor (they cost between $25 and $50; search for "formaldehyde monitor" on the Internet). You leave a vial open to your home's interior air for a specified period of time, and then cap the vial and send it to a lab. The lab makes the appropriate measurements and then mails you the results.

To avoid formaldehyde:

✔ Paint over old plywood surfaces with a water-based sealant or polyurethane varnish. Old kitchen cabinets are good candidates for repainting, as are old paneling and particleboard.

✔ Check before you buy. You can usually find out how much formaldehyde a product contains by consulting with the manufacturer, who is required to supply this information.

✔ Keep the air flowing. Formaldehyde is an airborne gas, so good ventilation can alleviate the problem to a great extent. Dangers are more acute in the winter months when homes are closed off.

✔ If you're buying composite wood or agrifiber products, get them with no added urea formaldehyde (look on the label, or call the manufacturer).

Volatile Organic Compounds (VOCs)

Volatile Organic Compounds (VOCs) is the name given to a class of carbon-based gaseous contaminants emitted from a wide range of home products:

✔ Solvents used in lacquers, adhesives, waxes, cleaning agents, cosmetics, paints and paint removers, and leather finishes. Common names are benzene, xylene, methyl collosolve, ethyl collosolve, methyl ethyl ketone, and trichloroethylene (TCE).

✔ Phenols found in household disinfectants, antiseptics, perfumes, mouthwashes, polishes, waxes, glues and, ironically, air fresheners. Phenols are also a byproduct of combustion, so they're more

151

prevalent in winter, when the windows are closed.

✔ Aerosol sprays propelled by propane, butane, and nitrous oxide gases.

✔ Permanent press fabrics, polyesters, and most synthetic materials.

✔ Pesticides, disinfectants, pet collars, and plant food. Pesticides are by far the worst source of contaminants in a home, and the chemicals last for years. Particularly noxious are the chemicals used by pest control companies, which spray heavy concentrations all around the outside of a house and often right inside. These companies have an incentive to make sure that insects don't appear, and the best way to do this is to use more than enough chemicals.

✔ Electrical equipment containing PCBs. This material is used because it is particularly fire-resistant. The problem is that when it's exposed to fire, some of it burns off. That's why whenever an electrical fire involves a utility company transformer, a special unit of the fire department is dispatched with high-tech equipment to protect the firemen. The same sort of contamination occurs in your home.

Avoiding VOCs

One of the easiest ways to avoid these chemicals is by not bringing them into your home. To do that, read the labels on the materials you buy. By law, manufacturers must list the contents of their products, particularly if potentially noxious chemicals are in the mix. Some prime culprits that you may want to include on your do-not-buy or be-careful-if-you-use list include

- **Chlorine bleach:** A component of most household cleansers. Many people use chlorine all the time without realizing it's unhealthy. If you must use it, make sure to allow for ventilation.

- **Oven cleaners:** Particularly bad news as they outgas for a long time. Buy an oven with a built-in cleaning feature, and when you're using it, make sure the ventilation is adequate. If you do need to clean your oven, use a mixture of baking soda and water and spread it around the dirty spots. Wait until it dries; then wipe it away.

- **Air fresheners:** These don't freshen air. They fool your nose into thinking the room is fresher. They don't remove the odor-causing problem; they simply overwhelm it with superior force. So now your room is completely full of swirling chemicals. Use an air-filter instead, or, better yet, find out what's causing the stink and get rid of it. Unless, of course, it's Uncle Albert.

- **Carpet:** Particularly risky, especially if it's old and dirty. In fact, carpet in general is a bad idea for people who are sensitive to chemical exposures of any kind.

- **Aerosol sprays:** Avoid these like the plague. Most household products that used to come in aerosol cans now come in misters, which are not quite as convenient and fun, but are much better for your family.

- **Oil-based paints:** Use latex paints instead. This makes life easier in a number of ways, in addition to health-wise.

- **Art supplies:** If you love to paint seascapes

and gorgeous landscapes, find out what sorts of chemicals you're breathing. You're right over the work for extended periods, so even if the chemicals aren't particularly strong, you're dosing yourself up more than you would with just about any other hobby you can find. Make sure the area you work in is well ventilated.

✔ **Ceramics:** Especially ripe for airborne abuses. If you insist on making ceramic artwork, do a lot of research before you partake.

✔ **Pesticides:** Come on now, do you really need pesticides? Insects are ugly — some have thousands of legs and eyes and furry little tentacles. Many of them can sting and cause other problems, plus they fly around and distract you when you're watching television. But the fact is, when you use pesticides you're exposing yourself to the same chemicals that kill the insects. Do you think you're any more immune to the assault than a bug? In fact, statistical studies have shown that the only difference between you and a bug is that you are bigger, although this may not be true in Florida.

✔ **Any product that doesn't list its contents on the label:** Products made outside the United States, for instance. Manufacturers in the United States are required by law to list the contents of their products, but manufacturers elsewhere may not have to follow the same rules.

Minimizing the risk

Despite your best efforts, chances are you won't be able to purge your home of all VOCs. In that case, you need to minimize the risk:

✔ **Ventilation is imperative.** Many noxious chemicals evaporate quickly, so exposure is only temporary. Always use glues and solvents in adequate ventilation. If possible, paint outdoors and leave whatever you're painting there until the paint is very dry.

✔ **Store paint, fuel, and pesticides well away from human habitats.** Or better yet, don't store them at all. Buy what you need and no more. Even containers that are sealed can still leak poisons. And admit it; when you seal a paint can and store it, you rarely, if ever, end up using the remainder. Most likely it just sits on the shelf until you move.

✔ **Wear protective clothing, safety goggles, and masks with appropriate filters when necessary.** Most of the stores where you purchase potentially toxic chemicals carry the appropriate equipment and can advise you accordingly. Work outside whenever possible.

✔ **Trust your nose; it's smarter than your brain.** In general, your nose will tell you when something is noxious. Trust your senses, and when in doubt, back off, read the label, open some windows, and start up some fans. You can also do the following:

- If you have some item of indoor furniture that has a chemical smell, seal it with polyurethane varnish.

- If your clothes smell really strong when you get them back from the cleaners, find a different cleaner.

✔ **Never eat food while working with chemicals.** This just makes the ingestion ten times worse. Also, never eat chemicals while working with food — this is somewhat intuitive.

✔ **Never use paint stripper indoors without ventilation.** Never. You may just as well drink a gallon of gasoline while playing with matches to accomplish the same end.

Asbestos

Asbestos has been used to provide heating and acoustical insulation and fireproofing, to strengthen building materials and make them more durable, to enhance the aesthetic value of a product, and even to make it easier to clean. Unfortunately, it's very toxic.

Finding asbestos

Around the home, asbestos fibers can be found

✔ In gypsum wallboard, textured paint, joint compounds, and spackling compounds in older homes (pre-1970).

✔ In older homes in insulation used around pipes, as well as in the paper wrapped around the pipe insulation.

✔ In a lot of old appliances, which use asbestos for insulation. In particular, the seals around doors in old wood-burning stoves are almost always made of asbestos. As they get old and crumbly, they're almost guaranteed to release fibers into the air.

✔ In siding shingles and sheet flooring, especially in older homes.

✔ In some kinds of floor tiles, particularly linoleum,

Alternatives to pesticides

To avoid pesticides, find other solutions. Following are some suggestions:

- Use steel wool to seal holes where insects come into your home. You can also use wood screws to cover holes.

- Screen off openings and keep your doors closed.

- Get used to the little buggers crawling around all over the place.

- Traps work well for mice, and you can get humane ones that don't even harm the little beasts. Or you can use the standard type, which propel them into the next life lickety split.

- Houseplants are prime culprits for the growth of insect colonies. Banishing plants from your home is tough because they create such a nice ambience, so take good care of them and pay attention. I've been in homes where the plants were literally crawling away, and the owners didn't even have a clue.

- Termiticides are the worst chemicals of all (probably because termites are the worst bugs of all, except for spiders that suspend themselves down from the ceiling right onto your forehead when you're sleeping). Keep those inviting wood scraps away from your house, especially underneath, near the foundation. Keep firewood away from your house. Hire professionals to get rid of the termites, and take a vacation while they're at it.

which have asbestos backing. This is not a problem until you decide to remodel and remove the tiles.

✔ Sprayed onto walls and ceilings for both decoration and insulation.

✔ Spun or woven into textiles, blankets, curtains, ropes, and lamp wicks.

How can you tell whether you have an asbestos issue? It's not easy, but if you're suspicious, finding out for sure may be worth the trouble. Consult an expert (look up "asbestos" in the phone book). Or check with the U.S. Consumer Product Safety Commission and the Center for Science in the Public Interest.

Solving your asbestos problem

In the 1970s, asbestos was largely banned due to its correlation with certain types of cancer and other diseases. But fortunately, asbestos is only harmful when the fibers become airborne. Here's what to do to make sure your asbestos stays grounded:

✔ **Simply leave asbestos products alone.** In particular, don't gouge them or tear them apart. It's the same as with mountain lions: Leave them alone and they'll leave you alone.

✔ **Cover them.** This is often better than tearing them out and installing new materials. For instance, if you have a floor with asbestos, simply install a new floor over that. If you have asbestos siding, install new siding over it or paint it with a sealant type of paint (ask at your paint store; a number of options are available). If you have asbestos insulation on pipes and it's starting to crumble, wrap it with a new coat of insulation and then paint that with latex.

You'll have much better insulation, and you'll have squelched the problem.

Removing asbestos

If you have to remove old asbestos products, the best bet is to hire a pro. Find one from a local environmental protection agency. If you do the job yourself:

✔ **Dress appropriately.** Absolutely get an approved asbestos mask from your hardware store. Wear it more than you think you should. A hat is a good idea, as well as clothes that cover all your skin. Plan on throwing the clothes away when you're finished. And use rubber gloves — this is a real hassle, as your hands will sweat and you'll lose most of your sense of touch. Too bad; you just have to suck it up for safety's sake.

Don't forget your shoes. If you step on asbestos dust and then walk into other parts of your house, you'll spread contaminants for sure. Dedicate a pair of old, throw-away shoes for the job and take them off when you leave the work area. Once you're done, throw them away.

✔ **Seal off the entire area and make sure it's well ventilated.** Before you do anything with the asbestos, seal the area with a floor-to-ceiling plastic tarp and close the area off to other parts of your house. For ventilation in the work area, your best bet is to have a fan operating, which refreshes the area with new air as well as carrying the dust-laden air out, where it disperses and doesn't present a problem.

✔ **Dampen the surfaces.** Get a good plant mister

159

and spray asbestos surfaces down with water before you work. This prevents most of the fibers from flying up into the air. Add some dish or laundry soap to the water for an even more effective solution.

- ✔ **Don't tear materials, and do *not* use a power saw.** Use tin snips and be gentle.

- ✔ **Clean up asbestos dust by using a mop and throwing the mop away when you're done.** An alternative is to use a vacuum with a special asbestos filter. *Don't* sweep with a broom.

- ✔ **Store discarded asbestos items in plastic bags and take it to a recycling center.** Don't discard them in your normal trash. You'll have to pay extra to take it to a recycling center, but you should do it to avoid exposing the sanitation workers to the very materials that you're so deathly afraid of.

Cigarette smoke

Cigarette smoke is full of hostile chemicals. If you smoke, you know exactly what you're doing to yourself and everybody around you, and I am not going to nag like everybody else is doing these days.

But consider this new angle (okay, so I'm nagging a little, but not like everybody else): From an efficiency standpoint, smoking is about the worst thing you can possibly do because not only are you introducing health hazards into your home and everywhere else you go, you're paying a hefty price for cigarettes at the same time. What do you get out of smoking? (Okay, I used to smoke; it was cool, and that first buzz is kind of dreamy. But this doesn't last long. And then it quickly turns into little more than an addiction.)

At the very least, go outside and hide behind the garage or something.

Burning Up with Combustion Products

If you have a gas-burning furnace, a wood-burning fireplace or stove, a gas cooking stove, or gas water heaters (in other words, any type of combustion device) in your home, you need to take extra precautions. This is also true if you have an attached garage, where exhaust fumes may enter your home.

Carbon monoxide (CO) is an invisible, odorless gas that's created by combustion (like carbon dioxide [CO_2], its more newsworthy cousin). In a well-designed home, chimneys and vents carry these gases away.

CO alarms are simple, inexpensive insurance policies to warn you if CO gas is building up in your home. They cost between $20 and $45, and work essentially the same as a smoke detector: They emit a high, shrill squeal when they detect high levels of the gas.

Buy an alarm, or alarms, that are UL-approved. You can get a digital type that plugs into your home's electrical outlet system and has a display that tells you what the concentrations are in your home. Even though the level in your home may be low enough for safety, you can see how the levels vary, and many times you can use this information to solve problems before they become extreme.

The best locations for CO alarms are near sleeping rooms on each level of your home. Position them away from drafts and solvents, which can inadvertently trigger a response.

If an alarm triggers, get everybody out of the house. Call your fire department and tell them what happened; then do what they tell you. Don't ignore an alarm. Always find out why it went off, and solve the problem.

Natural Hazards

Unfortunately, manmade chemicals are not the only noxious chemicals you need to contend with in your home. Mother Nature has a few of her own dirty tricks.

Slipping through the cracks: Radon

Radon can penetrate into a home when uranium is present in nearby soil or rock, thereby introducing radioactivity into your home. Granite, shale, and phosphate bedrock are the prime culprits, as well as gravel derived from these materials. The hazards of radon are the same as with exposure to any radioactive materials. Cancer is the worst.

Radon concentrates in basements where leaks through the foundation are common. The EPA did random tests across the entire country and found that up to 25 percent of all homes with basements are susceptible to radon poisons in potentially dangerous levels. Many states require radon tests to be performed when a home changes ownership.

The only way to know if a home is contaminated is to test, and a number of inexpensive means are available, the two most common being charcoal detectors and alpha-track devices.

- **Charcoal detectors:** You can find these on the Internet by entering "radon testing" into your browser. You place a charcoal detector in a cool, dry spot in your basement for no more than a week. Then you seal the container and send it to a lab.

You need to repeat the test twice to get a good result. The cost is around $10 to $25 apiece.

✔ **Alpha-track devices:** These give better results than charcoal detectors, and are recommended if your home fails the charcoal test. A strip of special plastic material is exposed to the air in your basement; then you send the plastic to a lab for analysis. Alpha-track devices require a minimum of four weeks of exposure but cost little more than the charcoal devices.

The good news is that, most of the time, radon infiltration can be contained rather easily. Two solutions exist: You can stop it from getting into the house, or you can dilute it once it gets in. When fresh air is imposed into a radon- contaminated region, the levels go down immediately. For ways to restrict radon entry, consult a professional or see Chapter 7 on sealing your home. You can also search the Internet for solutions. Enter "radon contamination" into your search engine. At the very least, if you have a radon-contaminated basement, seal the doorway between the basement and the ground floor of your home. This is a good idea in general, as you will also be preventing other airborne biological agents (keep reading) from entering your living area.

Operating in secret: Biological agents

Natural microscopic organisms include bacteria, viruses, fungi, molds, mildews, and mites. Pollen is a collector of spores from seed-bearing plants. All these can be either tracked in on shoes and clothing from the outdoors, or simply fly in on the wings of chance. And all multiply indoors and can cause irritations and illnesses.

The greatest source of nutrition for indoor microbes is the three or four grams of skin that flake off of the average human body once every day. (Did you know that most of the dust in your home comes from human skin?)

Symptoms of sensitivity include the usual retinue of allergic reactions: runny nose, sneezing, watery eyes, sore throat, coughing, and upper respiratory discomfort. Hives and rashes are also common. Flu-like symptoms can result, including fever, chills, malaise, muscle aches, and chest tightness.

No easy-to-use kits are available to measure for microbe contamination. If your family seems to suffer from any of the above ailments more commonly when the house is closed up (and wet or humid), you should do a bit of investigating.

The first place to look? Wherever there's water. Face it, water can be a big problem. Especially when left standing or combined with just enough warmth to create an oozy stew. Microbes *love* damp places. That's why the biggest front in your war on biological agents is in the marshes — wherever there's water. The following list tells you where to look and what to do to fix the problems you may find:

- Wet carpeting is a virtual breeding ground for all kinds of nasty little critters. If you have carpet in your bathroom, replace it with vinyl or tile, and make sure to seal the joints and edges extremely well. No carpet in the laundry room or kitchen, either. If you have area rugs, wash them in hot water occasionally or take them to the cleaners for thorough cleaning.

- Clothes dryers are hot and wet, perfect for microbe propagation. Make sure your dryer is vented well to the outdoors. If you have a leaky washing machine, especially if it's in your basement and it is perpetually wet underneath, you have a microbe farm.

✔ Clean all drains once a week with a strong disinfectant. Microbes love the filthy, wet environment down in a drain. If you have a drain in the basement that seldom sees water flushed into it, it's a prime candidate for a science-fiction movie.

✔ Repair all leaks in the roof or plumbing system. Leaks generally result in rotting wood or sheetrock. Not only does this cause contamination, but it also depreciates the value of your home.

✔ Repair leaky faucets. Every drop splashes and humidifies far more than you'd guess.

✔ Wet insulation materials are very fertile. If you have a leak in your roof or siding, you probably have wet insulation, which doesn't work very well and encourages rot, mold and infestations.

✔ If you have leaks in your grout, you have wet, oozing sheetrock somewhere beneath. You can fix leaks in grout very easily with silicon caulking. The clear stuff matches any decor.

✔ Never allow water to pool, especially in your basement. Find and fix whatever problem is causing the water to pool.

✔ Fix leaky toilets. These are just asking for it. Not to mention the fact that you're going to pay a lot more than you need to when you have to fix the rotted subflooring. And fuzzy toilet seat covers are simply nuts, if you value your health. (I could make a number of good jokes here, but I better not.)

✔ Install a vent (See Chapter 13) or a window in your bathroom. An enclosed bathroom with no ventilation equals microbe nirvana. You need to let your bathroom dry out thoroughly. Failing a vent or window, use a fan and keep the bathroom door open when not in use. Make sure the joints and cracks are sealed well.

 Moisture is essential for microbe propagation. Reducing the humidity in your home is always a good idea if your family is sensitive to skin irritations. See Chapter 8 for more details on how to keep the humidity low in your house.

Final Decluttering Tips

In an efficient home, there's a place for everything, and everything is in its place. Keeping a home neat and trim is not too different from keeping your body neat and trim. The best results come from cutting down on excess consumption. Here are sundry tips to get you going in the right direction:

✔ **Use the sun to clean and sanitize.** Put cushions, sheets, rugs, clothes, and so forth out into the hot sun. To find out just how well this works, try putting a sweaty shirt in direct sunlight for a couple of hours. It'll smell like new.

✔ **Use stove vent fans.** When grease mixes with dust in the air, it wafts around your kitchen and sticks. Over time, it makes a big mess.

✔ **Avoid humidifiers, if possible.** They encourage bugs and mildew.

✔ **Make sure to keep a good-sized, rough mat at each door.** When you come in, shed your shoes;

put slippers by the door and change into them.

✔ **Keep your plants healthy.** Healthy plants clean the air. Fake plants are dust magnets, and they launch colonies.

✔ **Seal the garage floor.** This makes for a cleaner garage, with less dust buildup that would eventually make it into your home.

✔ **Wax wood.** Doing so keeps moisture from permeating into the grain and keeps the dust down.

✔ **Use a battery-operated vacuum.** It's easy, lightweight, low-power, and you'll use it more often because it's less cumbersome. And make sure to change your vacuum cleaner bag. Full bags leak like crazy and waste a lot of energy to boot.

✔ **Clean curtains without washing.** Curtains don't need to be washed. Instead, put them in a clothes dryer, turn the setting to no-heat, and tumble the dust out of them in a matter of minutes.

✔ **Rent a high-pressure washer for exterior grime and dust.** Your entire house, inside and out, will be cleaner.

Chapter 7

Sealing and Insulating Your Home

You probably spend more energy on heating and cooling than you do on all the other energy-consuming functions combined. This means the greatest potential for energy savings lies in finding ways to make your heating and cooling efforts more efficient. In Chapter 8, I get into details about how to make your heating and cooling equipment run better and how to choose better equipment if you're in the mind-set to invest. But in this chapter, I show you how to seal and insulate your home.

Here is where you can find the biggest energy-efficiency improvements for the least amount of cash and labor on your part. Most homes have problems that can be fixed for

$100 or less — in fact, sometimes all you need to invest is a little time and labor.

Finding Leaks

By knowing where to look for heat loss, you can get a pretty good idea of where to find the problem spots in your own home. Table 7-1 lists the energy losses from heating and cooling equipment in a typical North American home. (**Note:** The first table entry refers to heat escaping or coming in through gaps. The other entries refer to heat moving through solid masses, like doors, walls, and so on.)

Table 7-1	Energy Loss in a Typical North American Home
Problem Area	**Percentage of Total Energy Loss**
Air leaks through gaps	35%
Through doors and windows	18%
Through floors and into basement	17%
Through walls	13%
Through ceiling	10%

Table 7-1 gives you a rough idea of where to look for problems and the order in which you should look for them. You can perform a leak test (as I describe shortly) to find the biggest and worst offenders: air leaks through holes in sheetrock and through hatches or trapdoors that lead into your attic or basement. The next logical place to look for leaks is in your doors and windows, and so on down the list.

Looking for cracks in your home

You can find a majority of leaks by simply taking a flashlight around your home and looking with a keen eye. Here are some details:

- Look at faucets, pipes, electrical wiring, and electric outlets. Cracks often exist around the junctions where pipes fit through foundations and siding. You can fix these with caulk (see the later section "Caulking your way to Nirvana" for advice on caulking).

- Check all interfaces between two different building materials. For example, check where brick or siding meets the roof and the foundation. Check where all corners meet and around the molding strips that are commonly used in corners of walls and between walls and floors. And so on. Plug all holes and voids with caulk.

Pay attention to where icicles develop. If they cluster around a particular location at your house, you have a leak somewhere above that's melting snow. It warms, drips down, then refreezes into icicles. These are usually pretty good-sized leaks.

- Look for cracks in mortar, foundations, siding, and so on.

- Check for cracks and voids around exterior doors and windows.

- Check storm windows for seal integrity. The interior window may be well-sealed, but the storm window will work better if it's also sealed just as well. To work properly, storm windows must fit tightly into the brackets. The way to ensure a tight seal is to check the weather stripping materials commonly fit into the gaps.

How heat moves

Heat is a form of energy. When a substance gets hotter, the molecules in that substance are moving faster, with more energy. When a substance gets cooler, heat is moving out of it into other nearby substances. The reason a hot substance can burn your skin is that heat moves very quickly in some cases.

Heat moves out of your home in the winter and into it in the summer — exactly what you don't want. That's why sealing your home is a good way to improve your energy efficiency. So how does heat move from one spot to another? Via the mechanisms explained in the following sections.

✔ **Convection:** In *convection,* heat is either transferred between a surface and a moving fluid (be it liquid, gas, or even the air itself), or it's transferred by the movement of molecules from one point to another. As opposed to conduction (see the next item), the hot molecules themselves move. Convection causes hot air to rise while cold air gravitates downward. Most people have heard of convection ovens; these work by using a fan inside the oven cavity to move the air and cook food faster. Cold air passing over a window removes heat from a home through convection. Wind in general causes a lot of convection loss. But all air is moving because the molecules are always moving, so even air that seems to be still is capable of a lot of convection. That's why convection is the most common culprit of heat loss in your home.

✔ **Conduction:** In *conduction,* only the heat moves, not the molecules. The material remains static while the energy moves through it. This is analogous to billiard balls, where kinetic energy is transferred from one ball to another, without moving the balls themselves. Heat can move through window glass via conduction. Window frames are also prone to conduction heat loss (particularly aluminum or metal frames), as are metal doors. And metal pipes are great heat conductors, too.

✔ **Radiation:** A hot object emits infrared *radiation,* any form of light energy, whether visible or not. The sun is a perfect radiator. Fires radiate heat, some of which you can see (a very hot fire glows white, for example, and as it cools down the color changes to orange, and then red) and most of which is invisible. When you can't see the embers anymore but can still feel the heat, the radiation is entirely infrared. In fact, there is far more invisible radiation than visible, but both versions are capable of heating. When you put blinds over your windows, you are keeping radiant heat from entering your home. On the other hand, when you raise the blinds to let in winter sunshine, you're inviting radiant heat.

Radiation is more of a problem in the summer, when you want to keep your home cool by keeping sunshine out than in the winter when you're trying to retain hot air (assuming you live in a climate where the temperature varies with the seasons). In the winter, you generally seek as much radiation heating as you can get.

Performing a pressure test to find air leaks

You can perform a pressure test on your home in rudimentary fashion. As I state in Chapter 3, you can hire a pro to do an audit that includes a detailed leak test, but you can do an easy one that's 80 percent as effective. The best time to do this test is when it's cold outside and warm inside, although it will work under any conditions if you have patience and tenacity.

To conduct a leak test, follow these steps:

1. **Completely extinguish any fireplace fires.**

   Close the fireplace damper as much as possible.

2. **Turn off your HVAC system and any furnaces.**

   If you have a gas water heater, turn that off, too.

3. **Close all the windows and doors in your home.**

   Also make sure to close any skylights or vents.

4. **Turn on all the exhaust fans in your home.**

   These are normally located in kitchens, bathrooms, and laundry rooms. If you don't have any exhaust fans, aim a portable fan out a single open window and turn it on. With the fans on, your house is depressurized, so any leaks will be readily apparent.

5. **Go around the house with a bowl of water, dip your hand in the water, and move your wet hand around the area you're testing.**

   You'll be able to feel a leak, especially if it's cold outside. Another way to do this is with a stick of incense — when the smoke fluctuates, you've found a leak. Or you can use a candle — in this case, flickering of the flame indicates a leak.

   Test the following areas and make a list of all the areas where you find leaks:

   - Test your fireplace. If it's leaky, you'll be

drawing in some stink. If so, turn the fans off and inspect your fireplace to find out why it's so leaky. If you can, fix it. If not, forge ahead if the smell isn't too bad. If the smell is really bad, call a fireplace specialist.

Fixing air leaks around your fireplace is vitally important. You don't want to pull in air from your fireplace because it contains a number of pollutants and volatile chemical compounds (see Chapter 6).

- Test windows, doors, molding interfaces, attic hatches, basement hatches, and so forth.

- Get a ladder or a chair and check for leaks in overhead lights. These are very common, but unfortunately a little more difficult to fix if you don't have good attic access.

- Check AC outlets and switch plates.

6. **After you've tested all the areas of your house, turn the fans off, and then fix the leaks.**

I get into details on how to fix leaks in the section "Fixing the Leaks You Find" later in this chapter, but here's an important safety tip that bears repeating: If you find a leak in an outlet or switch, flip the main circuit breaker off to turn the electricity off in the entire house before you fix it. You'll have to reset your clocks, but you'll be alive to do it, so don't complain.

7. **Once you've finished fixing leaks, turn the exhaust fans back on and repeat the wet-hand routine.**

Your house will be tighter now, and any remaining

leaks will be even more obvious.

8. **Repeat the whole process until you're satisfied.**

Finding attic air leaks

Attic air leaks are quite common. Following is a simple pressurization test that helps you locate air leaks in your attic as well as other air leaks through your ceiling:

1. **Completely extinguish any fireplace fires.**

   Close the fireplace damper as much as possible.

2. **Turn off your HVAC system, any furnaces, and if you have one, your gas water heater.**

3. **Close all the windows, doors, and any skylights or vents in your home.**

4. **Position a portable fan so that it aims into the house through an open window.**

   Now your house is pressurized (as opposed to depressurized).

5. **Go into the attic with a bowl of water, dip your hand in the water, and then move your hand around potential leak sites.**

   With a wet hand, you'll be able to easily feel the air pushing through from the inside of your house. Pay particular attention to these areas:

   • **The hatch you climbed through to get to the attic.** See the later section, "Weatherstripping," for details on how to fix this.

   • **Recessed lights in the rooms below.** Simply turn the lights on and, from up in the attic space, look to see whether light is visible. If so, you have a leak. You can fix it by buying a special kit at your hardware store that fits over the light from the top and seals the space.

- **Around chimneys.** If your chimney flue is not sealed, you likely have a leak here.

The good news is that most attic leaks are straightforward, if not easy, to fix. On the down side, most attics are a hassle to move around in, and some are just plain dangerous.

If you climb into the attic to check for leaks or to fix things like leaks in your overhead light fixtures, you'll find out what it's like to be a human pretzel. Although you may not be able to avoid contorting yourself into all sorts of odd positions, you can take these steps to keep the mess down and make your trek up there more bearable and safe (attics are notoriously cold in winter and hot in summer):

- ✔ Do it in the morning when it's cool.

- ✔ Wear a lightweight, disposable coverall (from the paint department).

- ✔ Wear a dust mask or particulate respirator.

- ✔ Wear knee pads, which you can get at any hardware store.

- ✔ Use a flashlight that clamps around your head and shines down onto your work.

- ✔ Plan ahead. Stage the job before you try it so you'll know which tools you need, and take the right tools up with you.

- ✔ Be careful where you step. Otherwise, you may fall through the ceiling.

Fixing the Leaks You Find

When your windows are all open, your home is basically a part of Mother Nature's fantastic domain. When you shut your windows and doors, it's another matter entirely — unless your house isn't well sealed. Some windows, for example, let in a lot of air, even when they're closed. Same with doors. And electrical outlets can leak air as well, just as can the light fixtures in your ceiling. Therefore, you can improve energy efficiency just by closing up these gaps. In this section, I present some valuable tips on how best to fix leaks. There are basically three kinds of fixes: weatherstripping, caulking, and expandable foam. All three have their time and place.

When sealing any home, be careful about indoor air pollution and combustion appliance back drafts. *Back drafting* occurs when the various combustion appliances and exhaust fans in a home have to compete for air because there simply isn't enough to go around. An exhaust fan may pull combustion gases back into the living space, for example, in which case you want to make sure you are ventilating combustion gases into the great outdoors rather than your home's interior. If your home burns fuel, you can avoid back drafts by making sure that the combustion system has an adequate air supply. (One way to tell whether your home is sealed too tightly is to note whether you get condensation on your windows during the winter. If so, you don't have adequate ventilation.) Go to Chapter 13 for more information about how to adequately ventilate your home.

Weatherstripping

Weatherstripping works great around doors and windows and where seals can't be made permanent (as with caulking). The trick is to get the right stuff, and the best way to do this is to take a sample of the existing seal (if there is one) to your local hardware store, where the salespeople will be able to sell you the appropriate new material. Foam and wrapped foam (a layer of vinyl or plastic wrapped around a foam core) are usually best and cheapest. Whatever weatherstripping you buy, be sure to follow the directions on the label. Here are a few other suggestions to make weatherstripping a breeze:

- Make sure to measure how much length you need before you buy. And if you end up with too little, don't stretch the material: It'll pull back over time and come loose.

- If you can, buy a kit to seal a door or window straight from the manufacturer of that door or window.

 The biggest culprits for air leaks are double-wide sliding doors, and the seals for these usually are best purchased straight from the manufacturers because they're very specific to a particular style of door.

- If you can't buy the same type of weatherstripping (because it's no longer available, for example), have no fear. Weatherstripping is pretty versatile stuff. You may need to use your imagination to figure out ways to cut it to fit into strange spaces, in which case you'll find that a good, sharp box-cutting knife is just the thing.

- Sometimes shutting a door or window right after weatherstripping has been applied is difficult, but this usually tapers off in a week or two. If it doesn't, give it another week or two. If *that* doesn't do the trick, get out the ubiquitous box-cutter and hack away.

- Most garage doors have a rubber seal on the bottom called an *astragal.* These are expensive, but in some cases they can make a big difference in your home's comfort. If your garage is well sealed from the home, you probably don't have to worry about this seal. But if you get drafts or your garage is perpetually cold, changing the seal may be worth it.

Expandable foam sealant

Expandable foam sealant is great stuff and horrid stuff, all at once. Via a long, straw-like wand, you squirt a yellowish foamy liquid into tight spots where there are air and insulation gaps. The foam expands and fills in the gap, and then it dries, hardens, and solidifies. Very effective. The problem is that expandable foam sealant sticks to everything, and nothing works very well to get it off. So a bit of a mess can easily turn into a big mess, accompanied by a lot of swearing and remorse (two things you want to avoid in the name of efficiency).

 If you're going to use an expandable foam sealant, practice first out in your garage, a barn, or an outbuilding before you try to fix anything inside your house. You'll quickly figure out how to work with it and how *not* to work, and you can also get the swearing part out of the way, which is especially wise if you have kids around.

Foam sealant works best for:

- **Leaks between jambs and wood:** Remove the trim molding from around leaking windows and doors, and you'll often find an air gap between the jamb and the frame wood. Squirt foam sealant in the gaps, wait until it dries, cut off the excess with a sharp knife, and then replace the trim molding. Many old houses benefit greatly from this simple, cheap fix.

- ✔ **Plumbing feed-throughs:** Squirt foam in the gaps around plumbing feed-throughs (where the plumbing goes through exterior walls to the outside world).

- ✔ **Plumbing vent pipes:** Squirt foam around plumbing vent pipes that pass through your attic.

- ✔ **Small gaps in insulation:** Squirt foam into any small gaps in insulation to stop air leaks.

In general, if you can, use foam sealant instead of caulking because it provides both a seal *and* insulation.

Caulking your way to Nirvana

Caulking is fun. Squirting beads of thick, sticky goo just seems to resonate with the human spirit. So get out your caulking gun, because caulk can be used in a lot of places:

- ✔ Around all exterior joints that may be in contact with water.

- ✔ Around doors, windows, decks, frames, and anywhere wind can push water in.

- ✔ On horizontal surfaces where water may pool and seep in over time.

- ✔ Wherever you think water can't get in (because it can, and it will).

- ✔ Around your teenager's bedroom door (because heaven knows the trouble a teen can get into when out of your sight).

- ✔ When in doubt, caulk. Why not?

As fun as caulking may be, you still need to know a few

fundamentals to make the job easier. I explain these in the following sections.

Getting the right tools

Buy a good caulking gun. A pro-style gun may cost $20, but it's worth it, especially if you're doing a lot of caulking. Look for larger handles, a smooth ratcheting action, pressure relief, and a hook on the end to hang on ladder rungs or rafters. An attached wire that pokes a hole in the tube's seal is especially convenient.

Use good-quality caulk. Three types are available:

- **Acrylic (latex):** Water-based and by far the most common. It skins over (dries on the surface) almost immediately, so you can paint it within minutes of applying (with latex paint, not oil-based).

- **Silicon acrylic:** More flexible (and expensive). Use this type if you're caulking between two surfaces that may expand and contract with weather. Make sure to get the kind that you can paint, if that's what you intend to do.

- **Polyurethane:** Performs better than latex but is much more difficult to work with and clean up. Use it between concrete, masonry, bricks, or on a surface that's been painted by oil-based paints or varnish. Because it has better adhesion, you may also want to use it on surfaces, such as on roof lines, where a leak could be potentially costly.

 All caulk is rated by years, but don't use the amount of time you want it to last as a guide; instead, buy the best stuff you can afford. Fifty-year caulk works better than 20-year over the course of its entire lifetime. If you must use the cheap stuff, use it where nobody will ever see it and where you need to simply build up mass to fill a space or void.

Applying the caulk

The key to success is in the application. The idea is not to squirt as much material into a joint as possible, but to lay a nice smooth bead across a joint. Follow these steps:

1. **Prepare the base by cleaning the surface to be caulked.**

   Dig out any old caulk with a putty knife or a 5-in-1 tool (you can get these at a hardware store; ask the clerk in the paint department). If possible, work some paint primer (latex) into the groove where you're going to squirt caulk. However, if you're caulking surfaces such as concrete, brick, or any other masonries, use "self-priming" caulk instead.

2. **Run a smooth ribbon of caulk along the joint you want to seal.**

   Try to avoid laying down thick blobs of caulk, which tend to crack when they dry.

3. **Run your finger along the caulk and press it gently down and into the joint; then wipe away the excess with a damp cloth.**

   Don't use paper towels because they tear and fray, and watch out for sharp little shards of paint or cracked materials that can cut your fingers.

Here are some suggestions for getting a nice, smooth bead:

- If you're a first-time caulker, practice in a place where mistakes can be tolerated.

- Cut the caulk tube ends at an angle to get a better

beading action. You can also cut the tube ends of several tubes to squirt out different diameters of material, and then use the diameter which best suits the particular joint you're working on.

✔ Don't squirt a bunch of caulk into a wide gap because it simply won't stick in there when it dries (caulk inevitably shrinks and cracks when it dries). Use foam backer rods (ask for these in your hardware store), which you can jam into wide gaps between materials. Then caulk over the backer rods.

✔ You can use painters' masking tape to block off surfaces you don't want to get any caulk on, as well as to make nice, crisp, even lines.

✔ To get into hard-to-reach corners and tight spots, tape a flexible drinking straw onto the tip of your caulking gun.

Inspecting and Repairing HVAC Ducts

Most of the HVAC ducts in your home send heated or cooled air into the house; one large duct is the return to the HVAC machine itself. All these ducts need to be tightly sealed. Yet in almost every home I've been in, especially older ones, the HVAC duct system has some big problems: shredded insulation, broken junctions, holes chewed through insulation and ducts by rats and mice, and so on.

Leaks in the ductwork are worse than air leaks in your house because the ducts are pressurized, which magnifies the amount of air escaping through cracks and openings.

Fortunately, duct problems are usually easy to find and fix (although gaining access may be tricky). It's amazing how many problems you can find with just a flashlight and a

183

quick glance. You can also turn the HVAC on, so that the ducts are pressurized, and find leaks with a wet hand (refer to the earlier section "Performing a pressure test to find leaks" for instructions). Follow these bits of advice:

✔ If the ducts aren't well insulated, you can get a number of different kinds of insulation sealing kits at hardware stores to do the job. Tell your hardware clerk what kind of ducts you have (what they're made of, how they're suspended, and so on) and he'll help you find the right kit.

✔ If the insulation around the ducts has any rips or tears, fix it. For this, duct tape works well but may be a real hassle. Once again, ask your hardware clerk what will work best.

✔ If the insulation is thin, you may want to build it up. You can add a new layer directly over the old.

✔ Many leaks occur at the junction between the ducts and the registers that feed the air into your home. You can seal these with caulk.

When working with dusty ducts, wearing a good-quality dust mask is highly recommended. You can get one at your hardware store.

 Duct tape works wonders, but it doesn't stick to dusty surfaces very well. If you've got a dust problem, wrap the duct tape around and around and just cover up the dust. It's easier than trying to clean it off.

Insulating Your Home (Not Insulting It)

The previous sections in this chapter deal with things that are responsible for convection losses, where warm (or cool) air escapes from your home. The other way to experience unwanted heat loss is through conduction, and that's where insulation comes into play. A well insulated house is comfortable and efficient, with just enough moisture in the air.

If your insulation is less than three inches thick, it's probably worth spending money to increase the R-value. If your insulation is over three inches, you should probably spend your money on some other efficiency improvement.

Capacity to resist heat flow is called *R-value.* County building codes have minimum R-values for homes, and you can check with them to find out what's right for your area. You can also get more information on insulation levels from your local utility, who may come out and do a home energy audit for you and check your insulation so that you don't have to (they'll usually do these audits for free, and they know what they're doing).

Insulation is generally an expensive fix that you should address only after you've taken care of air leaks. So if you haven't tested your house for air leaks, refer to the earlier sections "Finding Air Leaks" and "Fixing the Leaks You Find"; then come back to this section.

Types of insulation

There are dozens of different types of insulation schemes, but for most homes only a few are practical. The vast majority of homes use fiberglass insulation, and most people have a good idea of what this stuff looks like (cotton candy). In a distant second comes foam board, a type of insulation that is generally used when a home is being constructed. If you're remodeling or improving existing insulation, you'll probably use some form of fiberglass.

The best bet is to discuss your plans with the salespeople at your favorite hardware store and ask them what type of insulation is best for your application.

Owens Corning is the leading manufacturer of insulation. Visit its Web site at www.owenscorning.com to determine the number of square feet of material you'll need to insulate an attic or a wall in your home. Also check out www.certainteed.com.

The following sections describe the most common types of insulation, along with the pros and cons of each.

Fiberglass

Fiberglass, which is made of glass fibers, comes in at an R-rating of R-3 to R-3.8 per inch (thickness). Fiberglass is by far the most common type of insulation, and it is what you should use if you can. It's readily available and comes in spun rolls which you can easily cut and lay into place.

- **Pros:** It's low-cost, easy to install (once you get the hang of cutting and placing it into the gaps), and can be pressed into place without the use of glues or chemicals. It comes in standard widths and is available with kraft paper backing, which also provides a moisture seal.

- **Cons:** It's very irritating to your skin and lungs and is susceptible to air gaps. When you get big plastic bags full of it, and cut the plastic packaging off, it expands to three or four times the size and is difficult to move around and place.

Loose fill insulation

Loose fill insulation is chopped fiberglass material that is "blown" into place, as opposed to cut and fitted. It comes in at an R-rating of R-2.2 to R-4 per inch.

✔ **Pros:** It's low-cost and gives much better coverage in irregular spaces where the one-piece fiberglass format doesn't fit well. It can be poured or blown into walls and odd spaces, which makes working with it much easier than fiberglass.

✔ **Cons:** It's messy, and the quality varies even within the same lot. It can shift or settle over time so that gaps may grow rather large. You can't use it for under floors without a complex web of nets, which are not worth the hassle. Depending on the size of the job, you may need to rent a special blower.

Extruded foam insulation

Extruded foam insulation is solid, rigid material made of the same type of foam as a drinking cup. It comes in flat sheets, with an R-rating around R-5.2 per inch.

✔ **Pros:** It's high-strength, easy to tack up, covers well, and works underground and in wet basements. It's good for covering a house, then tacking up siding over it.

✔ **Cons:** It's very expensive and needs to be covered up with siding.

Sprayed urethane foam

Sprayed urethane foam is held in a metal container, under pressure, and then force sprayed onto walls where it sticks. It comes in at an R-value between R-6 and R-7.3 per inch.

✔ **Pros:** It forms a tough, seamless barrier that seals well over all types of surfaces, especially irregular ones.

187

✓ **Cons:** It must be professionally installed, and it needs to be covered up.

Checking and fixing your home's insulation

Visually check insulation wherever you can. Most gaps will be readily evident. Also look for spots where water has damaged insulation or spots where the insulation is very thin. Small problems, like gaps or voids in your insulation, usually occur around light fixtures and where somebody (like an electrician or plumber) has been working and pushed it aside. You can fix these voids by hand tucking some loose insulation into the gaps.

If you find your insulation wholly inadequate, you've got a big decision on your hands. Putting in new insulation is expensive — the payback time is going to be way out there. But if you don't, you'll continue to waste money and leave a big carbon footprint.

If you're on a limited budget and want to make the biggest difference for the least cost, insulate your family room (or the room you spend the most time in) first. In particular, if you don't have any insulation under your family room floor, adding insulation there is usually easy to do and doesn't cost that much. You'll get the biggest bang for your buck.

The following sections outline the different areas to check and explain how to remedy the problems you may find.

Attic

Insulation makes the most difference in the attic simply because heat rises. If no heat can leak out of your home through the attic, your home will be very well sealed.

The easiest thing to do is have the insulation in the attic thickened. You can do this yourself (use a dust mask at all times), or you can find a company to come in and spray loose fill insulation. Unfortunately, when the insulation in your attic is substandard, it's most likely also substandard in the walls. See the next section.

Completely seal up the attic for air leaks from the home *before* you apply insulation because once the insulation is in place, taking care of attic leaks is much more difficult.

Walls

Substandard insulation in your walls is not as easy to remedy as substandard insulation in your attic. The best bet may be to simply put new siding on the outside of your house. You can get good-looking siding with great insulation properties, and at least when you spend money like this, you can accomplish a visual remodel as well.

Basement

If you have a basement, check to see whether the ceiling is insulated. If not, putting insulation in is a relatively easy job, probably even easier than working in your attic.

If you need to insulate a basement, it's usually best to use foam sheets and then cover them with sheetrock. You can either glue the sheets directly onto the concrete basement walls, or build a wall up with 2 × 4s, which will make the room smaller.

Pipes

Hot water pipes should be well insulated. It's easy to see when they're not. You can also feel the pipes (after you've turned the hot water on in the house for a minute or two)

Insulating old homes

In some old homes, it pays to blow loose fill insulation into the walls. Normally this works when the existing insulation is so poor that air gaps are more common than insulation. Sound absurd? It's a lot more common than you think. Some homes have no insulation at all, like the old homes back east. Energy was so cheap (ah, the good old days) that insulation was not cost-effective.

Having a pro do an energy audit of your home to get a second opinion is a good idea. If you decide to go ahead, you'll need to rent a blower, which will come with detailed instructions. You'll need to cut a number of two- or three-inch-diameter holes through your exterior siding so that the blower head can get into each individual cavity between the beams.

A better way may be to simply cover your home with insulation sheets, and then cover that with new siding. This way, not only do you get the added insulation, but your home also gets a nice facelift.

to determine which pipes are for hot water and which ones are for cold. A number of easy options work well for insulating pipes, the easiest being a three-foot-long foam section with a longitudinal slit. You simply slide the piece over the pipe, and you're in business. Ask about your options at the hardware store.

Tips for applying insulation

Putting in insulation isn't particularly difficult, but it can go more easily if you keep a few things in mind.

✔ **With fiberglass insulation, wear a one-piece jumpsuit, along with a face mask and gloves, and make sure ventilation is adequate before you begin.** You don't want to breathe a lot of fiberglass dust, and you don't want to get it on your skin because you'll be scratching up a storm. Also, in old attics, the dust that collects on insulation can be very nasty. Try not to disturb it, if possible.

✔ **Fiberglass insulation is itchy.** Some versions come with plastic covers to reduce the risk of itch — if you're really sensitive, look for these.

✔ **Apply insulation carefully and evenly.** Fill entire cavities, but be careful not to cover up vents or other means for attics and basements to breathe.

✔ **When you come across electrical wires, arrange half of the insulation in front of them, and half behind.** You will have to tear the insulation open, but this works much better than leaving big air gaps without any material at all.

If you leave a gap unfilled, you're wasting money. Filling only 80 percent of a cavity prevents only 20 percent of the heat loss.

✔ **Always buy the right width and thickness to fill spaces.** You don't want to piece insulation together to fit a space if you don't have to, because you risk creating air gaps. Still, you can press fiberglass insulation tight into narrow gaps and cracks, and it will perform better than nothing at all even though it's compressed a bit. (Using expandable foam is best, but this may not always be practical, and it's not worth a lot of extra hassle.)

Compressing insulation reduces its R-value. When you squeeze it down to make it fit into gaps, you're accomplishing the opposite of what you intend. You're actually reducing the effectiveness of the insulation. So press it down only when necessary.

You can get one-piece seals for plugs and switch outlets for about $4 a dozen at your hardware store. Simply remove the plastic cover, set a seal into place, and replace the cover.

✔ **If you have moisture problems in your home, you may want vapor barrier facing on the insulation** (it comes prefaced on some versions, so look for that type when you buy). It doesn't cost much more, and it makes the insulation easier to work with to boot.

Use hedge shears to cut insulation, not a knife.

Working with Windows

Of all the investments you can make in your home, windows have the potential to make the most impact. Not only do they provide insulation (and sealing), but they also affect the aesthetic ambient like nothing else in your home. But installing new windows is very expensive, maybe one of the most expensive projects you'll ever take on. A typical residential window costs anywhere from $150 to $400, plus another $100 to $300 for professional installation. And you can easily spend a lot more than this.

If you have very poor insulation in your home and you're looking for the biggest bang for your buck, you're better off improving the insulation before buying new windows. See the earlier section "Insulating Your Home (Not Insulting It)" for details on insulation.

Do you really need to replace your windows? Answer these questions:

- ✔ **Are your windows single pane?** This may not matter, or it may be a huge factor in your energy bill. With homes in mild climates, the number of panes doesn't matter much. However, if you're living in extreme climates, single pane windows are almost always worth upgrading. Besides, single pane windows are always old, and you can buy something better looking.

- ✔ **Are your windows old?** Old windows can be especially problematic. If they're difficult to maneuver, you're less apt to open and close them, and you lose out on some of the ventilation tricks I detail in Chapter 13.

Simple, inexpensive solutions for problem windows

If you have substandard windows (basically, any windows you don't like or aren't performing well for you), you can always use blinds to help solve the problem. In this way, you also get a nice aesthetic effect as well. See Chapter 12 for more details on how to use sunlight to warm up a room.

You don't need to change all the windows in your house to make a significant improvement. One single, large window in a family or living room may make a big difference in both energy efficiency and aesthetic beauty. Or maybe a couple rooms' worth of windows, like the breakfast nook, the living room, and the family room, will do the trick. You can also put up heat-sealing cloth barriers in the summer or storm windows in the winter, and both of these solutions are much cheaper than changing windows.

Replacing windows

Before you replace windows, take your time researching all the options. Visit some window stores and check out the different types, like wood, plastic, fiber, and so forth (you'll probably be confounded by the variety), and get a number of bids. In particular, pay attention to the following:

- ✔ **Glass:** Ask about different types. Some glass selectively filters sunlight for UV; some has low-E coating and argon gas between panes.

- ✔ **Appearance:** Does the style blend in well with your existing home decor? Do the colors match your home, or are you going to be painting?

  You can get windows that require paint so that they'll match anything, but you don't want to because every five years you'll have a big, tedious job. (Painting windows is very time-consuming. You can't just roller — or even spray — it on.)

- ✔ **Cleaning:** Are they easy to maneuver so that you can clean them? A lot of new window designs enable you to clean from the inside. This is particularly handy for second-story windows.

- ✔ **Operation:** Are the windows smooth and easy to open and close? It pays to invest in quality bearings and movements. No one wants to have to remember a complicated schematic just to let in a little summer breeze.

✔ **Maintenance:** Where are you going to get parts when you need them?

✔ **Warranties:** The seal between double-pane glass inevitably gives out, so make sure you understand who is going to pay for this expensive repair.

Chapter 8

Getting the Most Out of Your Heating and Air-Conditioning System

. . . .

In This Chapter

▶ Seeing what contributes to your comfort
▶ Reducing your energy requirements the easy, cheap way
▶ Getting the most out of your existing system
▶ Determining when it's time to get new equipment

. . . .

Most homes have both heating and cooling systems. Together, these account for a large portion of your total energy use. (To find out just how much of your energy consumption is devoted to heating and cooling your home, do a home energy audit. Refer to Chapter 3 for details.) In Chapter 7, I show how to seal and insulate your house so that when you turn on your heating, ventilation, and air conditioning (HVAC) system, you can maintain a comfortable environment with less energy. In this chapter, I give you general advice about how to use your equipment more efficiently.

Note: This chapter doesn't present specific details on how to tune up your existing equipment for several reasons:

- Far too many different types of systems are available — so many that this book doesn't have enough room to include even the most common ones.

- Many adjustments involve quite a bit of technology and require the expertise of a pro.

- Combustion systems are inherently dangerous, and you don't want to mess around with them. Call a pro instead.

Understanding Human Comfort

Human comfort is not simply determined by room temperature, but by a variety of other factors as well, such as air movement, humidity level, and so on. Yet most people still erroneously think that the best way to make a room more livable is to set the desired room temperature on the thermostat. You can do much better than this, of course, if you're willing to learn some tricks and change a few habits. This section explains the factors that affect how comfortable a room feels and offers a few pointers on how to exploit these factors so that you can use your HVAC less frequently and still maintain — or even enhance — the comfort level in your home.

Getting air moving

In the summer, people like the feel of air moving over their skin. Just the phrase "summer breeze" generates a cool sensation. Even a warm breeze on a hot day can cool things down. That's because it's not air temperature that's important, but the actual temperature of your skin. Moving air removes heat, so skin temperature goes down. Essentially, a breeze cools you by convection (see Chapter 7).

Fans move air and, in the process, cool you down. They don't change the air temperature (if anything, they make the air hotter), but their effect is still pronounced. Fans, like breezes, cool by convection. You can make a room more comfortable just by installing fans to improve the ventilation (see Chapter 13 for details).

Don't use fans when no humans are present, because all fans do then is heat up the air. Fans do not cool a room; they just make the people in it *feel* cooler — there's a difference.

Helping or hindering: Humidity

On humid days, people feel much hotter than they do on less humid days, even if the temperature is the same on both days. Why? Because humid air doesn't carry heat away from your skin nearly as well as dry air does.

For this reason, equipping your home with a dehumidifier that you use in the summer can make the air feel much cooler. As an added bonus — and one that's particularly relevant to this book — dehumidifiers are much cheaper to operate than air conditioners, so they save money. Conversely, in the winter you *want* humid air because your skin can draw heat more readily from it than from dry air. In the winter, people don't want to feel moving air from fans because that removes heat.

Sweating is your body's way of eliminating heat and cooling itself down. Many people think the evaporation of sweat is the key, but that's only a small part of it. The truth is, water holds much more heat than air does; sweating is your body's way of expelling this hot water. In other words, the sweat itself cools you down — if you can get it off your body (otherwise, sweating just moves the hot water

The lowdown on portable heaters

Portable heaters are heaters you can move around to wherever you like. You see them underneath people's desks at work when the boss is a miser. If your HVAC system isn't working consistently from room to room, a portable heater may be just the thing.

But here's what's quirky about most of them: They come with fans that move air over a resistance coil. If the fan wasn't moving the air, the coil would get really, truly hot and probably burn up, which is clearly not something you want in your home (unless you want to collect on your fire insurance). The fan also tends to make you feel a lot cooler. So with traditional portable heaters, a conflict exists between their purpose (to generate warmth) and their design (the inclusion of the fan, which cools you down).

The best bet is to use a radiative type of heater, which uses parabolic reflectors with a heating element at the focal point, or something akin to this. These heaters spread heat by radiating it rather than by convection, which is the way a portable heater with a fan works. Radiation heaters are also more efficient, and they feel more natural because they're supplying heat the same way the sun does; through radiation.

Remember, though: Either type of heater is dangerous if used incorrectly, and in no case should a portable heater be used around children.

from *in* you to *on* you). That's where evaporation comes in and why humid days feel hotter than dry ones. When it's humid, the air is already full of water and simply can't hold any more, so sweat doesn't evaporate. It just hangs around, making you feel sticky and hot. Contrary to the way it may feel, you don't actually sweat more on humid days.

The following sections tell you how to keep humidity levels comfortable throughout the year.

In the summer

Use a dehumidifier in the summer. Keep the filter clean and try placing it in different rooms to get the maximum effect. The best bet is to place it in your family room (or wherever your family congregates the most). Other things to keep in mind include:

- **Clothes dryers absolutely must be vented to the outside world.** This is the single biggest source of humidity in a home. If you use a clothesline to dry things (like delicate garments) and you can't put it outdoors for some reason, put it in the garage, not inside the house.

- **Install exhaust fans vented to the outside in all bathrooms, the kitchen, and the laundry room.** Use them when you're showering or cooking to get rid of humidity in the summer. You can even install a humidistat to turn the vent fans on when humidity levels exceed a certain threshold.

  When you use a vent fan with the whole-house air conditioner on, crack a window near the vent fan. The fan will draw its air from that location instead of the cool air from the house.

- **Don't put carpet in the bathrooms.** It sucks up moisture and then releases it all day long, producing a musty smell through the entire house — which may be a good thing if you want fewer houseguests.

- **Don't allow water to pool in your basement.** Use a sump pump or find another way to get rid of it.

✔ **Ventilate your attic and basement.** This lets fresh air in and reduces humidity.

In the winter

Use a humidifier in the winter. This lets you decrease the load on your heating system (you don't need to turn the heat on nearly as much to maintain comfort levels). You can make a humidifier by simply hanging clothes to dry in your bathroom (keep the door open).

In the winter, don't use vent fans in the kitchen. You want both the humidity and the heat that you generate when you cook.

Capitalizing on the chimney effect

Heat rises. That's why your house doesn't fill with smoke when you're burning wood in the fireplace. When a fire is burning in your fireplace, cool air from the room is drawn in and the oxygen combines with the biomass in the firewood to create a flame. The heat from the flame moves up into the flue and out the chimney (unless something is preventing it, like a home that is too tightly sealed or a closed damper). Hence, the term *chimney effect*.

In the same way, hot air rises within the confines of a single room. The temperature of the air near the ceiling is always higher than that at the floor. If you live in a two-story house, you may notice that the upstairs gets hotter than the downstairs — that's due to the chimney effect.

Heat rising is a passive effect; you don't need a fan to make this air move. Passive effects are the absolute best when you're looking to maximize efficiency because they're essentially free. To take advantage of them, you just need to exploit physics. So how do you take advantage of the chim-

201

ney effect? In any of these ways:

- ✔ **Install ceiling fans.** Depending on whether the blades push air up or down, ceiling fans can move heat either up into the ceiling, thereby making the ground level cooler, or move heat down (in the winter). By using them to move the air in a room around, you can maximize the comfort level (see Chapter 13 for more details on fans and ventilation).

- ✔ **Adjust your registers.** During the winter, adjust the registers in your home so that much more heat enters the downstairs than the upstairs. Due to the chimney effect, the home will even out very nicely. During the summer, do just the opposite: Open the upstairs registers and let the majority of cool air enter there. Over the course of the day it will gravitate down to the lower floors.

Going for the greenhouse effect

Why does a greenhouse get so hot when the sun is shining? The answer is found in the *greenhouse effect.* Essentially, sunlight transmits through the greenhouse's glass walls and is converted into heat on the interior surfaces of the greenhouse. The same glass that transmitted the radiation into the greenhouse now serves to insulate that heat from getting back out into the great outdoors. The same effect causes cars to get hot when they're sitting in harsh summertime sunshine. To take advantage of the greenhouse affect, follow these suggestions:

- ✔ **Open all your blinds when you want to heat your home and the sun is shining.** Blinds prevent sunlight from entering, so you can't exploit the greenhouse effect when they're drawn.

✔ **Blinds work very well for insulating, so close them whenever you need to retain heat or cool air.** In general, closing your blinds at night is always a good idea. Close them on cold winter days, when the sun is dull, to make your heater work more efficiently (by increasing the insulation of your home).

Making more small changes for even bigger benefits

One of the best ways to reduce your energy costs is with a programmable thermostat. This is a great do-it-yourself project, and it costs less than $100, in most cases. Find a unit compatible with the equipment you have in your house. Consult your owner's manual to find out what types are compatible, call a heating and air specialist, or ask at your hardware store. Make sure to get one with easy-to-understand instructions. Avoid thermostats that seem complex to operate because that's an indicator that the design just isn't a good one.

Available options on programmable thermostats include the following:

✔ A reminder when it's time to change the filter

✔ The ability to automatically change programs between heating and cooling seasons

✔ A low-battery indicator

You can get as complex as you want, but in my book simplicity is always a premium.

Most homes don't need every room to be maintained at the same temperature. In general, rooms where you don't spend a lot of time or that tend to warm up or cool down

quickly (because of size or design) are good candidates for blocking off. Bathrooms, for example, don't need HVAC very much at all, nor do laundry rooms. The following list shares advice on how to vary the temperature of different rooms:

- ✔ **To block off rooms, close the registers and the door.** You can further seal the room off from the rest of the house by laying an old towel across the threshold at the bottom of the door. (Note, however, that the thermostat that controls your system needs to be in a room that isn't blocked off!)

- ✔ **Use window air conditioners to cool rooms individually.** A portable air conditioner is much cheaper to run than a big, whole-house unit. Perhaps you only need to cool your family room or a single bedroom upstairs so that your sleep will be more comfortable.

- ✔ **You can easily heat a single room using portable heaters.** If you set up a couple portable heaters in your family room, for example, you may not need to turn your whole-house system on at all.

Here are a couple other ways you can reduce your energy costs while maximizing your comfort:

- ✔ **Use your grill more.** If possible, do all your summertime cooking outdoors. Gas barbecues are the most efficient and convenient, which may motivate you to cook outdoors more often.

- ✔ **Adjust the lighting.** The human mind is subliminally sensitive to certain sensory effects, one of which is lighting tone. A harshly lit room (bright, silver, or yellow light) makes people feel hotter. A shady, dull room makes people feel cooler.

Candlelight makes people feel warmer. And so on. I get into more lighting details in Chapter 9.

Solving Some of the Most Common Inefficiency Problems

In order for any system to be efficient, it needs to be running well and smoothly. Sometimes, though, problems creep up that can decrease the performance of the system. This is certainly true of HVAC systems. If your existing HVAC equipment isn't working the way you think it should, here are some of the most common problems that you can solve yourself.

If you have a combustion system, I recommend you have an HVAC pro inspect and tune your equipment every few years. It pays, believe me, as these systems are prone to carbon buildups and other soot issues that can drastically affect their performance. Heat pumps can work nicely for a decade without being serviced, as can solar water heaters, space heaters, and so on.

Restoring air flow

To work at their peak efficiency, HVACs need adequate air flow. That means that the filters must be clean, and the airflow path must be unobstructed. When air flow is obstructed, the machine basically uses up the same amount of power but does less work for that power, and so it has to be on longer to get the same job done. You waste energy, and your house is noisier to boot. Following are some of the most common problems impeding air flow:

✔ **Blockage in the air ducts:** Construction debris sometimes falls into the ducts, as do kids' toys,

Window air conditioners for a single room

If you're buying a window air conditioner, get one with a Seasonal Energy Efficiency Rating (SEER) between 10 and 17. The higher the rating, the more efficient the air conditioner is. Check with your utility company to see whether they offer rebates for units with high SEER numbers. They may have a list of recommended units you can get at a discount.

You can also buy a stand-alone unit that sits on wheels and move it around your home as you see fit. You can use it in the family room during the evening hours, and then push it into your bedroom when you sleep.

When you install your air conditioner, put it in the shade. The cooler it is, the more efficiently it will run.

Fortunately, you can easily do the maintenance yourself:

- Clean the fins, evaporator coil, fan, condenser fins, and tubes. Be sure to unplug it first, and don't make a big mess. You can use a jet spray to clean out the fins.

- Air conditioners also have filters that get clogged. You can replace these inexpensively, or you may be able to vacuum the dust and debris from the filter material.

- Buy a cheap fan comb to straighten bent fins. Using the comb to straighten the fins out can make a big difference in the unit's efficiency.

carpet segments or pads, and so on. Small items are easy to remove (perhaps with the help of a small hand — the same one that's responsible for that Barbie doll being in there in the first place). Larger items can be more of a problem; you may need to pull the duct from the register either from underneath the floor, or from the other side of the wall.

✔ **Blocked registers:** Something may be sitting over a register, like curtains, drapes, furniture, or decorations. You may not even realize that the register is closed off. Or maybe the air is flowing freely, but it's headed in the wrong direction. You may be able to add a plastic reflector to aim the air better into the living quarters.

✔ **Loose joints:** To repair joints, use aluminum tape rather than duct tape. Wear a face mask to protect you from the dust, or you'll be sorry about an hour later.

✔ **Dirty coils, fins, and filters:** You can take the outer cover off of your condenser unit and jet spray the fins to remove debris and crud buildup. If you're still not sure whether enough air is passing through, get your system inspected.

✔ **A blocked return air path:** A forced-air system can't heat a closed-off room. You must crack the door open or cut an inch or two off the bottom of the door so the air has a gap to move through. Louvers work, but they're difficult to use and neither cheap nor easy to install. If you absolutely need to close off a room, look into a portable heating or air-conditioning unit for that room.

✔ **Too many bends in the ductwork:** When this is the case, air has a difficult time passing through. Not only are you not getting much air through the maze-like ductwork, but the air you *are* getting is expensive (because the machine has to work harder to push the air through all the turns). If you can't change the ductwork, consider installing a portable heater or air conditioner and simply closing off the inefficient ductwork entirely.

Repositioning the thermostat

Your system's performance is governed by the location of the thermostat. The temperature you set is maintained wherever the thermostat is located. Sometimes systems work poorly because direct sunshine hits the thermostat, resulting in a temperature reading that doesn't accurately reflect the actual temperature of the room. If the thermostat is located directly over a heating duct or in a remote corner of the house, its temperature is not indicative of the house in general. A well-designed system will have the thermostat near the center of the home, usually near the air intake vent.

You can have your controller moved, and sometimes doing so is cheap and easy. Or you may be able to find one that uses a remotely located temperature sensor. This works well unless your kid takes it to school for show-and-tell.

When Your HVAC's on the Blink

Something's wrong. Your house isn't staying as warm or as cool as it should, even though you've taken steps to maximize your HVAC system's efficiency. What do you do? Well, if you're like many people, you curse the Fates (because these things tend to break down on either the coldest day of the winter or the most searing day of the summer) and then call in the HVAC repair pros. But before you do, make sure you really need their expertise. Although some problems definitely need the attention of an HVAC expert, other problems are relatively easy to fix yourself.

What to check before you call a repairman

You know that your wallet is going to take a hit as soon as you call in a pro. So when your system is down, check out these things first. If you're lucky, you may just solve your own HVAC problem:

- ✔ **Check the thermostat and make sure it's on.** Fiddle with it, moving the temperature up and down. Give it a little time, like an hour or so, because sometimes there are fail-safes (timers, clocks, and so on) that go off.

- ✔ **Check breakers at your main panel.** Often when servicemen are called out, it's not the HVAC that's down, but the circuit panel, in which case you've wasted money on a call. Many furnaces also have an on-off switch somewhere on the chassis. Somebody (kids . . .) may have flipped it off, so check to make sure it's on.

- ✔ **Change the filter.** HVACs need flowing air to work properly. It's amazing how many times servicemen are called out only to discover that the filter is totally clogged up. They don't mind; they love to charge $80 to change your filter. But you can do it for much less.

- ✔ **Make sure the gas is on.** (Or if you have a tank, make sure it's not empty.) Check all the valves by closing them and opening them back up. This may not seem like it makes any sense, but valves can stick and by opening and closing them you may be able to get the fuel flowing again.

✔ **Check to see whether the chimney exhaust flue is clear.** This may or may not be an easy thing to ascertain because many chimneys meander back and forth, like an accordion. In other cases, you just plain can't see up into that dirty, black hole. If in doubt, call for service.

✔ **Make sure the line that drains water isn't clogged.** Many furnaces drain off several gallons of water per day in heating season. If the line becomes clogged and the water can't drain properly, the furnace shuts down due to a fail-safe switch. If the drain hose looks dirty, remove it, fill it with a mixture of bleach and water (30 percent bleach to 70 percent water), wait 15 minutes, and flush it.

✔ **Look for blocked or leaking ducts.** The big ones going into the furnace from the house/filter port are especially problematic. If you can get to the ducts, you can usually fix them yourselves (see Chapter 7). Or you may need to contact an HVAC pro (if you do, have them do a complete inspection).

✔ **Clean the outdoor equipment.** Remove debris like leaves and twigs from fins or intake and exhaust ports.

Symptoms that call for a pro

If your HVAC is exhibiting any of the following symptoms, you need the help of a professional HVAC repairperson:

✔ **Short cycling, or going off and on a lot:** When the thermostat is out of adjustment or the internals are out of balance, a fail-safe shuts the system off. Turn it off and get it repaired.

Different kinds of HVAC filters

The most expensive problem you can encounter with your HVAC system happens when either the filter or the fins get clogged up, in which case your machine runs, but little or no air passes through. Changing filters prevents both filter and fins from clogging. When buying filters, keep these things in mind:

- ✔ **Fiberglass filters** are woven and often blue, and they're the cheapest filters you can get. If you buy them in bulk, they're even cheaper, and you'll change them more often as a result. These only screen out debris that could damage your unit. Large dust gets through, as well as mold, mildew, toxins, and so forth. This may or may not matter to you. If you open your windows a lot, a high-tech filter on your HVAC input isn't going to change the average air quality in your home enough to merit the extra cost.

- ✔ **Pleated paper filters** have smaller porosity (so they filter smaller particles), as well as much greater surface area so they don't get clogged as fast. Use these if you only want to change the filter every three months or so. They're worth twice the cost, if you change them one third as often.

- ✔ **Electrostatic filters** get rid of smoke residues, allergens, and asthma-causing agents ($20 to $45 and up). Be aware, however, that simply installing these does not remove all particles from the air. You need to use your system a lot to get the effect. You also need supplementary systems like air purifiers (see Chapter 13 for more on ventilation).

- ✔ **Irregular flame from the burners:** This indicates a problem with dirty burners or a cracked heat exchanger. The flame should be nice and even

211

over the entire burner surface. Many times you can tell at a glance whether your burners are running optimally.

✔ **Strange sounds like rumbling, clicking, and so on:** These are okay in hot-water or steam-heating systems, but in a furnace with a forced-air system, they're a sign of trouble.

✔ **Inexplicable illness in your family:** You may have a combustion leak somewhere in the system. Call a pro right away. Get a carbon monoxide alarm right now and use it. Check out Chapter 6 for more on carbon monoxide poisoning, or better yet, check with your doctor.

✔ **Sooty accumulations:** Deposits usually appear near where the flame is burning. A good clean burn leaves very little residue, and it appears more brown than black. Sooty black grunge, on the other hand, is a sign of incomplete burning — you're not getting all the heat you could be out of your fuel — and you're paying for the inefficiency. Plus, you're going to have to clean the soot out of the system, which can be costly.

Buying a New System or Supplementing the One You Have

If your HVAC system is old, it's probably inefficient compared to newer technology. You're likely to be disappointed with your system's performance. Maybe it doesn't cool the house well enough in the summer, or it's on all the time in the winter and the air isn't hot enough when it comes out. Or perhaps you're getting tired of the twice-a-year service call, in which case you need to add these costs to the payback analysis. Either way, if you're like most people, you may be considering changing your HVAC equipment.

If you're thinking about replacing your current HVAC system, your best bet is to call an HVAC service company and have them come out and analyze your equipment. They can tell you how much better new equipment will perform (although you should keep in mind that their motive is to sell new equipment). Armed with this information, you'll have a payback decision on your hands. You'll be saving a certain amount of energy per year, which you can translate into cost by using your rate structure (see Chapter 3). What you'll probably discover is that, because HVAC equipment is expensive, you're not likely to get a payback in less than 20 years, which is a dubious investment.

Before you spend the big bucks, first try all the little things I present in this chapter and in Chapter 7. If you still decide to change, take your time. Do your research, and get at least three quotes.

Rather than replacing your existing HVAC, you can install supplemental heating and cooling equipment. You can do this in all sorts of ways:

- **Take advantage of the sun:** You can use the sun to heat your home, and prevent it from doing so when you want to stay cool. Details are in Chapter 12.

- **Improve ventilation:** This chapter has all sorts of little tips about getting the air moving in your house, and Chapter 13 offers much more detail.

- **Incorporate alternative energy sources:** A number of energy sources — solar, stoves, biomass, and others — can supplement your current HVAC system. All these are explained in detail in Part III. Before deciding that you want to change your existing equipment, take a quick stroll through this information. You may decide that you can solve your problem one step at a time and save a lot of money.

One of the best bets is to install a stove in your family room or living room. You can use the stove to heat the room locally, which means you won't be heating your entire home. This is inevitably cheaper, as long as you install the right type of stove and use it appropriately. I did this in my home: I installed a gas fireplace in the family room and it actually heats the entire home so well that most of the time I don't have to turn the whole-house system on at all. To be honest, I can't say that I saved a whole lot of money considering how much the equipment and installation cost, but the home is a lot friendlier because a fireplace flame is burning almost constantly in the most-used room in the house. The aesthetics are much better, and the gas fireplace is a cinch to operate. All it takes is the press of a button on the remote controller.

Hiring an HVAC Contractor

Whether you decide to replace your existing HVAC system with a brand-new one or supplement the one you have with additional heating and cooling equipment, you need to hire a contractor. Every contractor uses a standard contract and follows approved practices. Contractors can

✔ Obtain permits

✔ Manage the schedule and get the parts when they're needed

- Deal with all the inspections, and assume responsibility for a failed inspection

- Solve problems quickly and efficiently

To find potential contractors, your best bet is to ask friends who have the same kind of system you want to install for referrals (or warnings to stay away, as the case may be). You can look contractors up with the Better Business Bureau, or you can get information from state regulatory agencies. The Internet contains a lot of referral sites, but beware — these may be paid for by the contractors themselves. Enter the name of your city or county and the kind of project you want to do.

Never use a family member or friend. You may think they'll give you a better price (they'll probably be thinking they can charge you more since there won't be competitive bids) and better service (they'll be thinking they can work your job when it's convenient because you won't fire them), but the reality is you'll (both) probably regret it.

Getting bids

When hiring an HVAC contractor, always, always, always get multiple bids. There's a possibility that you may only be able to find a single contractor who can do the job you have in mind. In this case, try to get some information about how much the job costs in other areas so you'll have something to compare your bids against.

Always let contractors know you're going out for competitive bids. Never make a commitment of any kind when they first visit.

Comparing bids

After you get the bids, the problem becomes one of comparing apples to apples. Choosing the contractor comes down to three things:

- ✔ **Cost:** This may seem very important, but ultimately it may be the least significant factor. Why? Many things can go wrong, and problems generally add up to more cost. If you get a bid that's much lower than the other ones, beware. Your contractor probably doesn't understand what he's doing, either technically or competitively. Or maybe you're getting a contractor with a much lower overhead rate. Why? Does he not carry insurance? Is he working out of his truck, or off of his bicycle? Will he be around in three months to provide warranty coverage?

- ✔ **Craftsmanship:** Get referrals. Although this may not seem important, it reveals experience and efficiency. How long has the contractor been in the business?

- ✔ **Compatibility:** Let's face it. Some contractors are just dubious characters, and some are living in a different universe than you and I. Having a good relationship matters — a lot. Not only does it foster cooperation and increase the likelihood that problems will be ironed out quickly and effectively, but a contractor who doesn't like you is simply not going to go the extra mile for you (that's right — it can go both ways). You may get the work done as per spec, but extra time won't be spent to get the pipe joints just right. Or your phone calls won't be returned until it can't be put off any longer. The bottom line is that you want a contractor who is happy to answer the phone when he sees your phone number on his Caller ID.

 Make sure to ask about workmanship warranties. If the contractor is only offering the warranty that comes from the manufacturer, beware. Ask about bonding, insurance, licenses, and so forth too. If your contractor doesn't like these questions, beware. Good contractors are glad to hear these questions — it means their shady competitors are being weeded out.

Interviewing a contractor

All the contractors you contact want the job, for the most money they can get. Here's how to wade through the quicksand:

- Let the contractors do the talking during the interviews. If you're talking, you're not getting information.

- Ask the same questions of each contractor.

- Ask them what problems they foresee.

- Ask them whether they get their supplies from multiple sources. If they're stuck on a single system supplier, ask them why.

- Ask them what conditions would merit the contract being tossed out.

 You always have the right to negotiate, and they always have the right to refuse.

Sealing the deal

A contract should include prices as well as a schedule of

217

events that can be easily established and approved between the two of you. You also need to specify the cash flow: when payment is due and how much it will be.

Never pay a contractor until the work is finished. The best bet is not to make any payments at all until the entire job is finished.

Get *everything* in writing. Make it clear that throughout the entire project you expect everything to be in writing. Any decisions or changes made will be in writing only. E-mails are okay, but print them out and keep them in a file folder. I shall repeat: Get everything in writing. It's not that people are to be distrusted; it's that verbal communication is like that children's game Telephone, where the message gets garbled each time it's spoken. Writing forces clear articulation (although some readers of this book might argue that point).

Working with a contractor once the job begins

Once you're on the go, you need to work with your contractor as effectively as possible. Now is not the time to express doubt about your contractor's abilities. Now is the time to follow the Golden Rule: Do unto others as you would have them do unto you.

- ✔ **Always be completely square and decisive.** You may not want to express disappointment about how a job is turning out, but you should do so if that's what you're feeling.

- ✔ **Be friendly no matter what.** Don't get emotional. Problems happen. Be cool when they do, and your contractor will be more honest with you about everything.

✔ **Offer cold drinks.** Make a cooler available. Go the extra mile.

✔ **Don't forget the need for a restroom.** Make it nice and easy, and keep it clean.

Chapter 9

Lighting Your Home More Efficiently

• •

In This Chapter

▶ Understanding the differences between various types of light bulbs

▶ Considering the aesthetics of your lighting schemes

▶ Calculating cost savings that you can achieve

▶ Maximizing your efficiency with special light switches

• •

The typical North American home spends between 8 and 10 percent of its energy budget on lighting (not including the bulbs and equipment). In any given night, the average home uses 32 light bulbs, including not only lighting for rooms, but lighting inside refrigerators, ovens, and microwaves. Most of these light bulbs are the standard, 50-cent, screw-base style using a technology that has been around for over a hundred years. People have spent the vast majority of their lives with Thomas Edison's original brainstorm. But things are changing. A number of choices are available now that, while more expensive, provide much better economics and performance over the lifetime of the product. They also offer lower pollution, which is very important to many people.

In this chapter, I show you how to review your lighting arrangements and make sensible changes geared toward realizing payback. New lighting technologies can be very expensive, and you may be better off spending the money on other efficiency improvements. I show you how to make the right decisions. If you're interested in exploiting the sun for some of your home-lighting needs, head to Chapter 12, where I tell you how to let the sun shine in!

Picking the Right Light: Your Options

When you think of lighting, you may automatically think of Thomas Edison and his incandescent bulb. In fact, you may be reading this very book by the light of a bulb not too different from the one Edison first invented. But lighting options have evolved over time, from natural light to firelight to candles to incandescent bulbs to the energy-efficient products of today. Each has its plusses and minuses when it comes to ambience and energy efficiency. In this section, I review the most common light alternatives in use today.

The prevailing question is whether, by reducing the lighting component of your utility bill, you can actually achieve better overall efficiencies. This depends largely on why you're using lighting and what sort of climate you live in. There's a fundamental notion that lighting is inherently inefficient, but the story is not so simple. If your main energy issue is heating your home, for example, burning inefficient light bulbs will simply mean that your furnace is on less, so the process is not really as inefficient as it may first appear. In fact, you could conceivably heat your entire home exclusively with old-fashioned, inexpensive light bulbs.

Plus, incandescent bulbs shed a nice, warm color that has the psychological effect of making you feel warmer. The point is, you need to understand how and when the new technologies should be used because they're not universal solutions, as some would have you believe.

 Visit a good-quality lighting store to see all kinds of lighting options. Stores dedicated to lighting have better displays and a broader range of products than big hardware stores. The sales staff is also able to explain energy-efficient products better.

Natural light

Natural light includes sunlight, firelight, and candlelight. Sunlight has been around a lot longer than humanity, and it provides the overwhelming bulk of our lighting needs. Sunlight has a very broad *spectrum,* or many wavelengths of light — what most people think of as "color" (think of the colors of the rainbow and you get the idea). Sunlight's spectrum goes from ultra-violet, which we can't see, through the visible range (the rainbow colors), and on into the infrared and far infrared, which are also invisible to the human eye. Sunlight gets filtered as it transmits through the atmosphere, and that's why it can look very red in the morning and evenings. But mostly sunlight is white and bright, creating a jaunty mood that people associate with the best of Mother Nature.

Candlelight and firelight preceded all our fancy, electrical light bulb schemes. Flames cast a rich tone of reddish hues and make people's skin tone appear deep and attractive. Candles are popular because of the benign, tawny tint they cast on a room.

You can increase the lighting efficiency in your home by taking advantage of these natural light sources. Following are some ideas:

- Sunlight is the most efficient way to light your home because it's free and creates zero pollution. Sunlight also creates a specific mood, which can't be beat by manmade artifices. I go into a lot of detail on how to get sunlight into your home in Chapter 12.

- Candles don't require any utility power. If you want to light your whole house with candlelight, use natural beeswax candles with minimal scent and lead-free wicks, and try to find the long-burning style, which translates into less crud outgassed into the air in your home. Candles of this type can light your house very nicely and save a lot of money. (You don't want to use regular candles to light your whole house. Doing so can become very expensive, not to mention polluting.)

Don't blow your candles out when you're finished with them; use a snuffer (a long handle with a cone shape on one end) unless, of course, you like the look of wax-spray on your walls. Blowing out candles also causes more pollution in the air than a snuffer because you're blasting the wick with oxygen (the snuffer is much gentler). Notice how much less smoke a snuffer creates and you'll get the picture.

- If you want to light your home with firelight, let the kids play with matches in the living room. Be sure to have the fire department, your insurance company, Child Protective Services, and a good lawyer on stand-by.

Old-fashioned incandescent bulbs

Standard-style (incandescent) light bulbs work by using electricity to heat up a narrow, high-resistance filament until it glows very bright. The filament is enclosed in a vacuum-drawn envelope (called the bulb) so that when the filament glows, it doesn't burn up from being combined with oxygen. Incandescent bulbs cast a warm, reddish tint, especially when a dimmer is used. You can get them in a thousand different configurations, and they're inexpensive and widely available. Their widespread use is not going to diminish anytime soon, but the trend is toward other lighting sources simply because incandescent bulbs are so inefficient (at least in terms of lighting; they do make great heaters).

An important specification for a light bulb is how much light it puts out divided by the amount of energy it consumes (an efficiency standard). Incandescent bulbs are the worst of all lighting options in this regard: Most of the energy an incandescent bulb gobbles up is converted into heat — nearly 90 percent. That doesn't mean, however, that you can't use incandescent bulbs more efficiently.

When considering light bulb efficiency, pay attention to the bulb's intensity and spatial focus. A round light bulb emits its spectrum pretty much in all directions at once, while a laser beam, for example, is extremely focused on a specific spot. A 10-watt gooseneck lamp with a highly focused reflector can cast enough light onto the page of a book to make reading easy and comfortable on the eyes. A 100-watt light bulb in a broadly emitting lamp, on the other hand, may be so diffuse that nothing shows up clearly. So when you choose incandescent bulbs, remember that higher wattage doesn't necessarily mean brighter light. Rather than buy the highest wattage you can find, buy the bulb that's labeled a floodlight. These are usually conically shaped and have some reflective material on the inside of the glass envelope.

Halogen bulbs

Halogen light bulbs operate almost the same as incandescent bulbs, but with a few small differences. Inside a halogen bulb is a peanut-sized glass envelope that contains a tungsten filament and halogen gas (essentially, it's a light bulb inside of a light bulb). As the tungsten filament burns (the same way an incandescent does), the halogen gas catches the tungsten molecules and redeposits them back onto the filament, yielding a longer lifetime and better lighting uniformity. Halogen bulbs also emit a whiter, brighter, and more easily focused light, comparable to sunshine itself (this may or may not be a goal you have in mind, but in my book it sounds like a good idea).

Halogen bulbs are good for reading because they're easier on your eyes (due to color, intensity, and so on). They're also good for store displays or for artwork illumination where you want the light to have a color-neutral affect (and let the artwork do its own talking). They work well outdoors because the light is more noticeable. Although they may yield the same *lumen output* (a measure of how much light a bulb emits) as an incandescent, the light works better with the human eye, so the spectrum is more efficient.

Halogen bulbs burn hotter than regular incandescent bulbs, so you need to be more careful how you handle them. If you use one for a reading light, you may not like having the intense heat source next to your head. Or you may love the heat source, if it's a cold, winter night. Like incandescent bulbs, the overall efficiency of halogen bulbs depends on whether you want heat.

Halogen bulbs can be much more efficient than incandescent bulbs because they last twice as long. Use them in locations that are hard to reach, and you won't have to reach so far so often. You can also use them in locations where you're looking for more heat. Perhaps the most important advantage of halogen bulbs, however, is their benign appearance, particularly when dimmed. Having each bulb appear exactly the same may also be important in track lighting. Incandescent bulbs tend to change over their lifetimes, while halogen bulbs are very uniform (unlike you and me).

Flickering fluorescent bulbs

The wave of the future, fluorescent light bulbs (CFLs) use a gas-filled tube and a ballast with electronics. A high-voltage signal excites phosphors on the inside surface of the bulb, which, in turn, emit light. The main difference between CFLs and incandescent or halogen bulbs is that CFLs are far more efficient because they don't put out a lot of heat. A typical 15-watt CFL puts out as much light as a 60-watt incandescent light bulb, meaning CFLs are four times as efficient.

If you plan to replace an incandescent bulb with an equivalent fluorescent bulb, in general, you can divide the wattage of an incandescent by four to get the wattage needed for an equivalent CFL. But the best bet is to compare the lumens, an actual measure of the light output (wattage is simply the input power the bulb will take). Almost all light-bulb packages now include lumens in addition to wattages.

CFLs are more expensive, although the gap is closing due to the fact that so many more fluorescent bulbs are now being manufactured. The typical lifetime of a CFL is around four times that of an incandescent bulb, and herein lies their real benefit: They don't need to be changed nearly as often, so the lifetime costs are actually less than incandescent bulbs, making them cheaper in the long term. One caveat: You should only use CFLs in fixtures that you use at least two hours per day; otherwise, the extra cost and diminished appearance probably isn't worth it.

 The fact that CFLs have much longer lifetimes makes them useful in hard-to-reach places because you don't have to change them nearly as often. If you have a bulb that's on a lot and hard to get to, use a fluorescent bulb.

CFLs aren't without drawbacks. The chief one is that they tend to flicker like a strobe light (this may or may not be noticeable). Plus, their light spectrum (the color they broadcast) is often a bluish tint, which does not tend to flatter skin tone or food appearance. However, new technologies that solve these problems are becoming more common. Here are some other things to be aware of about CFLs:

- ✔ They can be dimmed, but only if you buy the right dimmers, and these are not cheap. Plus, some people don't like the pronounced flickering that dimmers create.

- ✔ CFLs don't like very hot environments, where their lifetimes are drastically reduced. Don't use them in enclosed spaces without ventilation because they'll heat up and grow old quickly, thereby negating the longevity advantage.

- ✔ CFLs often take a few minutes to reach maximum brightness. If you're shopping for a bulb and sampling the possibilities, allow some time for it to warm up before you decide whether you like it or not.

Around 5 milligrams of mercury are contained in each CFL light bulb (big bulbs have more, of course). Mercury is a very poisonous substance, although 5 milligrams isn't much at all (about as much as the tip of a fine-point pencil). The fact that CFLs contain mercury means you have to be particularly careful when disposing of and handling these bulbs:

- In most municipalities, you can't simply throw a CFL into the trash; you must handle it with special care. This boils down to an even higher cost, which must be weighed against the efficiency gains you may realize. Some options for disposing of CFLs include hazardous waste sites (most accept CFLs, but some don't) and stores that sell CFLs (many take back old, used ones; IKEA, in particular, has gone out of its way to be environmentally friendly). To find a suitable disposal option, contact the U.S. Environmental Recycling Hotline (877-327-8491) or check out www.lamprecycle.org.

- Never send a CFL product to an incinerator, as the mercury becomes airborne when the bulb burns.

- Never use a vacuum to clean up a broken bulb; the mercury is aerated into your home environment through the vacuum filter, which is too porous to catch the molecules. Use a wet paper towel, and stick both the bulb parts and the paper towel in a sealed, plastic bag.

Light-emitting diodes

Light-emitting diodes (LEDs) are extremely efficient — even more so than CFLs — and they have incredibly long lifetimes. However, they're much more expensive than other lighting sources. At present, LEDs are used where ultra-high efficiency or ultra-long lifetime are required, for instance, in off-grid homes that run off of batteries or remote cabins that run off of generators. In these applications, LEDs are actually cheaper in the long run, despite their high cost, because they enable smaller batteries. (In off-grid homes, the battery banks are the fundamental power source. Batteries are very expensive, so smaller batteries are economically desirable.) LEDs are also used in stoplights (due to their ultra-high reliability) and in auto taillights.

Portable devices that use batteries also benefit from using LEDs. The availability of LED flashlights and camping lanterns, as well as boat and RV lighting systems, is increasing. You can buy LED-based light modules that interchangeably plug right into existing screw-type light fixtures, but they cost over $25. Furthermore, the light is thin and silvery, which is not the friendliest hue. Before you buy LEDs, check them out at a lighting store because light bulbs, like kids, are not returnable items if you're not happy with their performance.

Going for Efficiency without Sacrificing Aesthetics

Lighting does more than illuminate. It also creates mood, or ambience. While one type of light produces a warm, cozy glow, another type produces a harsh glare. Either can be just the type of light you need or want, depending on your lighting needs, the area you want to illuminate, and the mood you want to create.

Most lighting is not for "seeing," but for mood and for making your home feel homier. By being imaginative —

moving your lights around in different setups and trying different light bulbs — you can probably find an optimum configuration that takes less energy than you're using right now without sacrificing a thing. Here are some ideas for your consideration:

- ✔ **Find a style of lamp that creates the mood you want.** The lamp is usually more influential than the type of light bulb in creating a mood. Lamps with dimmers are always good, and a lamp that focuses light lets you use a smaller light bulb and attain the same effect.

You can find a lot of very interesting lamps at garage sales, often for less than a dollar apiece. Be on the lookout for such a find. It can save you money twice: on the purchase price and on the energy costs. The best finds are gooseneck lamps with dimmers so you can focus the light on your work and turn the intensity up and down as desired.

- ✔ **Avoid metal or heavy paper lampshades.** Lampshades are very important in terms of focusing and directing light. Many of them cut off most of the light from a bulb. Look for ones that have the effect you want, but allow most of the light through. Diaphanous films are best.

- ✔ **Vary the intensity of lighting as much as you can.** Vary light bulb intensities to create texture and depth in a room. Disperse the lights around your house to highlight the good and ignore the not-so-good.

- ✔ **Vary wattage where you can.** The higher the wattage, the colder the light (bluish light "feels" colder than red; it's a human perception thing);

the lower the wattage, the redder the light, and the friendlier the tone. The wattage you choose depends on what you're trying to achieve. A number of smaller light bulbs distributed around a room makes for a soft color and even lighting. Plus, lower-wattage bulbs have longer lifetimes simply because they're not being so stressed by heat.

Always use the smallest wattage possible. Experiment instead of just plugging in what you have on hand. You'll probably find that you can use smaller bulbs in most instances. For example, a gooseneck lamp in the bathroom that focuses in on your face gives you the lighting you need *and* keeps wattage down.

✔ **Use lights creatively.** For example, vary the lights on tracks; they don't all have to be the same type or wattage, nor do they all have to be focused on the fireplace. A small spotlight on your favorite picture will bring those colors into play in the room. A small, 10-watt picture light can completely change a room for the better.

✔ **Try candles.** Use them alone or in combination with electric lights. You'll get hooked, and you'll save money if you do it right (see the earlier section "Natural light" for details on what makes candles energy efficient).

✔ **Lower the lights before bed.** Too much light right before bed creates a bad sleeping mood. Start to dim the lights or turn them off well before you retire. You'll find yourself gently relaxing into sleep mode.

✔ **Use night lights.** Having strategically placed night lights relieves you of the need to flip every light switch on when you get up in the middle of the night to go to the bathroom or nursery. Besides, blasting yourself with light in the bathroom in the middle of the night wakes you up, and it's a proven fact that it takes you longer to get back to sleep than if you simply use a very dim night light.

✔ **Make your lights do double duty where (and when) possible.** CFLs have a reputation for being more efficient than incandescent bulbs, but in certain situations that's not the case. In the winter, for example, incandescent bulbs are more efficient than CFLs because they're cheap *and* they help heat your home (because of the heat they emit). In fact, they

---

Creating an outdoor "room" with light

Here's a great way to leverage your lighting investment to the hilt. Create a "room" in your yard by strategically placing outdoor lights. You can use solar lights, which can be moved wherever you want, or you can use low-voltage lighting systems available at any hardware store. (Low-voltages are safe, so anybody can do the project without the need for an electrician.) You can also use torchlights, which are like big candles.

Establish the room's boundaries with lights: Shine them on bushes or trees and that's where your eye will subliminally see a "wall." Highlight features like fountains, flower beds, furniture, and so on. Use colored lights to vary the texture and create moods and aesthetic spaces.

By doing this, you can achieve an effect that makes your home seem larger, more spacious, and certainly more in tune with Mother Nature.

---

heat more uniformly and also cast a warmer mood. They may be more efficient at heating your home than your central heater or your stove.

Calculating How Much You Can Save

To make a long story short, your potential cost savings (and the payback of installing a more expensive technology) are entirely dependent on how much you use a light (the average number of hours per day). Obviously, the easiest way to save money is to simply use less lighting; you don't need to invest in new bulbs. The minimum lighting you need to function is one light bulb turned on per person in your home at any given time. (I don't mean this to be a lifestyle guide; I simply want to make a point.)

Of course, most people don't restrict themselves to turning on one light per person. In most homes, some light bulbs are literally on all the time, particularly outside lights or garage lights. And someone who likes a bright room may have every table lamp on as well as the book light he's reading by.

Consider the lights you use. Do you really need all of them? You'd probably answer no if you knew how much each one costs. Fortunately, lighting costs are easy to calculate. Here's how to determine how much you're spending on a particular light each month:

1. **Figure out how many watt hours (Wh) the bulb is on per day by multiplying the wattage by the number of hours the light's on daily.**

   You can read the wattage from the light bulb. The value is expressed in watts; 60-watts is very common. Then ask yourself how many hours you typically use that light per day. Two hours? All day (24 hours)?

2. **Multiply the total daily Wh by 30 to get the total Wh per month.**

3. **Divide the total Wh per month by 1,000 to get the total kWh.**

    Why are kWh important? Because your utility bill is calculated based on kWh.

4. **To get your monthly cost, multiply your kWh by the amount the electric company charges you per kWh.**

    Look at your electric bill to find out how much you're being charged for electricity. Fifteen cents per kWh is typical, but your rate may be a lot higher. (See Chapter 3 for more details. In particular, if you're on a tiered rate structure, use the highest rate.)

Here are some examples of calculations and the cost savings you may be able to achieve by changing your lighting schemes.

✔ A 60-watt bulb left on for an hour consumes 60 Wh, or .06 kWh per day. Ten 60-watt bulbs in recessed lighting in your ceiling turned on for four hours consume 2.4 kWh per day. At a rate of 15 cents per kWh, this costs 36 cents a day. For a month, the total comes to $10.80, or $130 per year. Add to that the cost of new bulbs, and you may be spending over $150 a year to leave those overhead lights on every night. Is it worth it? Calculations like this can be surprising.

✔ A 15-watt CFL costs around $4, while a comparable

60-watt incandescent bulb costs around 75 cents. For a light fixture that is turned on four hours per day, at a cost of 15 cents per kWh, the CFL costs $3.24 per year to operate. The incandescent costs $12.96 per year, for a difference of $9.72. Going with the initially more expensive CFL is actually more cost-efficient, easily paying you back the difference in original equipment cost and saving around 130 pounds of carbon dioxide pollution.

- Do you have an outside light that burns all night? If it's 600 watts, it's costing you: 0.600 kW × 10 hours/day × 30 days/month × $.15/kWh = $9 per month, or $108 per year. You could add a motion detector, which turns the light on only when something moves through the viewing area, and save $100 per year while still having light whenever you really need it. (See the next section for more on motion detectors.)

- A 15-watt CFL bulb costs $3.00, whereas a 60-watt incandescent bulb costs 50 cents. In a garage where the light is on all the time, a CFL costs around $20 per year to operate, whereas an incandescent bulb costs $80. However, if the CFL is put into a bathroom light socket that's only used for an hour a day, the annual cost difference is only $2.50, which is the difference in the prices of the bulbs. (Plus, in the bathroom, the hue of the CFL light is not very flattering.)

To calculate the savings you can achieve by installing a smaller bulb or a different type of bulb, do this:

1. **Figure out the wattage difference between the replaced bulb and the new bulb.**

   Simply subtract the wattages: If you replace a 60-

watt bulb with a 40-watt bulb, take 40 away from 60.

Keep in mind that you may not be getting the same amount of light, or lumens, when you change bulbs, but the cost on your utility bill depends only on the wattage.

2. **Figure out how many hours per year the light is on.**

   Multiply the number of hours the light's on daily by 365.

3. **Multiply the yearly value (Step 2) by the wattage difference (Step 1) and then divide by 1,000 to get the annual kWh.**

4. **Multiply what you got in Step 3 by your electricity cost, in $ per kWh.**

5. **Compare this to the difference in cost of the bulbs. Also take into account the expected lifetime of the bulb.**

For an easier way to calculate how much you'll save if you plug in different types of light bulbs, go to www.getenergysmart.com. For an online catalog of energy-saving lighting options, go to www.energyfederation.org.

Using Clever Switches to Reduce Your Bill

As earlier sections explain, you can use different types of light bulbs to increase your energy efficiency, but a better option may be to use clever switching systems that simply and automatically turn your lights off when you don't need them.

Motion detectors

Motion detectors are devices that switch light bulbs off and on when they detect something moving in their *field-of-view,* basically the area where the motion detector is set up to "look." Motion detectors are the exact same technology used in burglar alarms, except that they don't trigger an alarm; they simply turn on the light. Most motion detectors are integrated with a timing switch, so when motion is detected and a light is switched on, it goes off after a set amount of time (a couple minutes is typical — most devices are adjustable for time delay).

Motion detectors offer all sorts of benefits, some relating to efficiency and some relating to safety, but all relating to convenience. Burglars, for example, hate being suddenly illuminated while they're sneaking around. When a light is simply left on, a burglar doesn't mind so much; it's when things suddenly change that they get nervous and decide to vamoose. Mount a motion detector light over a porch or on the side of your house where a burglar is most apt to approach (like a dark garage side). Motion detectors aren't valuable just for their "gotcha!" effect, though. They turn on when anyone is there, which can be helpful when a neighbor comes up to your porch for a friendly visit, you pull into the driveway at night, and so on.

You get the best return on investment when you combine motion detectors with high-wattage lights, which are usually the kind employed outdoors. Here are some options to consider:

- ✔ **Solar-powered outdoor floodlights with motion detectors:** You can mount them anywhere so you get light exactly where you want it, and you don't need an electrical outlet so you avoid the cost of outlet installation. The unit includes a battery that is charged during high intensity solar hours, and so the amount of available energy is limited. At around $65, the potential exists for huge cost savings if you need light in a remote location. Plus, you can move the lights around at will, which you can't do with a standard hard-wired light fixture.

✔ **One-piece outdoor systems:** These include one or more motion detectors along with light fixtures in one complete package. These come in flood, decorative, and remote arrangements.

✔ **Motion detector switches:** These fit right into the standard switch socket you already have in your home. Whenever somebody walks into the field of view, the light goes on for about 30 seconds. These are great for utility rooms where your hands may be full of clothes or groceries, and flipping a switch is inconvenient. They're also good for basements and attics.

✔ **Screw-base-style motion detectors:** You install these between a light bulb and the socket that the bulb would normally be screwed into. At around $40 they're not cheap and the payback isn't very good, but they may be just the ticket for a utility room or laundry room where your arms are full of groceries or clothes and you can't grapple around for the switch. Go to www.sportys.com/shoptool to see a number of popular arrangements.

 Before you buy a motion detector, pay attention to the field of view, which is the area over which the motion detector operates. With some units, you can adjust the field of view; with others, it's fixed. Getting one with an adjustable sensitivity is best; you don't necessarily want your lights to go on when a cat crosses your yard (then again, maybe you do).

When in doubt, save the packing materials and receipt, and be prepared to buy something else.

Dimmer switches

Light dimmers are used for decreasing and increasing a light's intensity. Although they aren't particularly efficient, the net effect of using them is that you do use less energy. There's another benefit as well: The bulbs on dimmer switches last longer because they're operating at lower temperatures. In general, you get a friendlier, richer color, and you can vary the mood in a room like nothing else.

You can change almost any light switch in your house to a dimmer switch, but beware: You need to know a few basic rudiments about electricity before you start poking around inside your electrical junction boxes. You need to understand the difference between the white wire, the black wire, and the green (or bare) wire. The task isn't difficult, but explaining everything you need to know about electrical wiring is beyond the scope of this book. If you're motivated and want to give it a go yourself, keep the following advice in mind:

- **Before you do anything, the safest bet is to simply turn the main breaker switch off in your house.** You'll have to do your work during daylight hours or with a flashlight, but you won't be able to shock yourself. After you do the work, make sure you cover the dimmer switch with the faceplate. If you turn the main breaker back on and a circuit breaker trips, you've messed up somewhere, at which point I recommend you call in an electrician to find out what's wrong and do the job right.

- **Ask for instructions and guidelines at your**

hardware store. Someone there can probably tell you how to install a switch and show you the actual hardware to use. When you're getting instructions, make sure you understand how to maintain the proper grounding scheme, which is very important. You may need to be aware of local electrical codes, so ask your hardware store clerk about those as well.

Another option is to refer to *How To Fix Everything For Dummies* by Gary Hedstrom, Peg Hedstrom, and Judy Ondria Tremore (Wiley) for general information and instructions on common electrical wiring jobs.

If you have aluminum wiring in your house (it's shiny or dull gray, instead of the usual coppery or orange color), don't wire a dimmer yourself because there are technical problems you don't want to deal with. (Specifically, when two dissimilar metals come into contact, the potential for corrosion exists.) So when working with aluminum wires, call in a pro.

Whole-house lighting controllers

Whole-house lighting control systems basically switch all your home lights off and on from a central console. For instance, you can turn off all your lights from one location when you go to bed. Or when you enter your house, you can turn on a certain preset number of lights so you don't have to go around and individually activate each light. Some can be turned off and on by a timer. You can even get a system that you can call from a remote location (though why you'd want to, I haven't figured out).

If you program one of these contraptions for efficiency, you can achieve some significant cost savings. For instance, you could turn all your lights off at a certain time of night. You could also turn lights on and off according to a clock so that you capture exactly the right mood at different times of the evening.

Chapter 10

Watering Down Your Water Consumption

The minimum human requirement for water is only around four gallons per day, and that's for both consumption and cleaning. So how much does a typical family (2 adults, 2 kids) use? Between 200 and 350 gallons of water a day. That's 73,000 to 128,000 gallons per year. Landscaping, swimming pools, and spas take even more water. A small, working ranch may use over 270,000 gallons per year. Bluntly put, that's a well of a lot of water.

In most homes, water has four main destinations: faucets, showers (baths), dishwashers, and washing machines. In each case, water heating may be required, which consumes around 20 percent of a typical home's energy costs. Other

242

uses of water include outdoor irrigation, pools, spas, fountains, and so on. This chapter tells you how to save in these areas.

 The vast majority of homes get their water from the local utility, some with metered rate structures, some not. If you're not operating off of a water meter, your water utility may give you a better monthly rate if you voluntarily go to a metered rate structure. The utility will come out and install a meter, usually free of charge. If you're frugal, you can save money, and by having a meter you'll be more conscious of how much water you're using.

Drinking to Your Health

Most of the water used in a home isn't consumed. Instead, it's used for tasks like cleaning, watering, and so on. Yet many people today spend much more money for water they drink than on water they use for these other purposes. Why? Because our society is fixated on bottled and/or purified drinking water, which is almost always a waste of money and resources, and generates far more pollution than is necessary. In fact, evidence increasingly indicates that drinking purified water may lead to health problems. So what's the deal?

To help you sort out what you need to know about your water supply and to give you ideas for reducing the amount of money you spend on drinking water, I offer the following sections.

Wading through a flood of choices: Tap, well, bottled, and purified

Most homes have a number of choices for their water sources. In this section, I review the most common choices.

Your best bet is to use the cheapest source for each of your various applications. Most of the time, this is very easy; simply use tap water.

Tap water

Most homes get their water from local utilities, which have stringent quality requirements. In fact, federal standards for tap water are actually higher than those for bottled water. In addition, most tap water already contains minerals important to your health — minerals that some purveyors of purifier systems and bottled water deliberately add to their products and charge you more for. Bottom line: The government provides you with safe, healthy water, without the hassle and expense of bottled water.

Local utilities are required to make public their testing process and results. If you want to know exactly what's in your water, call the customer-service number on your utility bill and ask to be sent the data. There shouldn't be a charge for this.

Well water

Some homes get their water from wells. Although these sources are generally very good, they may not be the best source for drinking water because contaminants do make their way into wells, and you may have to pay for testing. Well water is especially prone to change over time. If you have a well, you're very likely getting the requisite minerals and other natural components. But you may also be getting pollution and other contaminants like dumped pesticides or other chemicals.

If you have a well, test it at least once a year; if your well fails a test, test more often. Look in the yellow pages under "Water Well Drilling."

Bottled water

Bottled water costs 240 to 10,000 times more than tap water. The costs show up in bottling, packaging, shipping, retail, sales, advertising, and so on. If you're paying this price for bottled water simply because you think it's cleaner, you may want to consider these facts:

- ✔ **Quality isn't guaranteed.** Unlike the water provided by utilities, the quality of bottled water isn't regulated by the federal government. That means when you buy bottled water you have no guarantee that you're even getting water that's as good as your home supply.

- ✔ **"Enriched" may not provide enrichment.** Some bottled water is advertised as "oxygen enriched." Absolutely no evidence exists to support the notion that this does anything whatsoever to help you.

- ✔ **Transporting water is costly.** Bottled water takes a great deal of energy to transport to your store shelf. Think how far that water from the Italian mountain lake has come, and then think of the pollution generated in the process. It doesn't matter that the water is cheap; the cost of pollution is not reflected in the cost of a product (although this is rapidly changing).

America's appetite for bottled water gobbles up more than 47 million gallons of oil and produces one billion pounds of carbon dioxide per year (that's right — billion!).

- ✔ **Plastic bottles stick around for a very long time.** It takes 1,000 years for a plastic bottle to degrade in a landfill. You can recycle the bottles (see Chapter 14), but if you don't need them in the first place, recycling isn't the best answer. Not using them is.

If you want to use bottles of water because they're convenient, use reusable bottles. You can fill these up with tap water. Alternatively, buy purified water at a grocery store that lets you bring in and fill up your own bottles and charges you by the gallon.

Purified water

Many people use water purifiers, systems that in most cases remove impurities but in some cases add minerals and other positive substances.

We humans don't necessarily need perfect water. In fact, evidence suggests that a pristine lifestyle leads to increased immune deficiency. Certain types of minerals and bacteria are required by the human body to enable digestion. And recent studies indicate that children raised on purified water are statistically more likely to suffer from childhood diseases than those brought up on tap water. The reason? The immune system needs to be constantly exercised in order to achieve optimum conditioning (just like muscles). Humans that live in sanitized, pristine environments don't get the necessary exposure.

Having said that, sometimes having a water purifying system is a good idea. The next section explains how to tell when your water supply is problematic and what you can do about it.

Getting the goods on suspicious water

In rare cases, you may actually have good reason to be suspicious of your water source. Potential contaminants include pernicious bacteria, *cysts* (parasites with protective coverings that make them very tenacious), heavy metals, chlorine, sediment, poisons, and many more.

Signs of a potential problem

Signs that your water supply may be contaminated include

- **Age of your pipes:** In old plumbing systems, some contaminants reside right in the pipes and are very difficult to get out. If your city water supply is pristine but you have an old home, you may still have a problem because you're running clear water through contaminated pipes.

- **Clarity:** Although unclear water is not a sure indicator of contamination, you should find out what the cause is. Most of the time it's only minerals, which isn't a problem.

- **Poor taste:** Bad tasting water may be a sign of a contaminant. But determining whether the bad taste indicates a real problem or just tastes different than you're used to is difficult (it's very common to go into other cities and find that the water tastes poor, even though it's just fine). If in doubt, get your water tested.

- **Smell:** The human nose is very sensitive. If your water smells bad, get it tested (although a bad smell isn't necessarily an indicator that it's unhealthy).

Testing options

If you're suspicious about the quality of your water, the best bet is to get your water tested. Here are your options:

- ✔ **Have your water tested by an independent company.** Check the Internet or your phone book for "Water Testing." For around $100, you can get a detailed analysis. (They send you a sterilized container; you fill it and send it back.) You need to do every testing sequence twice, at different times of the year, to get reliable results.

- ✔ **Have your water tested by a not-so-objective company.** You can get tests done by water purification companies (probably for free). But beware: Their goal is to sell you water purification equipment or services. They probably won't tell you that humans do better with impurities in their water supply. And — surprise, surprise — every water company that I've ever talked to has assured me that their water is the best.

- ✔ **Test your water yourself.** Although you can buy your own equipment and test your water yourself, I don't recommend it. First, it's expensive. Second, and more importantly, you probably don't have the expertise to interpret the results sufficiently. It's best to trust the experts.

Purifying your drinking water

So you've decided to improve your drinking water. Two types of home-based equipment are widely available:

- ✔ **Distilleries:** Distilled water is boiled, and, in the process, the water separates from the impurities. This type of purification is expensive and energy-intensive, but it's very thorough.

- ✔ **Filtration systems:** Filtering involves forcing the water through some kind of porous device that removes the impurities. Aerator filters that attach to faucets are the simplest type of filter.

As you consider your water purifying options, look for a system that only treats the water you plan to consume. After all, it makes no sense to filter water for your shower or your dishwasher. In addition, make sure the system targets the impurities you want targeted. Some systems only improve the water's taste and color. Others get rid of contaminants. Make sure you know what your system does.

It makes no sense to invest in purification equipment if you haven't had your water tested. Simply buying a filter because it sounds good is a waste of money, although most filters are purchased for this very reason. Purification equipment targets very specific types of contamination. Before you make an investment, make sure the equipment you're getting is designed to remove the contaminant you're interested in removing.

All systems take effort and maintenance. If you don't want to hassle with water purification, consider one of these alternatives:

- ✔ **Contract with a bottled water company.** A bottled water company will rent you a dispenser and come out twice a month to refill it with a big jug of distilled or filtered water and do the regular maintenance. The cost is around $8 per month. You can get dispensers that will heat the water, which is more efficient than using your water heater but less efficient than using your microwave.

- ✔ **Get a bottle with a built-in filter.** This is the cheapest way to go, and you only use this system when you need it. Fill the bottle with water from your tap, screw the filter/lid on, and, when you drink, the

249

water is filtered. Three micron porosity is good for removing bacteria and giardiasis. This simple scheme will satisfy most people's desire to filter their water.

Mechanical filtration

Mechanical filtration occurs when water is forced through a porous medium, like a screen or a chunk of carbon. These strainers use mesh with particular hole sizes. The size of the holes determines the strainer's *porosity,* which is usually specified in terms of microns (a *micron* is one millionth of a liter, on the order of size of mineral chunks). As you would expect, strainers with finer porosity remove smaller-sized contaminants than strainers with higher porosity.

To get an idea about what type of porosity you need, you have to determine what type of contaminant you're trying to remove. Sediment filters, for example, remove smaller particles like suspended dirt, sand, rust, and scale (known as *turbidity*). Once again, filters are always very specific to the type of material you are attempting to filter. Look on the filter label (or get on the Internet and research a particular filter's specifications) to see which types of contaminants it's good at filtering.

 If you need a filter with a very fine porosity, it's generally a good idea to remove the biggest impurities by using a higher porosity filter first. Larger porosity filters are generally much cheaper than smaller porosity filters (and easier to clean), so by catching the big stuff first, your overall filter expenses will be less.

Activated carbon filtration

Carbon absorption filters are the most widely used because they offer high performance at a low price. They remove many types of contaminants as well as chlorine, but they

250

Making your own solar water purifier

Here's a great project for the do-it-yourselfer. If salty or contaminated water is left in an open container, the water evaporates, leaving the contaminants behind. If the water is heated, the process speeds up considerably (this is the basis for a distillery). Here's a simple solar water purifier you can build for next to nothing, if you're clever and good with tools.

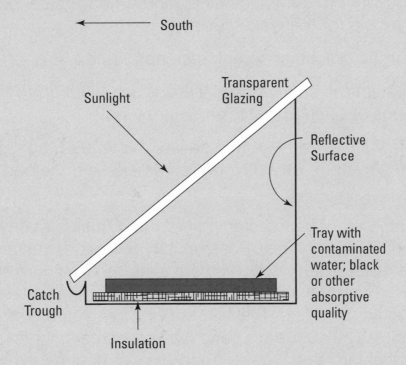

When the water evaporates, it condenses on the glass window and drips down into the catch trough. Tilt the catch trough just slightly and put a bottle or other container underneath the low end, and voilà! Purified water. (Large, efficient versions of this device capable of purifying hundreds of gallons a day are used in third-world countries.)

- ✔ You can make your system as cheap or as expensive as you want. You don't need glazed glass; you can use plain old window glass. You can get pieces of discarded glass from window shops for nothing but a smile.

- ✔ Reflection is easily accomplished with aluminum foil, shiny side out.

- ✔ Use sheet metal (the best option) or wood for the enclosure. If you want to get imaginative, find a good metal box and cut a hole for the glaze cover.

- ✔ Paint the box black to enhance absorption.

- ✔ A system the size of a small stove can yield up to three gallons of purified water on a sunny day.

The first few times you use this device the water may taste a little odd. Let the system "sweat" for a few weeks and the bad taste will go away.

Here's a little tip: When designing your unit, make it convenient to fill the inner tray with water. Position it by a hose, for instance. Then you won't have to carry water to your system. Configure some kind of funnel through the sidewall so you can pour the water right into the tray without spilling. Make it so you can remove the glazing top and clean out the tray, because the contaminants are going to remain behind. You'll get a good idea of how mineralized your tap water is when you see what's left in the tray over a period of time.

don't affect water hardness. Few carbon systems work with lead, asbestos, VOCs (dissolved organics), cysts, and coliform, so if these are your issues, carbon filters aren't recommended. In fact, most of the impurities that carbon filters remove are not the impurities that you are targeting.

In addition, carbon filters need to be changed frequently, and this can be very costly.

Reverse osmosis (ultrafiltration)

This method uses pressure to force water through a selective, semipermeable membrane that separates contaminants from the water. Reverse osmosis systems are very good at removing turbidity, asbestos, lead and other heavy metals, radium and VOCs. But keep these things in mind:

- ✔ **Membranes are costly to replace.** Most are capable of having the membrane washed out (backwashing), but the membranes do eventually need to be replaced, and this isn't cheap.

- ✔ **They waste a lot of water.** They use 3 to 9 gallons of water to get one pure gallon. This is a dubious way to achieve efficiency.

Virustat filters

Virustat filters eliminate viruses from water sources in foreign cities or wild streams. For the most part, these viruses don't affect local folks because they are used to them and have built up a tolerance.

Caring for your filters

As the filter cruds up, its effectiveness diminishes, so when reading specs, always remember that you need to change filters as often as the manufacturer recommends or you may not achieve the required performance.

Also, as the filter gets older it traps impurities of all kinds, so it may actually become a breeding ground for nasty little critters invisible to the naked eye, making the problem worse, not better.

Weighing in on water softeners

Some water is very high in mineral content. This is termed *hard water*. Minerals can cause scaling and buildups of white crud within plumbing systems. Some people are also sensitive to hard water. In particular, you can feel the sediments in your hair when you're done with a shower. With hard water, you get a sense that you're never really all that clean. But hard water doesn't pose any health problems, so installing a water softener is always discretionary. People generally do it only when the scaly buildup gets out of hand — for instance, when valves begin to fail and kitchen equipment gets so scaly that nothing shines anymore.

Water softening systems simply remove mineral deposits from the water by passing it through a filtering mechanism. The vast majority of water softeners incorporate a filter self-cleaning cycle that uses salt pellets that you refill on a periodic basis. (Bags of salt pellets cost around $5 apiece and are widely available in grocery stores. You'll need a strong back to dump the 45 pound bags into your water softener — teenage boys are excellent sources for strong backs.)

Water softeners are expensive. Plus the backwashing of water softeners wastes a lot of water, and you need to have some means of getting the backwashed liquid to go to a drain (this results in salt buildup there, which can be a problem in its own right).

You can install a water softener yourself, but only if you're competent with tools. Look for features that make the periodic maintenance easier, like a low hopper for feeding salt and easy-to-understand digital programming instructions. Also consider connecting the softener to certain faucets only, such as those in the kitchen and bath. You certainly don't need softened water outdoors or in your garage.

Directing the Flow of Traffic with Faucets

The typical home has six indoor faucets, and another four or five outdoors. That gives you a lot of opportunities for improved efficiency. Just by making a few changes in your faucets, you can use water more efficiently.

Some relatively easy changes you can make include

- **Using a two-valve faucet.** A two-valve faucet is more efficient than a single-valve type (where you move the lever around until you get the right temperature). The latter inevitably wastes hot water.

- **Using aerator filters in the faucets.** These filters add air and keep up the pressure while reducing flow volume. Most of the time, people are looking for greater pressure, not flow volume, from a faucet. In fact, many building codes now require low-flow faucets because they make so much sense (they save water without being inconvenient).

Of course, dealing with leaks is a great way to not only increase how efficiently you use water but also to offset some other problems as well. Read on to find out more.

Leaks: Money and energy down the drain

Leaky faucets waste water. A faucet dripping once per second can waste 2,000 gallons per year. Beyond just the waste factor, leaking faucets can also cause increased health issues because mold and mildew just love damp environments (see Chapter 6 for details).

In addition, a dripping faucet can humidify your entire house. In the summer, higher humidity means less comfort. Do not underestimate this effect — it's much more

255

pronounced than you may think (see Chapter 8 for more on how to control the humidity in your home). So not only are you wasting water, but also your house is uncomfortable and your air-conditioner is running more (which means wasted utility costs).

The largest cost is the heat being wasted when hot water is drawn from your water heater. If a faucet is dripping, it may be drawing hot water. If it's dripping very slowly, you may not even know it's dripping hot water because by the time that water has come all the way from your water heater through the pipes to your faucet, it has cooled down. But heat is still being wasted.

If your water pressure is high, you probably experience dripping faucets, especially outdoors where leaks are more likely to go unnoticed. High pressure basically means higher force, which can push through questionable seals. You can have a pressure regulator installed on your water system, but it's probably not worth the hassle. If you have high water pressure, you need to be sure to provide adequate maintenance for your seals and gaskets.

Outdoor faucets are more prone to leakage than indoor ones because they're generally cheaper, plus they get beat up by the weather (constantly changing temperature is hard on metals). Replace outdoor faucets that leak. This is much easier than replacing indoor faucets, and anybody can do it with the right wrench and patience level.

Obviously, the only way to deal with a leaking faucet is to fix it. Before you tackle the job, though, keep these suggestions in mind:

- **Shut off all the water.** Shut-off valves are generally found below sinks and the like, but simply shutting the water off in your entire home when doing plumbing jobs is a good idea. You can find a whole house shut-off valve in the utility box either in front of your home or in your basement (most of the time it'll be right next to your water meter, if you have one). Many homes also have an underground container near the roadway (watch out for spiders when you stick your hand in).

✔ **Be careful to get it right.** Make sure you understand what you're doing before you start, and make sure you have the right tools (and good ones). To find out how to fix leaky faucets, ask at your local hardware store. They have tons of experience with dripping faucets and usually know the types used in your community. You can also find instructions for fixing dripping faucets in *How to Fix Everything For Dummies* by Gary and Pam Hedstrom and Judy Ondrla Tremore (Wiley).

Almost anybody can do plumbing, but if you don't do it exactly right, you have to do it over until you *do* get it exactly right.

✔ **Take a picture before you start.** Whenever you take a plumbing system apart for repairs or maintenance, use a digital camera to snap shots once in awhile so that if you forget where things go, you can look back at the pictures. Once the job is done, delete the pictures (unless you want to add them to your family collection).

Don't feel up to the job? Then hire a plumber and watch him fix the leak. Then next time you encounter a leaky tap, you can do the job yourself. (Of course, watching a plumber work, you may decide you never, ever want to do plumbing. Either lesson is worth the money.)

A few more tips for using water wisely

Beyond fiddling with the faucets and fixing leaks, you can do a few other things to use water more efficiently:

- ✔ **Avoid using your garbage disposal.** It requires a lot of water to run and ends up filling the septic or sewer system far more than is needed. Get a composter and start a little garden, or toss the waste into your garbage. See Chapter 14 for more details.

- ✔ **Don't waste cold water waiting for the hot.** When you need hot water, you generally run water down the drain until it shows up. Instead, put a pot, bowl, or other container under the faucet while you're waiting for the water to get hot, and then use the cold water you collect for cooking, ice cubes, or whatever. Just don't waste it.

- ✔ **Don't leave the tap running while you're doing something else.** Whether you're brushing your teeth or cleaning off the countertop, turn the water off. It's an easy habit to break, and you'd be surprised how much difference it can make.

Savings in Showers and Baths

When you're thinking about water consumption, you need to factor in two things: heat and water. Heating water accounts for around 20 percent of the power bill in a home, and showers and baths use 37 percent of that. That means that around 6 percent of your power bill is dedicated to heating water for your shower and baths. You can save in both areas.

- ✔ **Forget baths.** They'll become a thing of the past when energy rates get high enough. You simply can't take an economical bath.

✔ **Double up.** Put the kids (appropriately aged, of course) into the shower together. Or take a shower with your partner (I could make some wise comments here, but I suspect I don't really need to).

✔ **Use handheld showerheads.** These focus better, allowing much less water to do the job (if you think about it, most of the water flowing from a showerhead is wasted). The downside is you have to hold them.

✔ **Avoid showerheads that "mist" the water.** They humidify your home more than anything, and the mist does no good at all. This is especially inefficient in the summer.

✔ **Take shorter showers.** Lingering in the heat is nice, but it wastes energy because all you get out of it is, well, lingering in the heat. Find something else to linger in.

 Avoid things that make your shower a pleasant living quarters, like radios, TVs, nice views, and so on. In order to be truly efficient, a shower should be strictly functional.

✔ **Install a "greywater" recycle system on your shower and bath drain.** These systems basically recycle your home's water. A tank is connected to certain drains (usually everything but the toilet) and then a chemical sanitizing process is performed that brings the water up to cleanliness standards suitable for landscaping and even washing. The best systems can clean water well enough to be consumed. Not only does greywater offset the demand for treating water to the highest potable standard, but it also may actually be beneficial to plants as it's likely to contain nitrogen and phosphorous. Installing one of these systems when building a new house is a lot more economically efficient than retrofitting an existing house.

 Water-wise, baths take 20 gallons or more of water, but a five-minute shower takes around 10 gallons, making baths about twice as expensive as showers. On the other hand, a shower can consume more water if you have an old-style showerhead, which typically delivers 4 to 5 gallons per minute — quite a rich and wasteful flow of water. To address this issue, the Energy Policy Act of 1992 set maximum water flow rates at 2.5 gallons per minute, so new houses and new showerheads are almost always at or below this number. New showerheads are designed to use less water and create more water pressure so you aren't aware that you're getting less.

Solar showering

For fifteen bucks you can get a solar shower that works great. You fill a dark-colored plastic bag with water, hang it in the sun for an hour or so, and then hang it up in a tree or whatever's convenient. You open the little valve and get a nice, gentle flow of hot water, au naturel.

Of course, these are for particular locations (outdoors mostly, although not necessarily — you can heat one up outside and bring it inside), and you also need good weather, with plenty of sunshine. But they work great after workouts or by the swimming pool or spa. Once you try it a few times you can easily get hooked just because they're so natural. If you're into green, this is a great option.

And you can use one as a giant water bottle. Very soothing.

You can easily measure the flow of your showerhead. Simply get a pitcher with gallons marked on the side. While you count one-Mississippi, two-Mississippi, and so on, run your showerhead into the pitcher until you've got one gallon. Divide 60 by your Mississippi count and you have your flow rate in gallons per minute. As mentioned previously, 2.5 is the current standard, but you can do better than this without sacrificing much quality.

Wasting Water in the Toilet

Toilets consume (a bad word, I agree) 45 percent of indoor water use, or around 32,000 gallons per year for a family of four. A running toilet (one that makes a constant hissing noise — you know what I mean), can waste up to 4,000 gallons of water per year. Fortunately, you can solve these problems, if you're willing to do a little dirty work.

Parts is parts

Many people hate the idea of working on a toilet because, well, it's a toilet. But if you're going to work on your toilet, you need to know the difference between one part and another. Trust me. Here's how it all breaks down:

- **The tank:** This is the part above the throne (uh yes, it's called the throne). The tank is perfectly clean. (In fact, the water in the toilet tank is as clean as the tap water that's filling it.) Fortunately, that's where the working parts are.

- **The water pipes that feed the tank:** These come from the wall and there's always a valve which will shut off the water flow to the toilet.

- **The toilet bowl thingee:** The throne itself, fit for a

king, queen, prince, princess, or toilet-trained house cat, as the case may be.

- ✔ **The plumbing system:** This is the part that takes away whatever gets flushed down. Obviously, this is the part that you *don't* want to work on.

Easy ways to cut down on water usage

Following are a few tips for saving on toilet water:

- ✔ At least for number one (man, I love euphemisms), don't use the toilet at all — go outside instead. You think I'm jesting? The birds and the bees do it; are you better than them? (I remember a bumper sticker that was common in California back in the 1980s during a particularly tenacious water shortage: "If it's yellow, be mellow; if it's brown, flush it down.")

- ✔ Don't use the toilet as a trash can; it's very expensive compared to a waste basket. Toilets are for butts, not cigarette butts.

- ✔ If you put a couple quart bottles filled with water in the tank, each flush will use that much less water. Bricks or rocks also work.

What to do when your toilet runs

If you're toilet is running, you need to chase, er . . . I mean fix it. Fortunately, finding the problem is almost always simple. The most common problem in a running toilet is the flapper, which is a rubber disk that covers the hole where the water enters the toilet bowl. These are so ridiculously easy to change that anybody can do it. Go to your hardware store and ask the clerk to show you how (they must sell a thousand of these things a day).

Every single hardware store on the face of the earth has toilet parts because, well, every single home has a toilet or two. Some homes even have ten toilets. Your hardware store clerk will be more than happy to explain in great detail exactly how your toilet works and show you the parts. You can touch them and play with them to your heart's content. There are even clubs you can join.

You can completely rebuild the workings of most toilets with new parts that will probably work better than the old for less than $60. A plumber will charge a lot more than that, maybe on the order of hundreds of dollars.

If you have to work on the mechanisms in the toilet tank, first drain the tank by turning off the shut-off valve (all toilets have a shut-off valve where the water source comes out of the wall) and flushing. The tank will empty down to an inch or two. Now you can work on the working parts.

Updated toilet designs

Nothing is worse than flushing a toilet and looking back down to find that it wasn't 100 percent effective. (Okay, one thing is worse — when the toilet clogs up and overflows all over the bathroom floor, especially when you're in somebody else's house.)

The old standard technology in toilets simply uses gravity feed to rush the water down into the bowl and carry away the waste products and any residue left clinging to the toilet walls. This works well enough most of the time, but it uses a lot of water, so less wasteful designs that accomplished the same thing came into being.

Pressure-assist toilets

Pressure-assist toilets use much less water per flush and

actually work better. The water is held in the tank under pressure, and when you trigger the flush lever it explodes down into the toilet bowl, thereby removing residue that may otherwise cling. These toilets are costly ($250 apiece) and hard to fix, plus they're very loud so everybody in the house is going to know what you just did.

Most public facilities use pressure-assist toilets. If you're considering a pressure-assist toilet, you can decide firsthand if you want this loud noise in your own home by going into almost any public facility and sampling the wares.

Vacuum-assist toilets

Vacuum-assist toilets suck waste right out of the bowl (which is sort of the opposite of the pressure-assist method of blasting it out). They're cheaper than their pressure-assist counterparts and easier to fix. But the very idea is also much ickier! Imagine being a vacuum-assist toilet.

Compost toilets

Compost toilets don't flush at all. Hmm. You need to be a hearty soul to consider these devices, but they're very earth-friendly. They basically allow the waste products to decompose in a specially designed chamber. At some point, you can take the "materials" out of the "finishing drawer" and to your landscaping (probably not your vegetable garden, unless you're really hearty).

Watering Your Landscaping

Ah, the great outdoors. Most people have some form of landscaping, and many people have extensive landscaping, including a lawn, which is the most water- and energy-intense form of landscaping you can imagine. In a yard, you can conserve water through your landscaping choices and through your choice of sprinkler. The following sections tell you how to use less water and energy in your yard.

For green landscaping supplies, check out the following sources:

✔ Composters.com (www.composters.com)

✔ Hobbs and Hopkins, Ltd. (www.protimelawn seed.com)

✔ No Mow Grass (www.nomowgrass.com)

✔ TerraCycle (www.terracycle.net)

Considering lawn alternatives

The one thing you can do to conserve the most water and energy is to get rid of your lawn. Replace it with drought-resistant plants, and don't water them much (create a drought of your own!). You can also replace your lawn with native plants that grow and thrive in your climate without need for additional watering (above and beyond what Mother Nature provides). Barring that, you can

✔ Set the height levers on your lawn mower an inch higher. Less heat will hit the dirt beneath the grass, thereby allowing you to water less. And longer grass chokes out the weeds much better than short grass, so you won't have to use herbicides.

✔ Use a mulching mower, which helps fertilize the grass.

Picking the right sprinkler and watering at the right time

If you need to water your lawn, all sprinklers are not created equal. Some waste more water than they apply to the plants. And you can also control the time of day or night you do your watering to gain better efficiency.

- **If you need to water an large area, use rotary sprinklers, which work the best.** Avoid misting sprinklers because all they do is mist water into the air where it blows away into the neighbor's yard. That may be efficient for them, but that's not really what this book is about.

- **Use drippers instead of broadcast sprinklers for isolated plants, particularly when they're surrounded by bark or other ground cover that doesn't need any watering at all.** You may have to spend more money up front on hardware, but you'll save a lot of water and your plants will be much healthier because they're getting water right where they want it — in their root systems. Plus, they're fun do-it-yourself projects because you get to play with all these little parts that go very well together — at least in theory.

A drip system needs to be maintained. Check it once in awhile by turning it on manually and making sure all the drippers are working.

✔ **Water at night or early in the morning.** The sunshine will be less likely to evaporate most of the water before it gets to where it's used.

✔ **Use battery-operated valves.** They save water by regulating the amount that's delivered. If you turn your system off and on manually, you'll forget about it. Battery valves can be set to open for a predetermined period of time. These generally fit right onto the faucet for a good mechanically rigid mount.

You can get small, cheap valves that you set for a number of gallons instead of time. These work very well for gardens and when your water pressure varies.

✔ **Use barrels under downspouts to catch rainwater.** You can then use the rainwater for other purposes. If you can, position the barrel in an elevated position (for instance, set it up on some concrete blocks); then simply use gravity feed when you need water.

Chapter 11

Pigging Out on Power with Appliances

Including your domestic water heater, around 40 percent of your power bill is consumed by your appliances, big and small. And just because an appliance is small in stature doesn't mean it's small in energy consumption.

Understanding how much power your appliances consume is the first step toward recovering from the rampant disease of appliancism. You can lower your power bills by using your appliances more sensibly — or even better, by not using your appliances at all. For instance, a great way to lower your power bill is to set up a clothesline. As with all energy efficiency investments, you need to take the bull by the horns.

Looking at Typical Appliance Consumption Numbers

Aside from your HVAC system (which I cover in detail in Chapter 8), appliances consume the lion's share of power in your home. Some of the biggest culprits in most homes are water heaters, washers and dryers, and refrigerators, which are on all the time. There are exceptions, of course. Some homes have aquariums that collectively steal the spotlight. Other homes have an old freezer in the garage that cranks the kilowatts 24/7. Increasingly common are homes with large entertainment centers, and these can gobble kilowatts with the biggest and baddest of energy pigs.

So what does the typical home spend per year on various electrical appliances? Table 11-1 shows you how many kilowatts per hour (kWh) the average home uses in a year and the annual cost (based on an electric rate of 15 cents per kWh, which is pretty typical).

You can determine your own annual usage and cost by gathering your electric bills, which show kWh used and your rate (see the next section for details). If your rate is higher or lower than 15 cents, adjust it accordingly. If you use gas or propane for your dryer, water heater, or stove, the annual cost will be around the same as for electric.

Table 11-1 Annual kWh of Usage and Costs for Various Appliances

Appliance	kWh Used per Year	Annual Cost (Rounded to Nearest Dollar)
Domestic water heater	5,400	$810
Spa (pump and heater)	2,230	$335
Pool pump	1,430	$215
Refrigerator	1,200	$180
Washing machine	900	$135
Waterbed heater	850	$128
Clothes dryer	845	$127
Freezer	750	$113
Electric cooking	680	$102
Dishwasher	600	$90
Aquarium/terrarium	570	$86
Well water pump	500	$75
Dehumidifier	357	$54
Microwave oven	150	$23
Television	140	$21
Home computer	107	$16
Electric blanket	98	$15

Note: When calculating how much you can save by cutting back on the usage of your appliances, use your top tiered rate, not your average. Why: Because when you cut back, the top tiered rate applies first.

Analyzing Appliance Consumption in Your Home

To find out how much an appliance costs per month to run, first estimate how much time it's on per day. Then determine how much power it consumes. You can usually find this information on the label, but you may have to consult the instruction manual or go to the manufacturer's Web site.

Use this formula to estimate your monthly cost to run an appliance:

Wattage ÷ 1,000 × hours on per day × cost per kWh × 30 days = total cost per month

Say you want to know how much it costs you to run your washer, dryer, and iron (assume that your rate is 15 cents per kWh):

Washer: You run your 900-watt washing machine for

six hours a week. (Figure your daily usage by dividing the number of hours the washer is on by the number of days in a week: 6 ÷ 7 = .86.) Here's what you spend:

900 ÷ 1,000 × .86 × .15 × 30 = $3.48 per month

Dryer: Your clothes dryer uses 5,570 watts (that's a whole lot). If you dry clothes for six hours a week, you spend this much to dry your clothes:

5,570 ÷ 1,000 × .86 × .15 × 30 = $21.56 per month

Iron: If you iron clothes with a 1,200-watt iron each morning for 15 minutes, it's costing you:

1,200 ÷ 1,000 × .25 × .15 × 30 = $1.35 per month

Add up these numbers and you can see that for the appliances you use to keep your clothing clean and pressed, you spend a total of $26.40 per month.

If you put up a clothesline, you would save $21.56 per month (and around 1,748 pounds per year of carbon dioxide emissions). Plus, your clothes would smell better and you could pat yourself on the back for doing your part to save the planet Earth.

You can work this number stuff to death, but what you really want to do is simply make sensible improvements in your efficiency. Start with your biggest appliances and work your way down. Some appliances are easy to use less often; others are harder to do without. It also makes sense to start with the appliances you use the most. Just do your part where you can, and you'll be surprised at the difference it makes.

You can find out how much your old appliances are costing by visiting www.energystar.gov. Click on Home Appliances and enter the year, size, and other data for your old appliance. A calculator tells you how much your current unit is costing, as well as how much you could save if you switched to a new, energy-efficient model.

Keeping Water Heaters in Check

The water heater accounts for about 20 percent of the typical home's power budget. Dishwashers and washing machines use up to 80 percent of their energy on heating water, and only 20 percent running the mechanical equipment. The cost of taking showers and baths is almost entirely in the cost of heating water.

Unfortunately, the typical domestic water heater is wasteful. It holds a considerable amount of hot water, and when it's not being used, heat seeps out of the tank, which is sheer inefficiency. The best water heaters have thick insulation, but some heat is still lost.

So what can you do to save on water heating costs? Follow the advice in the following sections.

Paying attention to pipes

When you use hot water, not only do you drain the water you use from the hot water tank, but all the intervening

Making time stand still

Here's an educational project. Try to get your power meter to stand still. Find your meter and note the spinning wheel and the numbers. (These are kWh. When the utility people come to read your meter, they read this number, then subtract the number they read last month to get your monthly consumption.)

First, turn off the main breaker on your circuit panel. If your meter is still spinning, you have a ground fault, and you're paying for electricity that's basically going through the earth beneath your feet. This should not to be misconstrued as generosity; have your utility company come out and fix this right away.

If that checks out, turn the main breaker back on and check to see how fast it's spinning. Now switch off every one of the individual breakers in your box; the spinning should stop, once again.

Now start switching the individual breakers back on, one at a time, and see what happens. The panel should have a well-articulated legend that tells you what each breaker is for: HVAC, laundry room, upstairs lights, and so on. The biggest switches (those with the biggest numbers, such as 30 or 50) are for your HVAC system and your clothes dryer. You may also have a swimming pool pump or spa that's on a large circuit.

As you switch the individual breakers on, you can see how much power each of the individual circuits consumes. (Make sure each appliance you check is turned on so that it's drawing current.)

Here's where things get interesting. You'll probably find a circuit that draws current even when nothing is turned on in that room. In particular, note that TVs, computers, DVDs, and other digital devices draw current even when they're turned off.

You can take this a step further by plugging in various small appliances like hair dryers, portable fans and heaters, electronic games, and so forth. You can see how fast the meter spins for each of these. Some of these little gadgets can make the meter look like the Tasmanian Devil.

plumbing fills with hot water as well. The amount of hot water trapped in your pipes can be significant, depending on how you're using the water and how far away the faucet or tap is from the tank.

If you're taking a bath, the amount of water in the pipes is small compared to the amount in the tub, so you're not wasting a lot of hot water (aside from the fact that taking a bath is inherently wasteful compared to a shower). But if you're simply filling a cup with hot water, you're leaving a heck of a lot more hot water in the pipes than you're actually using. You're almost always better off heating water in the microwave oven than drawing it from a tap.

How much hot water are you wasting?

Here's a little experiment you can easily perform to demonstrate just how much hot water you waste when you turn on your hot water faucet. Get a large pitcher with measurement gradations. Hold it below your faucet and turn the hot water on. Now measure how much water fills the pitcher before you start getting hot water from the tap. You may be surprised to find up to two gallons or more have flowed through. This means that there are now two gallons of hot water sitting in your pipes, which is a big waste because all it will do is cool down and release the heat into your home's environment.

A number of high-efficiency dishwashers heat their own water for this very reason. Heating locally is almost always more efficient. In addition, machines that heat their own water work better because they can maintain the specific temperature that they need.

Staying on top of maintenance

Regular maintenance goes a long way toward maximizing the efficiency of your hot water heater. Like your HVAC system, you should have your domestic water heater tuned up periodically (the gas version gets especially gummed up). The following sections outline areas to pay attention to.

Draining the tank

Every four months or so, drain a quart of water from your tank. There's a valve near the bottom of the unit for this very purpose. Before you begin, consider where the drained water is going to go. If the heater is in your garage, you can broom the water outdoors. Otherwise, you may need a drain bucket. Be sure the bucket is shallow enough to accommodate the valve.

The water you drain from your water heater's tank can be very hot, so be careful.

Draining a quart of water directly from your water heater's tank prevents sediment buildup, which affects efficiency. If you haven't tackled this task in years, you'll be shocked at how much crud comes out.

Changing the heating elements

Change the heating elements in your electric water heater every few years (most of them have two elements, one on top and one on bottom). Use a stainless steel heater element if your old one is corroded. This makes the unit operate more efficiently and avoids untimely failures.

When you buy the heater element, be sure to buy a special wrench head that fits the element; ask the hardware store clerk to help you find the right wrench. (You may be able to borrow one from a friend and save some money. And if you don't return it, you can save even more.) Note that sometimes very old heating elements get stuck into place, in which case you can use WD-40: just spray it on, wait a day and then give it another try.

Finding more ways to save

Beyond regular maintenance, you can do several things to make your water heater more efficient. Temperature, timing, and insulation are all factors that come into play.

Setting the water temperature lower

Most domestic water heaters are set at too high a temperature. Scalding water is too hot. For each 10°F reduction in water heater temperature, you can expect to lower your heating cost by 3 to 5 percent. You may find yourself dialing more hot water in your shower to get to the same comfort level, but so what? The most common problem you may encounter if you lower the temperature is that your dishwasher may not clean as well. You can usually remedy this by changing to a detergent that requires a lower temperature (read the label). See the section "Lessening the Load on Your Dishwasher" for more information.

Using timers

Hot water heaters consume a lot of energy when they're on. Most of them aren't on all that much, but when they are, they gobble power up. Use a timer to turn off your hot water heater at night and during the day when you're gone. Specialty hardware stores sell special units for this purpose. The salespeople can tell you how to install them.

When you're away from home for extended periods, turn the hot water heater off before you go. Either flip off the appropriate circuit breaker in your fuse box or turn off the gas valve (in which case you'll have to relight the pilot). You may also be able to turn the temperature all the way down to minimum and then turn it back up when you return.

Adding insulation

Insulate the storage tank with a specially-made blanket. Your utility company may give you one free (call the customer-service number and ask). Or you can buy one for $10 to $20 at most hardware stores. A tank that's warm to the touch is a clear sign that you're losing heat and can save money and increase efficiency by adding insulation.

Insulating your hot water pipes is easy, and a number of options are available. The best is a long, cylindrical piece of foam with a slit lengthwise — you just slide it over a pipe and you're done. Don't worry about corners and inaccessible pipes — whatever you can cover helps increase efficiency. Another option is a fiberglass wrap that you roll around and around the pipe and then cover with a plastic tape material. This covers the pipe more completely than the slit foam, but it's a lot harder to install, especially if the pipe is close to a wall.

Considering a solar or tankless water heater

Most North Americans (almost 55 percent) heat their water with natural gas. About 38 percent heat water with electricity. (The few others heat with oil and liquid petro gas.) However, two types of water heaters are increasingly being used for their energy efficiency: solar and tankless water heaters.

- ✔ **Solar water heaters** are the best from an energy-efficiency standpoint, but the economics vary greatly from region to region and depend on your power rates and rate structure. From a pollution perspective, you can't do better than solar. See Chapter 16 for details.

- ✔ **Tankless water heaters** have no storage tank; they heat water as it is being used. They are generally gas-powered because of the need for very high, instantaneous power. They're more expensive than conventional water heaters, but if you don't use much hot water, you can save big in the long run.

   Smaller units only work with a single tap or faucet at one time, so if you're interested in taking a bath while you're doing the dishes, forget it. Large-capacity units cost around $1,000 (a conventional unit costs only $300). Units can save the typical family $100 per year, so the payback in extra investment cost is around 7 years.

   Tankless water heaters are especially good if you have a cabin or second home that you don't use that often. In this case, you won't be continuously heating a big tank full of water while you're gone. (And although you could turn your water heater off if you're going away for a long time, if you're like most people, you'll forget. With a tankless water heater, you don't have to remember.)

Making the Most of Pools and Spas

Pools and spas can be very big expenses. They both require chemicals and filters. By definition, a *spa* — a hot tub with a whirlpool device — requires a heater. Many pool owners like to heat their pools, too. The following sections tell you how to save money on these energy hogs.

Making your pool energy-efficient

If you own either an above ground or an in-ground pool, there are a variety of ways you can achieve the same performance at far less cost in energy as well as chemical consumption. In my experience, most pool owners can do a few very simple things and save big.

Optimizing operations

One way to increase how efficiently your pool runs is to do routine maintenance and make a few changes for optimal operation:

- **Make sure all valves are working properly.** If you have gate valves (the kind that lets you dial in the amount of water flow you want), replace them with ball valves, which are more efficient (ball valves are either on or off, and when they're on they impede water flow much less than a gate valve). Make sure all ball valves are completely open or closed; it doesn't make any sense to adjust one to half open.

- **Keep the filter clean.** A dirty filter loads the pump, which costs a lot more in terms of power. If your filter is old, replace it. Cartridge filters are much better than diatomaceious earth, which use a big cartridge

280

full of loose sediment filter material that's difficult to work with and expensive as well.

✔ **Run your filter pump less.** Most people run their pool pumps much longer than necessary. Try running yours half as long as you do now and see what happens. If you calculate how much it costs to run the average pool pump, the hair on the back of your neck will stand on end.

✔ **Drain your pool in the off-season, and turn your pump off.** If you can't drain your pool, you'll have to leave the pump on because the water will get so filthy you'll need to drain it and change it. But you can't drain it.

✔ **Install windbreaks around your pool.** Convection losses from wind can increase water evaporation 300 percent or more, which wastes not only water, but heat as well. Windbreaks keep your pool warmer with less evaporation.

Sealing in the heat: Solar pool covers

Despite the fact that the surface area of most swimming pools is large, very little sunlight is converted into heat. Pool water is transparent (hopefully), so sunlight simply passes right through. In addition, during the night, a pool loses a lot of whatever heat it manages to store up during the day.

The cheapest and most effective solar heating system for your swimming pool is a solar cover. A cover converts sunlight into heat, which then transfers into water. Some covers are black for this very reason. But the most widely used are made of inexpensive clear plastic that looks like bubble wrap. The air bubbles work as insulation: Heat that goes in can't get out. You can get a cover for around 30 cents a square foot ($130 for an average-size pool).

Why do these covers work so well? Because they do the following:

- ✔ Prevent heat from escaping from your pool at night, when the air is cooler than the swimming pool. You can easily lose four or five degrees in temperature over the course of a cool night. If you use a heater to heat you water, it doesn't need to work as hard to maintain (or return to) the set temperature. If you don't use a heater, the retained heat just makes the water that much warmer.

- ✔ Limit evaporation and retain heat. Each gallon of evaporated 80°F water removes about 8,000 Btu (2.34 kWh) from the pool.

- ✔ Reduce chemical depletion, which reduces cost and may be considered a form of energy conservation.

- ✔ Increase the temperature of an in-ground pool by 5°F for each 12 hours of coverage.

You can extend your swim season a couple months just by using a plastic cover. For example, in the Midwest you may be able to swim in a covered pool from mid-April until mid-October, whereas a completely unheated pool would only be usable from mid-May until mid-September. You don't need to cover your pool during the hottest months, which is when people want to swim the most. Just fold the cover up and store it whenever it's not in use.

You don't need to cover your entire pool to reap the benefits. If you have a kidney-shaped pool, floating a rectangular cover over the pool will still help considerably.

Covers have to be placed on and removed from the water. Many kinds of systems are available to assist you in this process, some manual, some automatic:

✔ **Manual systems** cost around $300. These roll up the cover, much like a window blind. But you still have to pull the cover back out over the pool, and you may have to get into the water first. In either case, cranking the handle is not easy; women and children may have a hard time.

✔ **Automatic systems** can cost over $1,000, and the installation is a bear. But all you have to do is press a switch and voilà! The cover moves back and forth of its own volition — at least in theory — all mechanical systems are prone to failures.

As beneficial as pool covers are, they do pose certain problems:

✔ **Plastic pool covers:** When plastic bubble wrap covers get old, they fray. Plastic shards can get into the filter and may even cut the filter paper, necessitating a new, expensive filter. Storing these covers in the sunlight (when they're not wet) also causes the plastic to degrade.

✔ **Any pool cover:** Any pool cover can be dangerous! Anyone (particularly a child) who falls into a plastic pool cover will get "wrapped" by the cover, and getting out of this situation can be very difficult. Even automatic covers, which extend across the water surface and are secured by tracks, don't entirely eliminate the risk of drowning. These fill with water when it rains, and children have been known to fall onto the cover and drown in the standing water.

Using a solar swimming pool heater

Certain energy expenditures, like driving, heating in the winter, lighting and so on, are just plain necessary (although you can still reduce them). Other energy expenditures — like heating a swimming pool — are entirely discretionary. Strictly speaking, you don't need to heat your pool — at least not in the summer. You can even swim in the middle of winter without heat (talk about putting hair on your chest!).

If you want to become more energy efficient, not only to reduce your costs but also to reduce greenhouse gases, one of the best solutions is to use solar energy to heat your pool. It's the only solution that is completely free of pollution. See Chapter 16 for details on solar swimming pool heaters.

There are other options for heating your pool, like natural gas heaters (these are common) or electric. But these are so expensive that they shouldn't even be mentioned in a book on energy efficiency. You can save up-front money on an electric or gas heater, granted. But the steroid-bound utility bills they guarantee will quickly make your initial frugality seem foolish.

Getting into hot water with a spa

Spas are energy pigs, and you can't do much about it. Old spas are far worse than the new versions, which have excellent insulation and good covers. If you've got an old redwood spa without a cover, throw it away now and buy a new spa. Other than that, here are some tips for making your current spa more efficient:

- ✔ **Always use a cover.** You can waste 80 percent of the heat without a cover. Covers are cheap if you buy an off-the-shelf size — you just have to tolerate a little slop over the edges.

✔ **Insulate your spa.** You can use a box of expandable foam insulation or you can stuff batt insulation into the crevices. Either one makes a big difference.

You can often get old insulation for free. Contractors who remodel houses may let you scavenge their work sites to your heart's content. Who cares if it's cruddy old stuff? It's going outdoors, and nobody's going to see it anyway.

✔ **Run your filter less.** You can probably run your filter cycle less often than you think without sacrificing much quality. The vast majority of pool owners could halve their filter on time, without apparent loss of water quality. Give it a try. You may even be able to reduce it more.

✔ **Turn it off when you're away.** When you're on vacation, empty your spa and turn it off. If you time it right, you can make your vacation coincide with water-changing time.

✔ **Turn the temperature down in the summer.** Better yet, turn the heater off entirely.

Washing and Drying without the Crying

The average washing machine wastes more energy than any other appliance in the home. With due diligence, most households can save 50 percent on operating costs and use 50 percent less water (including hot water, which costs a lot more than cold) just by changing the way they do laundry. Following are some practical tips.

Running hot or cold: Changing water temperature

A great way to save energy doing laundry is to use hot water only when you need to. Eighty-five percent of the energy used in washing is consumed by heating the water. A lot of people simply run their machines on hot all the time. You can easily save 25 percent on your washing costs by using cold water most of the time — in particular, for the rinse cycle. Look on the label of your detergent for the best ways to use cold water. You can also effectively *wash* in cold water if you use detergent made for cold water. Check your detergent label to find its temperature requirement.

 Another way to save energy is to make every member of the household responsible for cleaning his or her own clothes. You'll see an instant decrease in wash-load quantity, especially if you have kids.

Adjusting load size, water level, and cycle

When you wash clothes, use as little water as necessary to get the job done. To that end, only wash full loads — it's much more efficient, per item of clothing, than partial loads. Always adjust the water level to the lowest possible setting for the load size. For the smallest loads, use a mini-basket insert that fits over the agitator.

You can also take advantage of the cycles your washer offers. If yours has a pre-soak cycle, use it. Presoaking cycles save energy. They take more time, but so what? Some washers also let you choose the speed of the spin cycle. Faster spin speeds remove more water, resulting in less dryer time. If you're using a clothesline, faster, longer spins make your life much easier because the clothes weigh less and pull the line down less.

Don't use too much detergent. Contrary to what you may think, more is not necessarily better, especially if it doesn't get completely rinsed out. The more detergent you use, the more you have to rinse.

Saving drying costs

Dryers use more power than every appliance save the washing machine and refrigerator. Saving money with your dryer is easy.

Avoiding the dryer altogether

The best way to save money on drying costs is to use a clothesline — you know, that thing in the backyard that your mother used when you were growing up so long ago. Clothes dried outdoors smell much better, particularly if they're in direct sunlight.

The best clothesline style for most users is an "umbrella" arrangement (true to its name, it folds up like an umbrella). You mount it into the ground and it rotates, so you can set your laundry basket down and move the line around as you pin clothes up. It features the most length of line for the least amount of space, due to its spiraling structure. Retractable mechanisms are great. I have a clothesline on my back porch, and when it's not in use, the line retracts so you can't even see it.

To determine the best location for your clothesline, consider the following:

- **Convenience counts.** If getting to the clothesline is a hassle, you'll be less apt to use it. Garages work well, and they're usually right next to the laundry. Open the garage door if you can. Otherwise, your garage will get humid.

✔ **Air movement is helpful.** A breezy spot with direct sunshine is ideal.

 Not convinced fresh air can freshen clothes? Try this experiment: Take some sweaty, smelly workout clothes and simply hang them up in direct sunshine. Check them out a couple hours later — they may feel and smell better than clothes you run through the washing machine.

Another way to avoid using the dryer is to hang clothes to dry indoors. A quick, easy way to dry small loads is to simply hang them over your shower curtain rod while you're at work. You need some ventilation in your bathroom or you'll humidify your home, but maybe that's what you want to do.

Timing is everything

If you time the use of your dryer just right, you can take the best possible advantage of the heat it puts out. Consider the following tips to decrease your drying costs:

✔ Over-drying is hard on clothes, and it wastes energy. Like pasta, clothes should be dried al dente (just enough).

✔ Moisture sensors are much better than timed drying cycles (using a timer makes no sense at all, if you think about it).

✔ Cool-down cycles are the most efficient because the dryer heater gradually shuts off and the residual heat finishes the cycle.

✔ Dry two or more loads in a row, thereby taking advantage of the dryer's retained heat.

Taking care of your dryer's ductwork

Dryers have vented pipes (around 4 inches in diameter) that lead outdoors. The purpose of these pipes is to vent the hot air to the outside environment (take that, Mother Nature!). To work most efficiently, this vent pipe needs to be free of obstruction.

- ✔ Clean the removable filter every time you use the dryer. Keep a small waste bin by the machine so you can toss the coagulated lint into it.

- ✔ Check your dryer ductwork. It may be clogged with years' worth of accreted crud, which causes inefficiency. New ductwork is cheap. You can find it at any hardware store; ask the clerk for help.

- ✔ Where your ductwork ends outside you'll find a vent, often with a flapping door that opens and closes when the dryer is on and off (to keep birds and rodents out of the line). These often get dented and smashed, thereby restricting flow and wasting money. If possible, just get rid of the vent. Or replace the one you have with a better-working model.

- ✔ You can buy a duct cleaner — a long, snaking wand with a big, bushy brush head that you cram down the duct line — but for the cost, you're probably better off simply rebuilding the ductwork, assuming you have easy access. Many ducts are built into walls, in which case you're stuck with cleaning.

- ✔ Use the straightest, shortest duct possible. Ninety-degree bends cause your dryer to work harder and longer to accomplish the same task. In fact, most ductwork can be rebuilt to good advantage.

Keeping Your Cool with Refrigerators

The number-one way to save money with your refrigerator is to keep the coils clean. On either the bottom or the back of your unit is a meandering line of narrow tubing. Air is drawn over this tubing, and, over time, dust accumulates and clogs the flow, decreasing your refrigerator's efficiency. You can get special brushes that enable you to brush the collected dust off the tubes, or you can simply use your vacuum cleaner.

Coils on the bottom of a refrigerator are harder to get to than those on the back, although for the latter, you have to move your refrigerator out. You're likely to be shocked at how much dirt and crud accumulate behind your refrigerator. This stuff causes health problems.

If your refrigerator is 15 years old or more, buying a new one is undoubtedly cost-effective. Look for a top-bottom model rather than a side-by-side. The top-bottom refrigerator arrangements use around 10 percent less energy than their side-by-side counterparts. The payback on a new energy-efficient refrigerator is less than five years.

Beyond buying a new refrigerator, you can do other things to make the refrigerator you have run more efficiently. The following sections explain.

It's what's on the inside that counts

How you arrange your food, the temperature settings you select, and how much ice buildup you have in the freezer all contribute to how well or poorly your refrigerator works. Some advice:

- ✔ **Check the temperature.** If your refrigerator allows different temperature settings for different zones, adjust the temperatures accordingly. Recommended temperatures are 37–40°F for the refrigerator, and 5°F for the freezer. Long-term freezer storage (deep freezers) should be set at 0°F.

Place a cheap thermometer in a glass of water in the center of the refrigerator. In the freezer, place the thermometer between a couple frozen packages. You can then check temperatures in different locations and see how they compare.

✔ **Defrost the freezer.** Ice buildup makes for inefficiency.

✔ **Eliminate overcrowding.** When the air inside a compartment can't move, the machinery has to work harder.

✔ **Cover all foods in the compartments.** Uncovered foods release a lot of moisture and make the compressor work harder. Besides, if you don't cover the food, it'll taste weird.

Close the door!

Keep your refrigerator's doors closed as much as possible — an obvious piece of advice, perhaps, but worth stating anyway. Of course, if you have kids like mine, this admonition goes in one ear and out the other.

Tight seals are a must. If they're tattered and leaking, you're wasting up to 25 percent of the refrigerator's energy (even more if your home is hot). If you can't change the seal, use some silicon sealant instead (the same kind you buy for bathtubs and sinks works just fine). Follow these steps:

1. **Spray Pam over the metal frame surface of the**

refrigerator where the seal should be located.

2. **Squirt the silicon over the seal.**

3. **Close the door and let the material dry.**

One or two?

Operating one large refrigerator is much more efficient than operating two smaller units. A lot of people have a refrigerator in their garage — usually the one that used to be in the kitchen. You may not want to throw it away, but old reefers cost a lot of money. That unit in your garage is costing you a lot more than the new one. Is it worth it? What do you have in there, anyway? Drinks for the kids? A whole pig? You can surely live without two refrigerators.

Lessening the Load on Your Dishwasher

Dishwashers use as much energy as clothes washers and dryers. Around 80 percent of this energy is consumed by heating the water — which means that one way to maximize your energy efficiency is to reduce the amount of hot water your dishwasher uses. Another way to save energy is to modify the way you rinse your dishes and load the dishwasher. The following sections explain.

Using less hot water

New dishwashers heat their own water, which is far more efficient than drawing hot water from the water heater the way older models do. Keep this feature in mind if you're in the market for a new dishwasher.

In addition, dishwashers get warm and heat your kitchen.

In the winter, this is fine. In the summer, it makes your air conditioner work harder. During warm months, use the no-heat dry option. If your machine doesn't have a no-heat option, simply stop it after the rinse cycle, open the door, and let the dishes dry that way.

In the summer, the dishwasher humidifies your house quite a bit. Get some ventilation going to get that humidity out of the house, and you'll feel cooler.

The temperature of the water from your domestic heater may affect the quality of your dishwasher's performance. If the water isn't hot enough, your machine will have a hard time doing the job. However, some detergents are rated for a lower water temperature. (For more information on water heaters, refer to the earlier section "Keeping Water Heaters in Check.")

Changing the way you rinse and load

The key here is to minimize how much water you use. Here are some suggestions to help you do that:

- ✔ **Rinse dishes as little as possible.** In fact, just scraping off large chunks of food without rinsing at all is often sufficient. Most dishwashers do a good job of getting rid of caked-on, hard stuff. New models have special cycles that steam-heat the crud and loosen it up.

- ✔ **Always run a full load.** Your dishwasher uses just as much water to wash a few dishes as a full load, so make the most of the water you use.

- ✔ **Try skipping the pre-rinse cycle on your dishwasher and using the economy wash cycle.** You probably won't be able to tell the difference.

Eating Up Power with Stoves and Microwaves

Depending on how much you cook in your home, energy costs for your stove and microwave can be significant. There are a number of easy things you can do to save costs, and in this section, I describe the best and easiest candidates.

Checking out efficient ovens

Some ovens (both microwave and conventional) are just plain more efficient than others. Some have features that offer extra efficiency, and some are more efficient even without the extra features.

- ✔ **Self-cleaning ovens:** These ovens are more efficient because they have higher insulation levels. What this means is that less heat is lost to the outside ambient while you're cooking.

✔ **Gas ovens with pilotless ignition:** One of these ovens saves you 30 percent over its lifetime, and the air in your home will be cleaner. With pilot lights, some gas is always being burned (you can usually see the little blue flame wavering near the burner). With a pilotless gas stove, a spark plug type device ignites the gas each time the burner is turned on.

✔ **Convection ovens:** Convection ovens incorporate a small, high-temperature fan that moves the internal air in the oven compartment thereby bringing more heat into contact with the food being baked. Convection ovens are very efficient because they allow you to bake in less time, with less energy. Use your convection feature if you have one.

Altering your cooking techniques

You don't have to use a conventional oven to cook a hot meal. Sometimes the following appliances can do the job more efficiently:

✔ **Toaster ovens:** Use a toaster oven for small jobs. Small toaster ovens (the kind that sit on your countertop) take much less energy than big conventional ovens. And if you know how to use them properly, you can get great browning effects. They don't cost much, but you're better off getting a good one with an automatic timer and temperature controls.

✔ **Barbeque grills:** Use your barbecue as much as possible in the summer. From an efficiency standpoint, gas models are the best. Charcoal grills waste a lot of energy (you can't turn them off and on, as needed), plus they put out far more pollution. Small propane barbecues work very well and, contrary to what some people claim, they don't make the food stink. Burning petro-based charcoal is no different than burning petro-based natural gas.

- ✔ **Crock pots and portable pressure cookers:** In the summer, put them outdoors to save air-conditioning costs and lower humidity.

Even when nothing but a conventional oven will do, you can employ energy-saving strategies like the following:

- ✔ **Bake dishes simultaneously.** Try to fill your oven with a number of dishes at the same time. This will lower the per-item cooking cost. If different items call for different temperatures, relax; there's wiggle room. Put the items that need higher temperatures on the top rack, and items that need lower temperatures on the lower rack (that's easy to remember).

- ✔ **Don't preheat.** Let your food warm up with the oven. And turn your stove off a few minutes before the allotted cooking time — the residual heat will finish the process.

- ✔ **Don't lay foil on racks.** Foil obstructs the natural flow of heat.

- ✔ **Use glass or ceramic pans in the oven.** The food cooks more efficiently, and the texture is better.

- ✔ **Match the pan to the size of the heating element.** This way, no heat escapes around the edges.

- ✔ **Contain heat in the summer.** Putting a lid on that boiling pot reduces the amount of heat and humidity that's released into the air. Rinse pans out as soon as practical to cool them down.

✔ **Release heat in the winter.** In cold weather, let hot pots and pans release their heat into your home. Don't rinse them out because that washes the heat right down the drain.

Enjoying the Fine Life with TVs and Computers

Although the new flat-screen televisions reduce power consumption, the trend toward gigantic screens drives consumption right back up. Combine a big screen with a big sound system, and your entertainment center may be costing you an arm and a leg. Computers and their various components and accessories constitute a similar category of common household energy-eaters. What's a modern man to do?

For starters, be aware that "off" doesn't always mean what it implies. Even when your TV, entertainment system, computer, monitor, DVD player, and so on are sitting idle, they're still drawing power. (Check out the earlier sidebar "Making time stand still" to see this for yourself.) You can put a halt to this energy drain by plugging these appliances into a power strip and turning the power strip off when you're not using them.

In the same vein, always use the power down feature on your computer, and turn your computer off at night and on weekends. Remember, even in the sleep mode, power is being wasted. Don't forget to turn your printer off when it's not in use, too.

Some processors use a lot more juice than others. Do you really need all that speed and power? Probably not, although computers have now taken over the role that big muscle cars used to play for macho hard guys. Laptop computers use a lot less power than desktops, so if you can, opt for a laptop.

Old CRT monitors draw considerably more power than the new, flat-screen versions. They also put out a lot of extra heat, requiring more air conditioning in the summer. So you may want to update (unless, of course, you're looking for heat in your home office, in which case you may want to keep your old CRT).

Buying New Appliances

Most of the time you don't have a choice over whether to buy a new appliance. The old one breaks, it can't be repaired, and you come to the difficult conclusion that it's time for a funeral. Many people also decide that upgrading to a more energy-efficient model is worth the investment.

Fortunately, the government has made your decision process easy for you with the Energy Star program (yes, a government program that actually works the way it's supposed to — take advantage of this rare opportunity!). The Energy Star is only awarded to appliances that significantly exceed the minimum national efficiency standards, typically by 20 percent, and by as much as 110 percent. Energy Star ratings apply to all major appliances, plus HVAC systems, natural gas and oil systems, programmable thermostats, and so on. Even windows are certified with Energy Star. You can easily find the Energy Star Label on those products to which the standard applies (see Figure 11-1).

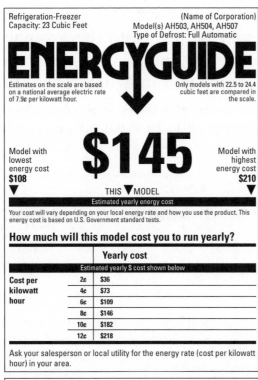

Refrigeration-Freezer
Capacity: 23 Cubic Feet

(Name of Corporation)
Model(s) AH503, AH504, AH507
Type of Defrost: Full Automatic

ENERGYGUIDE

Estimates on the scale are based on a national average electric rate of 7.9¢ per kilowatt hour.

Only models with 22.5 to 24.4 cubic feet are compared in the scale.

$145

Model with lowest energy cost
$108
▼

THIS ▼ MODEL

Model with highest energy cost
$210
▼

Estimated yearly energy cost

Your cost will vary depending on your local energy rate and how you use the product. This energy cost is based on U.S. Government standard tests.

How much will this model cost you to run yearly?

		Yearly cost
		Estimated yearly $ cost shown below
Cost per kilowatt hour	2¢	$36
	4¢	$73
	6¢	$109
	8¢	$146
	10¢	$182
	12¢	$218

Ask your salesperson or local utility for the energy rate (cost per kilowatt hour) in your area.

Room Air Conditioner
Capacity: 5400 BTU/hr

(Name of Corporation)
Models 000XXX

ENERGYGUIDE

Models with the most efficient energy rating number use less energy and cost less to operate

Models with 5300 to 5799 BTU's cool about the same space

9.0

Least Efficient model
6.3
▼

Most Efficient model
9.0
▼

Energy Efficiency Rating (EER)

This energy rating is based on U.S. Government Standard Tests.

How much will this model cost you to run yearly?

Yearly hours of use		250	750	1000	2000	3000
		Estimated yearly $ cost shown below				
Cost per kilowatt hour	2¢	$ 3	$ 9	$12	$ 24	$ 36
	4¢	$ 6	$18	$24	$ 48	$ 72
	6¢	$ 9	$27	$36	$ 72	$108
	8¢	$12	$36	$48	$ 96	$144
	10¢	$15	$45	$60	$120	$180
	12¢	$18	$54	$72	$144	$216

Ask your salesperson or local utility for the energy rate (cost per kilowatt hour) in your area. Your cost will vary depending on your local area rate and how you use the product.

Figure 11-1:
An Energy Star label.

299

The Energy Star label shows the product's annual power consumption. Even better, note the annual cost estimates based on different utility rates. On these labels, the highest rate is 12 cents, which is somewhat anachronistic in light of rising energy rates. But multiplying the costs based on your own rates is easy enough. For instance, if you're paying 16

Playing it safe with combustion appliances

Nearly a third of water heaters and stoves (and many refrigerators) use natural gas. These units require a few extra precautions that are worth noting:

✔ All combustion equipment should be installed and maintained by knowledgeable personnel. Electrical equipment is inherently safer, and, as a result, it's cheaper because you can do most of the maintenance yourself. With combustion equipment, you assume some extra risks.

✔ Install a carbon monoxide detector near the equipment.

✔ Make sure your smoke detectors are working correctly.

✔ Yellow flames always indicate that the gas is being burned inefficiently, which causes soot buildup, as well as wasted money. If you see yellow flames, get a service technician to tune up your system.

✔ Combustion equipment always requires appropriate ventilation (the reasons are too complex for the scope of this book, but trust me on this one). Read the instruction manuals, and make sure that a qualified service person not only installs the equipment, but also maintains it. If in doubt, opt for the service call — your family's life may be on the line.

cents, simply multiply the result based on 8 cents by two.

You can easily compare different models of appliances using the Energy Star labels. Simply compare the estimated annual costs. You can then compare the difference in price with the difference in costs.

 If you want to buy an energy-efficient appliance, buy one with an Energy Star certification; it's that simple. You can get super-duper-efficient models, but they tend to cost a lot more than they're worth. These are generally for the off-grid crowd or those willing to pay any price to go green. For the most part, if you buy an Energy Star model and use it efficiently, you're doing very well.

Now if only the government would come out with an income tax form that made as much sense as Energy Star. . . .

Chapter 12

Controlling Solar Exposures in Your Home

Sunshine is free (at least until the government comes up with a way to tax it). And sunshine is natural and amiable, so it should be used as much as possible. In fact, most people do use sunshine, but not nearly as effectively as they could.

Using sunshine effectively isn't as simple as just letting the sun shine in. Obviously, in the winter, you want both the sunshine and its heat in your home as much as possible. In the summer, you want the sun's light but not the heat — two goals that are almost always at odds.

In this chapter, I show you how to heat your home in the winter and avoid doing so in the summer. I show you how to light your home with sunshine, and how to plan and build sunrooms that increase the value of your home and provide increased living area at an efficient cost. (For much greater detail on this subject, check out *Solar Power Your Home For Dummies,* also authored by yours truly and published by Wiley.)

Lighting Your Home with Sunshine

The more you use sunshine to light your home, the less you need to rely on artificial lighting. Using sunshine to your advantage also creates a kinder, more inviting atmosphere. The following sections outline a variety of ways to manipulate sunlight and reap all the benefits it has to offer. (For details on how to deal with the heat factor, head to the later section "Heating Your Home with Sunlight — Or Not.")

Planting a tree

By far the best way to control sunlight in your home is to strategically locate *deciduous trees* (those that lose their leaves in the winter) around your home's exterior. If you plant a single deciduous tree outside a southern-exposed window, particularly a large window, you benefit in many ways.

In the summer, the leaves block most of the sunlight, leaving the room with diffused, subtle, cool light. On a hot summer day, harsh sunlight makes you feel even hotter, but shade creates a sense of calm and well-being, not to mention relief. In the winter, with the leaves gone, direct sunlight enters the room, casting the interior with warmth (due to the greenhouse effect), as well as a bright, yellow tint that feels warm.

Making natural light more effective

You can make the most of whatever natural light is available to you. Here are a number of clever ways to increase the effectiveness of sunlight in your home's interior spaces.

Putting up mirrors to enhance existing light

Position your mirrors in corners to broadcast light around the entire room. In essence, mirrors magnify light. Two mirrors positioned catty-corner on opposing walls work even better and make the room seem much larger.

Before you nail a mirror up permanently, try it out at different times of the day to gauge its effect. If you want more effect in the morning than the evening, put the mirror on an eastern-facing wall. Also keep in mind that mirrored closet doors often work wonders to light a bedroom and increase its perceived size.

Using glass bricks to let light in

Cut some high holes through the solid walls of a dark hallway (it doesn't matter whether the walls lead to other rooms or outdoors) and put glass bricks into the spaces so that light enters the hallway. Doing so not only spreads light but also makes the hallway seem larger and less restrictive. In fact, your entire home will feel friendlier and more open. Installing glass bricks is a relatively straightforward and inexpensive do-it-yourself project (ask for more details at your hardware store).

Using windowed doors

Instead of the usual solid wood doors, install French doors between rooms. You can get French doors from most any building supply stores. Even if you use curtains for privacy, the light will still shine through, and your home will seem more spacious. You're likely to find one location in your home that's a perfect candidate for a French door.

Don't forget the front door. Glass panels can lighten up your entryway, and guests will find them more inviting than a solid, impersonal mass of heavy wood staring them in the face. Then again, maybe you don't want to encourage guests.

Getting rid of overgrowth

If vegetation is crowding the light through one of your windows, cut it back. This is especially important with windows facing east, because morning sunlight works much better than coffee, and it's not a laxative.

Cleaning or tinting your windows

Spotless windows make a huge difference in the way a room feels. Cleaning may not matter much in terms of the quantity of light coming in, but it definitely enhances the quality, which may be even more important.

If your problem is that a room gets too much sunshine (or you want to obscure a view to the outside without using blinds), apply window tinting. Tinting comes in sheet tape form, and anybody can put it up (well, pretty much anybody — it helps if you don't have ten thumbs).

Decorating to make the most of natural light

Decorating a room with light-colored carpeting and walls makes it seem like there's a lot more sunshine. Placing the right kinds of trinkets in the right spots can also make a difference. Here are a few tips:

- ✔ **Hang stained-glass window decorations to create a splashy mood.** The decorations dominate the room when the sun shines in directly, adding color, verve, and even some dynamics for a very low cost. You can also use sparkling crystals and ceramic art pieces for the same effect. Sunny breakfast nooks are ideal for spectral trinkets.

- ✔ **Whitewash dark trim molding.** This simple trick makes a big difference. Even in a room painted all white, dark molding can dominate.

- ✔ **Mount glass shelves on sunny windows and fill them with knickknacks.** This has the subtle effect of making the room seem much lighter. Glass shelves in a window can also block an undesirable view so you don't have to close the blinds. Your eye stops at the glass shelves instead of the view beyond.

Installing skylights and solar tubes

For those of you with more advanced ambitions, skylights and solar tubes can make a big difference in your home's lighting for a relatively small investment.

Traditional skylights are big, expansive channelers of sunlight, and the large openings in your home's ceiling will make a room bigger and airier, both literally and figuratively. If you're interested in skylights, consult with a contractor unless you're really good with tools and projects. You can find remodel books that detail the tasks, as well as the parts, tools, and skills required.

Skylights are very expensive to install. If you want multiple skylights, consider doing them all at the same time. Installing three or four skylights at one time takes around twice as much time and money (rather than three or four times as much) — food for thought when you're deciding how many skylights to install.

Solar light tubes, also known as tubular skylights, are a less expensive alternative. These let in natural light that varies with the clouds and the weather. Solar tubes, which can be installed by just about anybody in half a day for around $250, can have just as much effect as a traditional skylight for around one tenth of the cost. (The typical price, uninstalled, is $200 for a four-foot-long pipe. Extensions cost an additional $20 per foot.)

Here's how a solar light tube system works: Sunlight is collected up on the roof and transmitted down a shiny, silver pipe into a diffuser, which broadcasts the light into the room below (see Figure 12-1).

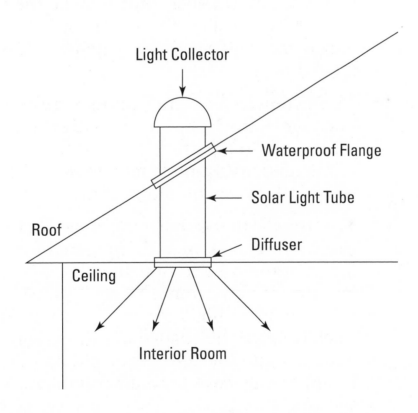

Figure 12-1: *A solar light tube system.*

If you're interested in solar tubes, keep these points in mind:

- ✔ **You can make most rooms bright enough to work in during daylight hours, even in the winter.** Large-diameter units (12 inches and more) can output as much light as a dozen 100-watt light bulbs, at one tenth the heat. Because they don't produce as much heat, you can use your air-conditioner much less.

One of the best locations for a solar tube is a dark corner in the family room, where the light will be well-used and have a dramatic effect. Solar light tubes are also good for dark, isolated bathrooms. The natural light is comforting, and you never have to flip a light switch during the day. If you have a dark kitchen, a solar tube may be the perfect solution, especially if a lot of people come and go during the day. The light switch won't be constantly flipped off and on.

- ✔ **The intensity of light changes quite a bit because solar light varies with the clouds and weather.** On a partly cloudy day, you can get a lot of fluctuation as clouds move across the sun, making you much more conscious of the outdoors.

- ✔ **The tubes themselves can drastically change the way decor looks.** Be prepared for a drastically different room because lighting is very influential in terms of how a room "feels." (I installed one in a bathroom and had to start a big remodel the next week because the change in tone simply made the old paint and tile colors look old and drab — okay, I didn't really *have* to, but my wife made me and she wears the pants.) Also, the silver color imparts a certain "cool" mood. Some types of solar light tubes come with filters for creating moods, but the filters cut out light as well.

✔ **Installation isn't easy (you have to go up into your attic space), but it's doable.** When deciding where to install solar light tubes, always keep the installation itself in mind. Just forget about installing these tubes in locations where you can't easily go: like shallow attic spaces or near the edges of the attic. If you plan to install solar tubes yourself, heed this advice:

- Don't try to buy separate parts. Get a complete kit, with however many extension tubes you think you need. Get an extra extension, and leave it in the box for return if you don't use it.

- The hardest part of the job is working in the attic space. Plan your route up and over to where the work is going to be done, and figure out how you'll sit and stand once you get there. Also determine what tools you'll need.

- Cutting through a typical roof takes more than a toy saw. Composite shingles eat jigsaw blades, so get extras. And take precautions to seal against the weather on the rooftop. Solar tubes come with detailed instructions for sealing; follow these instructions carefully or you'll be sorry. If there's any possible way for water to get in, it will.

Heating Your Home with Sunlight — or Not

In addition to being a great light source, sunlight is a great source of heat — which is wonderful when you want heat, but not so wonderful when you want to stay cool. Fortunately, you can regulate how much heat the sun generates in your home.

First, you need to understand the greenhouse effect. The best way to describe how sunshine heats a home is to explain how a greenhouse works. Sunlight enters the enclosed space through the *glazing,* or window material, and then gets absorbed and turned into heat. The heat stays in the enclosed space thanks to the glazing's insulation properties (see Figure 12-2).

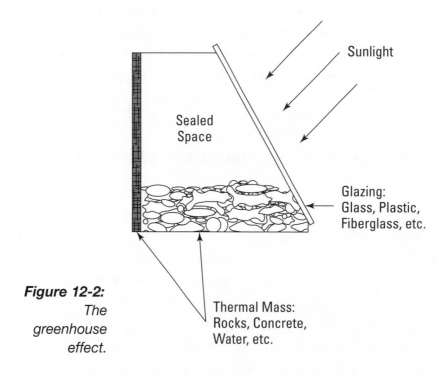

Figure 12-2:
The greenhouse effect.

You can enhance the greenhouse effect — and make your home warmer — by increasing the transmissibility of the window and maximizing its insulation. Double-pane glass works well for this, and a number of window coatings and other optical tricks can also be used to good effect. Inexpensive plastic materials that work well are available, although they tend to blur the view.

To maximize the heat generated, the space must be well-sealed to prevent air leakage, although the greenhouse effect is often powerful enough to work well even in relatively leaky environments. In fact, sometimes it works so well that the heat is intolerable. (The greenhouse effect explains why your car gets so hot when it sits out in the summer sunshine.)

So how do you reduce the greenhouse effect when you don't want all that heat? Easy. By controlling the amount of sunshine that enters your home.

Installing blinds and sunscreens

When you install blinds or shades, you control the amount of sunlight that enters your home. An added benefit is that these things can also increase the beauty of your home and, if you're really smart (of course you are — you're reading this book), you can use blinds and shades to *insulate*, or maintain heat storage, as well.

Bare glass lets the sun enter freely. Using blinds or sunshades (and even curtains) restricts the amount of sunlight that enters and, depending on how they're hung (whether on the inside or outside of the window, and how far from the window), affects the insulation properties, as Table 12-1 outlines. You can see your hanging options in Figure 12-3.

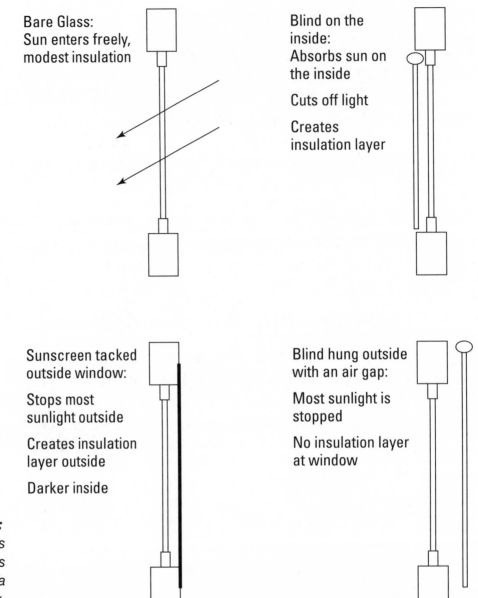

Bare Glass:
Sun enters freely,
modest insulation

Blind on the
inside:
Absorbs sun on
the inside

Cuts off light

Creates
insulation layer

Sunscreen tacked
outside window:

Stops most
sunlight outside

Creates insulation
layer outside

Darker inside

Blind hung outside
with an air gap:

Most sunlight is
stopped

No insulation layer
at window

Figure 12-3:
*Differences
in the ways
to cover a
window.*

312

Table 12-1   Window Covering Options

Type of Covering	Sun	Insulation
Bare glass	Sun enters freely	Minimal insulation
Blind on the inside	Absorbs sun on the inside; controls lighting and enhances decorative qualities in the room; may also completely block view and light	Creates excellent insulation layer inside — good for cold climates and winter
Sunscreen tacked outside of window	Stops most sunlight outside; darker inside but doesn't obscure view	Creates insulation layer outside; heat is stopped outside so that the interior of the room is cooler; best for hot climates
Blind hung outside with an air gap	Stops most sunlight outside, but doesn't obscure view	No insulation layer at window; maximum cooling effect, especially in breezy locations

Hanging blinds: Inside or out?

When you hang blinds on the inside of windows, the sunshine comes in through the window, strikes the blind, and gets converted into heat. The heat is trapped in the air gap between the blind and the window and can get very hot because of the greenhouse effect. Of course, heat is only desirable in the winter. In the summer, you may have a cooler room if you just leave the window uncovered and let the sun and air in.

- ✔ **To warm a room in winter:** Contrary to what you may think, the best way to heat a room with sunshine in the winter is not to open the blinds, but to use special blinds that capture sunlight and insulate at the same time. You can get interior blinds made to do just that.

- ✔ **To keep a room cool in summer:** Interior blinds made for summer reflect a lot of light back out the window. They are usually shiny and white, at least on the exterior-facing surface.

To get the best cooling effect, allow for some ventilation between an outside blind and the open window it covers. If you can't do that, use an outside blind that has a shiny, metallic exterior surface that simply reflects all sunlight and doesn't let any heat into the room at all. The room will be completely dark, but this is desirable on a burning hot day.

- ✔ **To maximize the efficiency of an air conditioner:** When your air conditioner is on, it's best to hang blinds so that they create as much insulation as possible *and* banish sunlight. You can achieve this by closing your interior blinds all the way. If you have outside shades, all the better. The best scheme for a sunny home that uses a lot of air conditioning is both solar screens (see the next section, "Putting up sunscreens") and interior blinds. The home will be very dark, but it will also be much cooler.

Infrared filtering glass

You can get special glass that filters infrared light out before it gets into your home. In fact, most of the sunlight's heat comes from light that is invisible to the human eye. Some animals can see infrared light (like owls and nocturnal hunters) but humans can't see it. Infrared filtering glass rejects up to 70 percent of the heat of sunlight, yet you can't tell the difference in the view because it transmits visible light as well as a conventional window. Solar screens and other sunlight-inhibiting processes inhibit the view, and you may not want this if your window is a centerpiece to a home that features lavish views.

You'll pay more for infrared glass, but it may be just the thing.

Putting up sunscreens

Sunscreens, also called *solar screens,* are an inexpensive and effective way to cool your home in the summer. They reflect a lot of sunlight — up to 90 percent — plus they create an insulation barrier on the outside. Most are dark, heavy-duty, fabric screens with a tacky surface. Some are a flexible, tinted plastic film. You can get sunscreens up to 8 feet wide, with unlimited length.

Only windows that get more than a few hours of direct sunlight a day are worth sun screening. The best candidates are tall windows facing south, but east and west exposures can also get very hot. With a solar screen tacked up on the outside of a window, most of the sunlight is reflected before it even gets to the window. The screen gets hot and an insulation barrier keeps that heat trapped, but it's all outside the window.

You don't want sunscreens in the winter, which means you

need to mount them in such a way that you can bring them down in the winter. Your options:

- **Use removable frames.** You can buy frames for sunscreens. Most are aluminum. You can get them either preloaded with screens, or you can load them yourself. They come in a range of colors.

- **Tack them up.** The fastest and cheapest way to cover a window is to tack the screen right onto the window frame. You don't need anything more than tacks, a hammer or a stapler, and scissors or a box cutter. Just cut the screen down to a few inches bigger than what you need, tack it up, and then trim it with scissors or a box cutter. In the winter, just pull the screen down.

- **Roll them up like blinds.** You can get automatic, electric controllers so that, with the push of a single button, you can command every solar screen in your home.

Sunscreens are easy to put up, and most people can do it themselves. Call a screen shop direct for tools, materials, and installation advice. Easy-to-use mounting hardware is essential. (For automatic sunscreens, you'll need a professional installation.)

 Before you go the do-it-yourself route, ask the shop what they would charge to install sunscreens for you. They can do a window in a few minutes, and their bid for the entire job may not be much more than what you'll pay for the material alone.

You can expect at least a three-year lifetime with quality sunscreen, at around 75 cents per square foot. For a 3-foot × 6-foot window, if a screen lasts five years, the cost is only $2 per year (with the cheapest installation method).

If your climate is hot and sunny, there's no question you'll get good payback on this small investment. Cheap screen bleaches out and looks perpetually dirty — avoid it unless you like cheap and perpetually dirty.

Covering your windows with exterior awnings

Awnings are great light shades because you can configure them in different geometrical relationships and control the light over the course of a day. They also drastically change the appearance of your home for the better. They add shape and break up monotonous flat surfaces, and complement the color scheme of your home's exterior. Two common awning styles are the Venetian awning and the hood awning (see Figure 12-4):

- ✔ **Venetian awnings** allow sunlight in the winter, when the sun is low in the sky, and block sunlight in the summer, when the sun is high. Venetians also allow you to see out of the top of your window, and the effect is much more open than that of hood awnings.

- ✔ **Hood awnings** are more decorative. They can be made of nice fabrics that match or complement the house. They work better in rainy climates because they keep cold water off your windows. (You can lose a lot of heat by water-based convection from rain.)

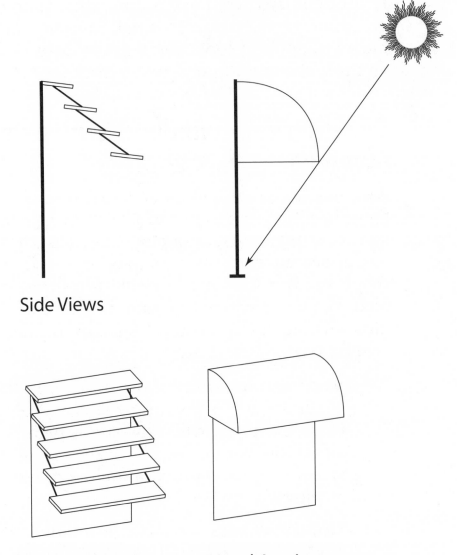

Side Views

Figure 12-4:
Venetian and hood awnings.

Venetian Awning   Hood Awning

 Do-it-yourselfers can build very nice-looking wood slat aw-nings that can be attached to most surfaces. You can buy designs over the Internet, but designing them yourself is even more fun. You can paint them to match your house, and you can use materials that last a long time. You can even devise an adjustment scheme that allows you to raise or lower the pitch, depending on conditions.

Installing outdoor window blinds

Outdoor blinds, which are designed to cover windows from the outside, stop the heat on the outside of the home. Plus in the winter, these blinds can act as insulators. Outdoor blinds are usually made of vinyl. Some are prettier than others, which may or may not matter to you. Import shops stock different sizes of roll-up bamboo shades, often priced as low as $5 apiece. You'll probably have to throw these cheapies out after a single season, but so what — they're cheapies.

These blinds are also commonly used overhead for patios and porches where late afternoon and evening sunlight can prevent you from using the area. In this case, leave them up all day or your floor will heat up (concrete or tile floors hold heat for a long time).

Most outdoor blinds have cords that you pull different ways, but if you don't want to raise and lower the blinds manually, you can find outdoor blinds that retract automatically. Automatic retractable shades are available from specialty suppliers. You can even find solar-powered retractors that work with a hand-held remote controller.

Putting up radiant barriers

A radiant barrier is a sheet of thin material that looks like reinforced aluminum foil. It's tacked up beneath your roof joists or simply laid over the insulation on your attic floor. It keeps a lot of heat out of your home, but it doesn't prevent your attic from getting warm in the winter (in the wintertime, heat rises from your home, and it's composed mostly of convective heat so radiant barriers don't have any effect at all).

The material itself costs around 20 cents per square foot. For a 2,000-square-foot house, the material costs $400, and the payback can be very impressive. In hot climates, radiant barriers cool the home down more than enough to pay for themselves in less than a couple years.

To install a radiant barrier, you simply staple it into place, regardless of whether you mount it overhead or lay it on the floor. (Make sure you have a good quality stapler.) The design of your roof impacts how easy installation will be. Open rafters are the best candidates; if you have complex trusses, forget it. Installation is also a snap if your attic floor is open and easily accessible.

 Even if you can only cover a portion of the rafters or floor, it's worth it. Try to cover an entire small area, rather than isolated spots in a number of different areas.

 Attics can roast you fast. They'll heat to over 130°F, easy. Don't kid yourself; if it feels real hot, it can be dangerous. One way to stay safe is to work in the morning, when things are cooler.

Cutting out summertime sunlight with overhangs

Overhangs, which are solid constructions built over windows, can provide both financial gain and aesthetic beauty. You can design an overhang to visually complement your home's roofline.

Here's how overhangs work (see Figure 12-5): In the winter, sunlight can enter the home because the sun is lower in the sky. If you have high thermal mass floors (like concrete or tile), your home will heat up nicely. In the summertime, when the sun is higher in the sky, the overhang stops any direct sunlight from entering the home.

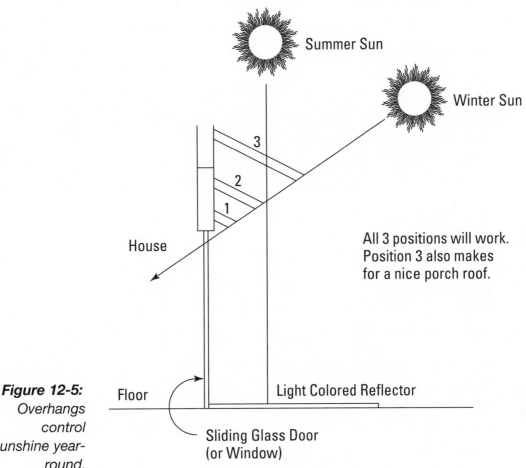

Figure 12-5:
Overhangs control sunshine year-round.

 Be sure the overhang you install changes your home's appearance for the better (the best looking overhangs mimic the pitch of your roof and use the same materials). Before you nail an overhang up and make it permanent, try to arrange it where it's going to go and see what it looks like. Alternatively, take a digital photo of the window and use a computer program to play around with different ideas. You can find overhang designs in home plan books.

Garnering Sunlight with Greenhouses and Sunrooms

There are two types of solar rooms: greenhouses and sunrooms. Greenhouses, which are either connected to your home or separate from it, can help warm your home as well as provide inexpensive, delicious, highly nutritious food or beautiful and soothing decorative plants. Sunrooms, which are always part of your home, add living space and square footage for a relatively low cost, increase the efficiency of your heating and cooling efforts, and brighten up your home's ambience and decor.

A well-designed solar room can provide up to 60 percent of a home's heating in the winter, depending on the amount of sunlight available. Even in very cold climates, a solar room can work efficiently. And particularly in a cold climate, a sunroom can provide needed relief from the gray doldrums of winter.

Most home additions cost more than your property value increases due to the improvement. But with solar rooms, the variety of designs and the reduced building restrictions make it possible to enjoy profitable appreciations, especially if you do it yourself.

Deciding between the different types of solar rooms

So which type of solar room is better: greenhouse or sunroom? That depends on what you want to achieve and which type of room you prefer.

Greenhouses invite the maximum amount of sunlight and generally require a glass ceiling or sloping glass walls. They are also very functional. They need a water supply, their temperatures need to be regulated (the difference between the hottest and coldest temperatures needs to be kept to a minimum, as dictated by the type of plants), they need adequate ventilation to provide oxygen for the plants, and they need floors that can withstand water leaks and mud spillage.

Sunrooms, on the other hand, are designed as extensions of your home's living space. You can leave them partially open to the outdoors, or you can completely enclose them and put in carpeting and fine furniture. Because too much sunlight is uncomfortable and sunrooms are meant to be inviting, they generally have water-tight, solid roofs. They may or may not contain skylights and vents, but both increase the livability factor.

In both types of solar rooms, most of the southern wall space is taken up by windows or some other suitable glazing material. In addition, both greenhouses and sunrooms can increase a home's privacy by providing a buffer between the outside world and the interior spaces.

Building a solar room yourself

A do-it-yourselfer can design and build a sunroom or greenhouse at a relatively low cost with relatively low risk. These rooms can be separate from the house and, as such, don't need electrical wiring or plumbing and don't require that you obey all the building code requirements that are unavoidable inside of a home.

 If you don't want to have to apply for building permits or have the property value reappraised (with the commensurate increase in property taxes), build the sunroom against a house, but don't actually nail the frame elements to the

323

home — in this case, it's just a free-standing porch. (Keep in mind, though, that if you ever sell your house, you can't advertise your solar room as part of your house's square footage.)

If you plan to add a solar room to your home, kits are the best bets for do-it-yourselfers. (Greenhouse kits made of plastic sheets instead of windows are easy, cheap, and effective.) Fortunately, an entire industry is dedicated to manufacturing and selling prefab kits that cost anywhere from a few hundred dollars to hundreds of thousands of dollars. You can see samples in showrooms. It's always best to touch things before you buy; photos are often misleading and rarely reflect reality the way you expect them to.

Alternatively you can build your own custom design and use the same materials (windows, framing, trim) as the rest of your house. If you have a good imagination, you can find very cheap materials, particularly glass windows and heavy beams. As much as a well-designed solar room can enhance your home's aesthetics, a poorly designed one can make your house look awkward and uninviting. The following sections offer some practical tips for creating a solar room you can be proud of and happy with.

- ✔ Make very good drawings done to scale before you begin building (use gridded paper and let one square foot equal one grid). Consider all the angles and, if you can, draw some perspectives (from the street, for instance). The more thought you give to the room's appearance before you start, the better the odds that your solar room will increase the value of your home.

- ✔ In cold climates, use between 0.65 and 1.5 square feet of double-pane glass for each square foot of building floor area. In temperate climates, use between 0.3 to 0.9 square feet for each square foot of building floor area. Even if you can't achieve these ratios, any amount of glass will work to your advantage. Solar rooms are usually compromises between the best physics and the best aesthetics and cost. In general, aesthetics should win for sunrooms, while physics should win for greenhouses.

- ✔ Always build your sunroom on a southern front. Put the absorbers and thermal mass on the north side. Otherwise, your room won't work to maximum advantage. Also, try to use as many of your home's existing walls as possible, preferably on both the east and west ends of the sunroom. These walls are already insulated, and they match the house.

- ✔ The best location in your house is adjacent to the kitchen for attached greenhouses, and adjacent to the living room or family room for solar rooms. These locations afford not only the most efficient use, but also the most use in general. Leaving the doors and windows open between your house and sunroom lends a sense of increased floor space and size to your home. (Building a solar room off your family room is the cheapest way to increase the square footage of your home.)

- ✔ Plant deciduous trees at the same time you build your solar room. They'll cut back the sun in the summer and allow it all in during the winter. Plus, the room will be much prettier with a view of some nice trees. Partnering with Mother Nature brings a benign continuity to the entire project.

- ✔ Use the same materials that your home is made of, if you can. Otherwise, don't try to match at all — just do something that's complementary but

325

totally disparate. Nothing mismatches more than an attempt at matching that doesn't quite cut it. For example, blue and orange match up much better than orange and a slightly different shade of orange, which just ends up looking cheap and classless.

 Easy and straightforward candidates for solar rooms are existing porches and decks that already have the basic support structures and flooring in place. All you need to do is build up and around them.

Chapter 13

Breathing Homes: Ventilation, Fans, and Air Filters

Unless you live in a perfect climate where it's never too hot or too cold, heating and air conditioning make up the largest component of your power bill. If you rely solely on your heater and your air conditioner to keep you comfortable, then you're missing a big opportunity for energy efficiency. The key to comfort is air movement. By moving air appropriately through your home, you can achieve a much higher level of comfort and save money by using your HVAC system less, particularly in the summer. This chapter tells you how.

Taking Advantage of Natural Air Movement

A small amount of air movement increases convective cooling quite a bit, which is why people like fans blowing when it's hot in the summer. A fan can make a room feel 5°F cooler, even though the temperature has not changed. In the winter, winds make air seem much colder, an effect known as the *wind chill factor.* People seek breezes in the summer and avoid it in the winter, not because air movement changes the actual temperature, but because it increases the rate of convective cooling. (Refer to Chapter 7 for a discussion on how convection heating and cooling works.) That's why ventilation is so important to your comfort.

Each house has a natural ventilation scheme, which is influenced by the following factors:

- ✓ **The prevailing winds,** as determined by the weather patterns in the climate in which you live

- ✓ **The chimney effect,** which dictates that hot air naturally rises while cool air settles

- ✓ **The vent patterns of your home,** as determined by the location of windows, doors, vents, and other openings in your home

Methods of heating and cooling that take advantage of these factors to increase energy efficiency are known as *passive* methods. The most efficient ways to move air always complement the natural ventilation scheme rather than work against it. By understanding your house's ventilation scheme, you can exploit the prevailing winds and the chimney effect and optimize air movement through your home's vents. You can passively cool your house well enough to avoid using your air conditioner on all but the hottest days.

Which way is the wind blowing?

Prevailing winds are the winds that are most common in your area. Wind has both a speed and a direction, and both are important. Some areas have very consistent prevailing winds, while other areas experience changes almost daily. You probably already have a good idea what the prevailing winds are where you live, but you can refine your understanding by paying more attention. In particular, how do the winds change over the course of a day? Over the seasons? (Typically, prevailing winds come from the southwest in the summer, and the northwest in the winter.)

Prevailing winds dictate the arrangement of fans and window openings that will work best in your house. Basically, you want to create a situation in which you take most advantage of natural air movement as possible because this comes entirely free of charge.

Figure 13-1 shows a typical situation. If all four windows are closed, there's no breeze in the house. If only one of the windows is opened, there's very little air movement in the house because air can neither enter nor leave. If only windows 2 and 4 are opened, there is very little air movement because the two open windows are at the same air pressure; the movement of the breeze is precisely the same at each window. However, if windows 1 and 3 are both open, a good breeze moves through the house, entering window 1 and exiting window 3. If all four windows are open, you'll get much the same breeze as you do when only 1 and 3 are open.

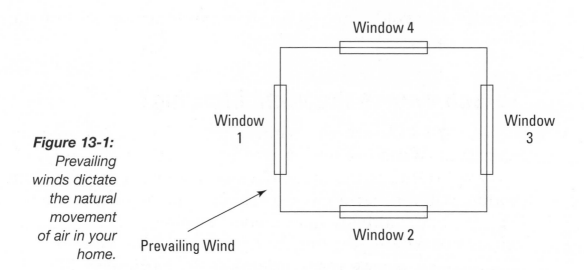

Figure 13-1:
Prevailing winds dictate the natural movement of air in your home.

Window 4

Window 1

Window 3

Window 2

Prevailing Wind

You can use a fan to work with or against the prevailing winds, as Figure 13-2 shows. A window fan aiming into the house at window 3 works directly against the natural ventilation scheme, and you may end up with no air movement at all. But aim the fan out at window 3, and you enhance the natural scheme. The same results can be achieved by mounting a fan in window 1 and aiming it either inward or outward. If you set a fan in the middle of the room with windows 1 and 3 open and with the fan facing window 3, you enhance the natural scheme somewhat, but you can enhance it even more by placing the fan right in the window.

The environment outside of the windows can affect the temperature of the air. If a particular window has a nice big tree overhead and lawn beneath it, the air being drawn into the house through that window will be cooler than that which comes through a window situated over concrete in the direct sunshine. In Figure 13-2, for example, a big tree over window 1 would have a cooling impact on the breeze entering the house.

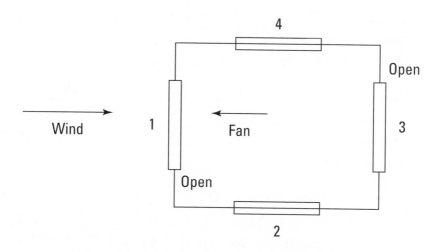

This destroys the natural ventilation scheme

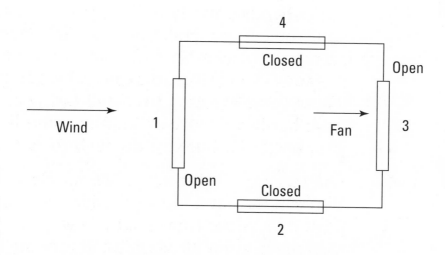

Figure 13-2:
Locating fans to enhance the natural ventilation scheme.

This fan location enhances the natural ventilation scheme

Up, up, and away: Chimney effect

The chimney effect accounts for the way hot air rises. In a closed room, the temperature at the ceiling is always higher than that on the floor. The differential in air temperature between the two areas can be over 15°F. You can achieve cooling, without any prevailing breezes at all, by arranging vents in your house to take advantage of the chimney effect (see Figure 13-3).

Many different types of vents are used in houses, as shown in Figure 13-4. Your home may or may not have these types of vents, but you can probably add them if you see the need:

- **Ridge vent:** Ridge vents work very well to ventilate your attic space because they make maximum use of the chimney effect while also exploiting prevailing winds. If you're in a hot climate, these types of vents are very efficient.

- **Roof vent:** Whether roof vents are efficient or not depends entirely on where you locate them on your roof. In general, you want to place a roof vent on the downwind side of your home's roof, as near the apex as possible to exploit the chimney effect. These vents are easy to install (ask a clerk at a large hardware store or building supply store about your options), but you do need to rain-proof them.

- **Gable vent:** Gable vents are simple to install. You can mount a big fan inside the gable vent and push a lot of air (make sure to work in conjunction with the natural air ventilation scheme, not against it). These vents are usually much better than roof vents when it comes to keeping rain out of your attic space. Plus you don't need to leak seal them with anywhere near the same integrity as a roof vent.

- **Soffit vent:** These vents are common in almost all residential constructions. The best way to ventilate your attic space using only passive (non-powered) means is with a number of soffit vents with a few strategically placed roof vents (or a ridge vent). Soffit vents don't need to be waterproofed because rain doesn't get to them.

✔ **Whole-house vent (with fan):** These are the best way to ventilate a house, providing the HVAC system isn't on. Not only do you ventilate your entire home, but you also ventilate your attic space with a whole-house vent. They make a lot of noise, but for the energy dollar you easily get the most bang for the buck. If you're reasonably skilled with tools and projects, you can install one yourself (aside from electrical connections, which may need to be done by a licensed contractor).

✔ **Kitchen and bathroom exhaust vents:** These vents get rid of humidity right at the worst sources in your home. In the summer, when you're cooking, always use a kitchen exhaust fan with a nearby window opened (even if you're running an air conditioner). If you take a shower in the summer, always use a bathroom exhaust fan to get rid of the humidity; otherwise, you'll feel hotter and run your air conditioner more.

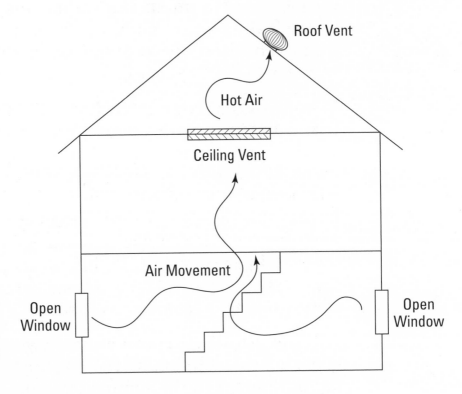

Figure 13-3:
The chimney effect moves air through your house.

Roof Vent

Hot Air

Ceiling Vent

Air Movement

Open Window

Open Window

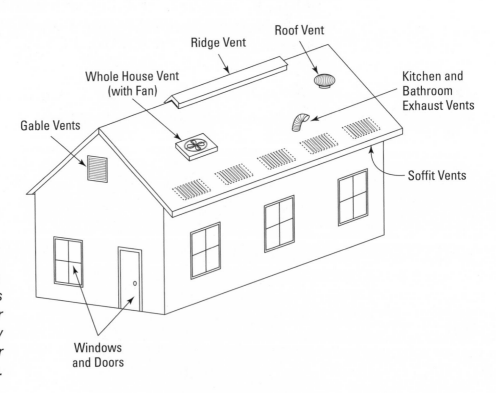

Figure 13-4:
Using vents to move air naturally through your home.

Ridge Vent

Roof Vent

Whole House Vent (with Fan)

Kitchen and Bathroom Exhaust Vents

Gable Vents

Soffit Vents

Windows and Doors

Getting Mother Nature on your side

Here are some tips on how to open and close your doors and windows in order to optimize the use of breezes to cool your home:

- **Leave interior doors open whenever possible.** This allows for better air circulation in your home. Even if you don't end up increasing air circulation, you still benefit because closed-off rooms are much more prone to wet spots and microorganism breeding.

- **Whenever possible, open your windows.** Surprisingly, many people simply don't think to open their windows. If you have multiple stories, opening windows on different floors can increase the flow of breezes. Experiment to see what works best. Unfortunately, what works best for one wind direction won't necessarily work for a different direction. But most locales have prevailing winds that don't often deviate.

 When you want breezes through your home, open windows and doors only on the windward and leeward sides of the house, and try to balance the openings. Don't just open every window you can. Experiment a little.

- **Add screen doors whenever possible.** Then open your doors, just like your windows.

- **Whenever you remodel, add some ventilation ports.** Remove interior walls whenever possible. Add skylights. Provide adequate clearance beneath doors so that air can move out of a room.

To gain the most advantage in moving air, you need to manage solar radiation entry into your home by using blinds and window coverings in conjunction with opening and closing windows. Chapter 12 addresses sunscreens, window blinds, awnings, and other shading methods.

Getting the Air Moving with Fans

Most homes don't do a great job when it comes to ventilation. Most people simply open windows and aim fans without rhyme or reason. A better idea is to strategically place fans so that you achieve the desired effect in both summer and winter. Some fans are better than others. What you want is to achieve the highest efficiency at the lowest cost (including both operating and equipment costs).

Unfortunately, achieving optimal ventilation year-round is a little tricky because requirements in winter are usually diametrically opposed to those in the summer. In the winter, you want to invite heat in and retain it as much as possible, whereas in the summer you seek to banish heat. Most homes are designed to optimize one season only, which creates problems in the other seasons.

A wide range of methods are available for moving air. Passive methods, such as exploiting prevailing winds and the chimney effect to cool your home, are the subject of the earlier section, "Taking Advantage of Natural Air Movement." In this section, I look at active methods, including ceiling fans, whole-house fans, and more. The next section, "I Need to Vent! Moving Air in Your Attic," delves into how improving ventilation in your attic can improve air movement throughout your house.

If you operate a fan without sufficient outside ventilation, you may draw combustion products, like smoke and carbon monoxide, into the living space of your home. Gas heaters and water heaters put out carbon monoxide. Always pay attention to where that gas is going. You may want to invest in a carbon monoxide alarm.

Fan efficiency and operation

The efficiency of a fan is determined by calculating the amount of air it moves divided by the power it consumes. Fans are rated for how much air they can move in a given amount of time. The most common spec is cubic feet per minute (cf/min). To find the proper size fan, calculate how many cubic feet are in the area you want to cool (just multiply length × width × height), be it your entire house, a room or the attic. Then buy a fan that's about 20 percent bigger than your calculations suggest.

To maximize a fan's efficiency, you must set it up properly. Consider the following:

- ✔ **The air route:** You need to consider the entirety of the airflow path, and make it as straight and clear as possible. Long, meandering hallways impede air flow much more than it may seem. Other efficiency-busters include the following: aiming a fan directly at a wall, setting a fan near a window that is only cracked open, and aiming a fan through a grate that is coated with dust (but I didn't really need to tell you that, right?).

- ✔ **A cowling:** The most efficient movement of air occurs when a fan has a cowling because a *cowling,* the metal ring around the outer diameter of the fan blades, directs airflow (see Figure 13-5). If all you're after is some air movement in a closed room, a cowling isn't so important. But if you're interested in moving a large quantity of air through your house, it's very important. Most heavy-duty work fans come with cowlings.

All fans are heaters. They dissipate power, which is given off as heat. If you put a fan in a closed room, the air temperature rises — it's a fact of physics. The room may feel cooler because of convective cooling, but the temperature goes up nevertheless. Fans used solely to stir air for convective cooling should never be turned on when no humans are present. Leaving an oscillating fan on all day long while you're at work only heats your house.

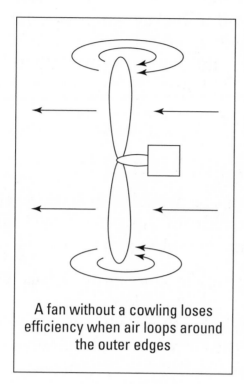

A fan without a cowling loses
efficiency when air loops around
the outer edges

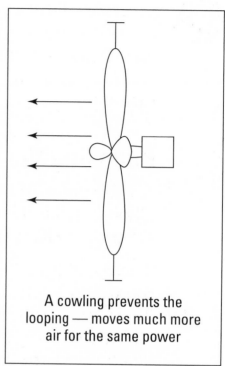

A cowling prevents the
looping — moves much more
air for the same power

An enclosed window
with a cowling is the
most efficient

Figure 13-5:
A fan with
a cowling is
more
efficient than
one without.

339

Thermostats are switches that open or close at a set temperature. They come in handy when you set up a fan in a remote location, such as an attic. When the attic reaches a certain temperature, the fan activates. When it's hot in the summer, you get ventilation. In the winter, the fan doesn't turn on.

Choosing the right kind of fan

A wide range of fans are available at a wide range of prices. Choosing the right unit for your needs will ensure you get the proper effect you're looking for.

The most effective fans in your entire house are your bathroom and kitchen vent fans. They remove tons of humidity, if used properly. Use them whenever you're cooking or taking a shower in the summer. Crack open a small window nearby and the fans will be very efficient, even if you're running an air conditioner. (Humidity in the summer is a back-breaker. It causes you to turn the air conditioner on, and when that doesn't feel like it's working, you run it even more. See Chapter 8 for details.) Following are the most common types of household fans.

Box fans

Box fans are portable units you can move around as needed. Most have some kind of cowling. Blade design also determines efficiency of air flow. You can find fans that are impressively efficient, but keep in mind that paying extra for a good fan may not be as worthwhile as simply using a smaller, cheaper fan the right way in the first place.

The noise a fan makes is an important consideration. Cheap fans are loud and clunky. Good ones make a smooth, even sound that may even be pleasing. The larger the blades (not power, blade size) the slower the blades can move to produce the same amount of air. If you have room, a large, lower-powered fan is better than a small brutish one.

Window fans

Window fans come with a sheet metal mounting arrangement that fits right into an open window and seals around the edges (a perfect cowling). Most of these are very efficient.

The best way to move air in your house is by using a good window fan mounted into the most appropriate window, probably upstairs on the downwind side of your house (aim the fan out the window). One small window fan mounted properly can do the same work as a number of large fans scattered about the house.

Exhaust fans

Exhaust fans in bathrooms and kitchens are important, but to ensure efficiency you need to make sure you use them correctly. If you turn on a bathroom fan without a bathroom window open, the exhausted air will be drawn from the house, and outside air will be drawn into the house through whatever openings are available (leaks in the insulation, open windows, and so on). Also, you shouldn't use exhaust fans when the HVAC system is running, but if you do, open a small window nearby to control air movement.

Oscillating fans

Oscillating fans move back and forth and are used for convective cooling only, a job they don't do very well. To get the most convective cooling for the least cost, get a small, stationary fan and aim it directly onto your uncovered body. Position it close, so you get the most benefit from the air movement. A big oscillating fan on the other side of the room is inefficient and may even make things worse by stirring up hot air near the ceiling.

Ceiling fans

Ceiling fans can accomplish two things: convective cooling and reversing or enhancing the chimney effect (see Figure 13-6). They may or may not bring outside air into the house, depending on how your vents are set up.

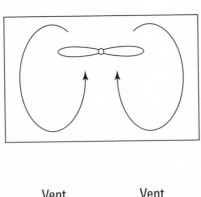

Closed room:
Enhances chimney effect

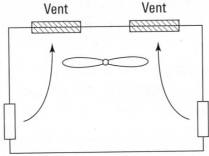

Vent   Vent

Venting to achieve maximum cooling

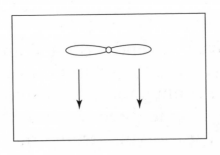

Winter: Pulls heat from ceiling, into room

Figure 13-6:
Ceiling fans move air inside of a room.

342

Ceiling fans work best when the fan blades are 7 to 9 feet above the floor and 10 to 12 inches below the ceiling. You may need several in a large room. Aesthetics are likely to dictate the size you choose, but keep in mind that the bigger blades are quieter because they move more slowly and achieve the same airflow. The maxim "You get what you pay for" is especially true for ceiling fans. Cheap ones make noise, are inefficient, and don't last long because they have shoddy bearings. In other words, cheap ceiling fans are very expensive, particularly if you factor in the time and effort it takes to install one.

Whole-house fans

Whole-house fans are mounted in the ceiling between a high point in your house and the attic. They draw air through open windows, exhaust it up through the roof, and cool the attic space at the same time. Whole-house fans are never run with the HVAC on at the same time, and they're rarely run in the wintertime. But in the summer, when the outside air temperature cools down at night, a whole-house fan works better than any other air movement scheme. With a whole-house fan, you can open any window in the house and get air movement in that room. Before you run out and buy one, here are a few tidbits to consider:

✔ In the winter, you need to cover a whole-house fan with some kind of insulation or you'll lose a lot of heat up into the attic. Some house fans come with metal vents that automatically open or close when the fan is on or off, but the insulation properties of these are very poor, and they generally leak a lot as well. You can buy covers over the Internet, or you can make a very effective cover yourself. (Cover your fan from the attic side rather than the house side, where aesthetics are important.) Alternatively, unplug your whole-house fan in the off season and simply cover the whole unit (on top) with a thick, old blanket from a thrift store.

✔ In the summer, turn the fan on when the sun goes down and leave it on all night. When the sun comes up, turn the fan off and close all the windows and drapes in the house to keep as much heat out as possible. Rule of thumb: Use a whole-house fan only when the outside air is below 85°F.

✔ Whole-house fans make a lot of noise because they're big and powerful; because they're mounted in a central location, you can hear the noise throughout the house. To reduce the noise, mount your whole-house fan on rubber gaskets. They also bring in a lot of dust and humidity.

✔ If your attic is not vented well, a whole-house fan will move very little air for the amount of power it consumes. Go up into your attic and check to make sure there are plenty of vents. If not, either make some or don't use a whole-house fan because it won't be worth it.

I Need to Vent! Moving Air in Your Attic

Attics can get to be over 160°F in the hot summer sun. This heat migrates down through your ceiling into your house. Even in the middle of the night, a poorly ventilated attic stays very hot. If you can somehow manage to continuously purge the air in your attic with outside air, your entire house will be much cooler. This is especially true of old houses with poor insulation. The following sections give you ways to move air out of your attic. (You can also purge the hot air out of the attic with a whole-house fan; see the preceding section for details.)

Adding attic vents for greater comfort

Attics need to breathe properly. They're usually built with vent systems either right through the roof or up in the walls below the eaves. When working properly, these vents let the hot air inside your attic escape. The most efficient of the attic vents is the rooftop vent (refer to Figure 13-4). It can be located right at the apex of the roof where the most heat collects due to the chimney effect. Unfortunately, attic vents can get completely clogged with dust. Dirty vents cause your attic to get much hotter in the summer. The solution? Clean them out periodically.

If you only have a few vents and they're in spots that don't enhance prevailing winds or the chimney effect, putting in a few more vents may be the answer. Most houses, in fact, could use a vent or two near the top of the roof to enhance the chimney effect. You can get inexpensive ones from most hardware stores, and they're relatively easy to install.

 Consider what the vents will look like from the street. You may want to locate roof vents so they won't be visible from the street level.

Using attic vent fans

Attic vent fans move air in your attic space only (as opposed to a whole-house fan, which moves air through both your home's interior and the attic). You can install an attic vent fan in a roof vent and move air through that vent. Or you can install one in a gable vent, which is the most common configuration. Many attic vent fans are activated via a thermostat switch. When the attic gets hot enough, the fan comes on. In addition, most attic vent fans are covered up in the winter to prevent natural ventilation and keep heat trapped in the attic space.

Installing an attic vent fan can be very expensive because you have to hire an electrician to provide the requisite 120VAC power to the fan's location and install a switch where it can be easily accessed. Additionally, accessing the attic space where the fan should be installed may be very difficult. Most electricians are not monkeys, so you'll pay if your attic space is a tough nut to crack.

A solar attic vent fan, on the other hand, can be installed anywhere and requires no county permits or electrician labor. The fan will run whenever the sun shines on the PV modules; this makes perfect sense because you want the most air pumping when the sun is the brightest.

To determine where to put an attic vent fan if you decide you need one, follow these steps:

1. **Figure out your attic's natural ventilation scheme.**

    Go up into your attic. Make a rough drawing of the attic's layout, including all vents and openings designed for ventilation vents.

2. **Pick the best location for the fan.**

    In keeping with the rule to always enhance the natural ventilation scheme, the most logical spot to put a vent fan is in the roof, with a cowling around the fan. Also, always try to locate a fan downwind in order to equalize ventilation throughout the attic.

3. **Select the type of fan and size for your application.**

Attic vent fans come in two forms, one-piece units and distributed units, as described in the following sections.

One-piece unit

A one-piece unit (see Figure 13-7) costs around $270. Installation is very simple; you don't even need to go into the attic space. Simply cut a round hole in your roof, pull the shingles back, slide the unit up under the shingles and drop it into the hole. Seal for weatherproofing and you're done.

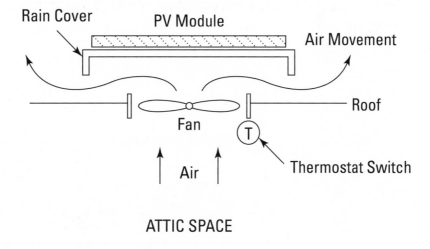

Figure 13-7: *One-piece attic vent fan units are very easy to install.*

The unit will only come on when the set temperature is reached. However, in the winter, air will escape through the unit and cool the attic space. It's best to cover the unit with a plastic tarp or something similar over the course of the winter.

A potential problem: The solar modules are fixed in place on the unit, and it may be that the best location for your vent fan is not the best location for collecting sunlight (if your solar modules aren't getting good sun, the fan won't pump good air quantities). In this case, you need to go with a distributed system.

A distributed unit

Buying separate components for a distributed unit, as shown in Figure 13-8, costs much less than a one-piece unit — you can buy a separate 12VDC fan powerful enough to do the job for around $100, and a PV module to run it for another $130 — but the installation is more expensive and difficult. You will need a hood of some kind over the fan to prevent rain from getting into the attic or soaking the fan itself. You could potentially install the fan on a horizontal surface, behind a grate, and avoid a lot of installation problems, like cutting through a roof (which always entails the risk of leaks).

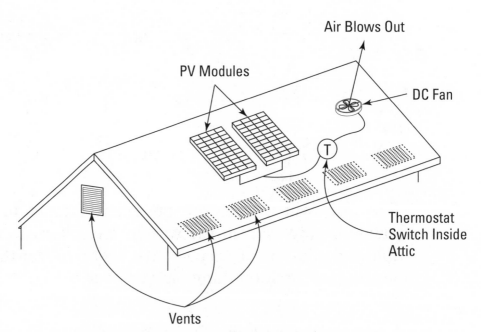

Figure 13-8:
A solar attic vent fan.

You can get better performance by tilting the modules to the west, because you want the most air movement in the afternoon. Tilt the modules to peak at around 2 p.m.

Strategizing Your Ventilation Plan

When opening windows, directing and installing fans, and installing or opening and closing vents, always work with the natural ventilation scheme, never against it. For instance, if you install a whole-house fan in the attic (refer to Figure 13-4), you need to direct the air up into the attic, never back into the house.

Making the plan

To determine the best way to direct air through your house, follow these steps:

1. **Draw a rough floor plan of your house.**

    Be sure to include all the windows, doors, sunlights, vents, fans, and so forth. Draw your attic, with all the vents and openings.

2. **Figure out what the natural ventilation scheme is for both inside the house and the attic.**

    Use what you know about prevailing winds in your area and the chimney effect. See the earlier section "Taking Advantage of Natural Air Movement" for details.

3. **On paper, note different combinations of doors, windows, and vents.** Determine how best to complement the natural ventilation to achieve comfort without the use of active devices.

As you devise your plan, keep these tips in mind (see the earlier section "Getting Mother Nature on your side" for more advice on how to enhance airflow):

- Use smaller openings for the inlets and larger

openings for the outlets; this increases the speed of the breezes.

- Make the air move over as long a path as possible. Windows a few feet apart don't do much, nor does opening all the windows at the same time.

- Air from cooler outside areas is best, but may not be practical due to prevailing winds. Try to get air intake on the north side of your home. If possible, get air intake from a shaded area — under a tree, for instance.

- Not all windows should be opened or closed concurrently; determining the best strategy ultimately boils down to trial and error.

- Determine a daily routine. What works best in the morning is rarely what works best in the afternoon or at night.

4. **Add fans to your plan to forcibly move air.**

   Imagine where one single fan would work the best, in conjunction with windows and doors. How big does that one fan need to be? One small fan in the right location can easily produce more comfort than a huge fan in the wrong spot.

5. **Put your plan into action.**

Accommodating seasonal variations

What works in the summer for cooling is almost always diametrically opposed to what works in the winter for warming. In the summer you want your attic vented as much as possible. But in the winter, you want your attic to retain as much heat as possible. Some means of opening or closing vents is needed to optimize for both seasons.

For instance, you may have a roof vent for purging hot air in the summer. But in the winter, you'll want to cover this vent up. Using a heavy plastic garbage bag with duct tape works well, but the neighbors may start a petition, so use your common sense.

 Look into installing a thermofor. A *thermofor* is a compact, mechanical, heat-activated device that opens windows, skylights, greenhouse vents, and so on at a certain temperature, adjustable by the user. No electricity or power is required, so it can be mounted anywhere. Multiple units can be configured to open heavy windows and vents. These are very handy for attic vents and windows where one single opening makes a big difference in the entire house. And you don't have to make special arrangements for winter versus summer because it's all automatic.

Venting in summer

In the summer, without the AC on, windows and vents can be opened and closed at will. You want maximum, cool breeze through the house, hopefully from a window that's under a big tree so that the air is cooler. You also want to maximize the breeze in your attic, which is usually accomplished by locating a vent at the highest point in the attic (to capitalize on the chimney effect).

In the summer, when the AC is on, you must close all windows. The best bet is to close all window coverings as well, to increase insulation and prevent solar heat from entering the house. But you also want to consider how heat will move in your house when the air conditioner is on. If you can arrange a fan to blow air over your body while the AC is on, you can turn the temperature of the AC down and get

Evaporative coolers

In the western United States where humidity levels are low, evaporative coolers offer very economical performance. They use around one-fourth the energy of a conventional air-conditioning unit, and don't require toxic chlorofluorocarbons (CFCs) or other refrigerants. They cool air by drawing warm outside air over a wet filter pad (they need a source of water). The water evaporates from the pad to reduce the air's temperature. A fan circulates the moist, cool air into the room and pushes warm air out through open windows. Portable room-sized units start at $100.

Perhaps the best bet is to buy a PV-powered unit that operates only when the sun is hottest in the sky. These don't cost a dime of utility power (nor emit an ounce of pollution), and they're easy to connect because you don't need to tap into your home's electrical system. They work hardest when you need them to work hardest (there's a certain poetic justice in this).

the same comfort effect, so small fans are always a good idea in an air-conditioned house.

Holding heat in during winter

In the winter, close all windows. Prevailing wind is not a factor inside the home, although it still is in the attic. You want to direct the heat to where you live in the house the most, probably the kitchen and family room. You also want to close off the attic space in order to retain heat up there.

Improving the Quality of Your Home's Air

Getting the air going in the right direction isn't the only

goal. You also want to make sure that the air your family breathes is clean and healthy. For the most part, Mother Nature will take care of the details for you. But in some rare cases, you may need to filter your air. You need to understand exactly what you're trying to accomplish in order to filter your air efficiently.

See Chapter 6 on indoor pollution sources. Many of these relate to air quality. If your family is having health issues, you may find the culprit and a solution there.

Air filters

The notion that the way to clean indoor air is to close windows and use an air filter is wholly mistaken. Once again, Mother Nature is far wiser than man and his meager inventions. The best way to condition your home's air is to keep a fresh supply of outside air moving through. But if you can't open your windows, or if it's simply too cold or too hot for good ventilation, an air filter is the only solution.

Active air filters work on much the same principle as water filters: they filter the air as it comes into your home. They are also very specific to the type of substances that you need to filter. For instance, if you need to eliminate pollens, you use a filter specifically designed to filter pollen. If you need to eliminate cigarette smoke, there are filters made for this specific purpose.

Filtering through the options

There are three types of active filters in use:

- **Mechanical filtration** methods use filters and move air by means of fans. Very simple. Filters can be made of anything from paper to tightly-packed fibers. You can put different types of filters on your

HVAC input port.

✔ **Electrostatic precipitation transfer filters** (whew) impart an electrical charge to particles in the air. The air then passes over an electrically-charged plate that works somewhat like a magnet to pull pollution from the air. Hmm. Sounds good, but unfortunately it doesn't work as well as it sounds. At the risk of sounding politically incorrect, the problem here is discrimination. Some particles simply don't want to be charged up.

✔ **Negative ion generators** form a high voltage field across air, thereby ionizing it (I could write an entire book on this, but let's just leave it at that). Charged particles then attract airborne particulates. In theory this sounds viable because of all the big words, but in practice, these generators don't work very well, so don't waste your money unless you like science fiction movies an awful lot. *Negative Ion Generators Run Amok!*

Consumer Reports (a very reliable information source in print and online at www.consumerreports.org) recommends mechanical filtration with HEPA (high efficiency particle arresting) filters. No, these don't pull particles over, read them their rights, and then haul them off to jail. They punch them in the gut and leave them to rot.

 Pollen, which causes hay fever, is the most common airborne irritant. Unfortunately, active air filters do very little to prevent pollen in a home (notwithstanding the elaborate claims you hear on infomercials). So don't waste your money on filters for pollen. Take hay fever medicine instead.

A word about size

In general, the larger devices are more effective because they move more air and have larger filter surfaces. If air doesn't enter the filter, it isn't filtered.

Puny little things like ionizers and plug-in style electric devices should be left on the store shelves where they will do just as much good, without consuming energy in the process. And those little devices sold in grocery stores called air fresheners? They do just the opposite; they load your air with synthesized chemicals that make your air smell a certain way.

Getting the most from your air filter

If you find yourself in the market for an air filter, keep these tips in mind:

- Get a filter that's quiet. No matter how good it may be, if it sounds like a garbage truck coming up the street, it won't get turned on.

- You absolutely have to change filters, and they generally aren't cheap. Old filters may even make your air worse because they can serve as breeding grounds for all kinds of insidious microbes. Imagine what an air filter is holding after it has been on for awhile — it catches everything in a room's air. Not only does it capture microbes, but it also captures microbe food.

- Air filters are often hard to find. Look for them at a surgical supply house or medical supply store.

- If your doctor prescribes a filter for you, you may be able to get your insurance company to pony up. Good luck with that.

Natural ways to improve air quality

You can do a number of things to keep the air in your home clean. Most of them don't require much, if any, effort at all.

Grow houseplants

Houseplants are by far and away the best way to filter indoor air. Spider plants, for example, love to gobble up carbon monoxide and dioxide, and they're easy to grow. In fact, they're so prolific you'll have a thousand little baby spider plants in no time, whether you like it or not. And elephant ears and heartleaf philodendrons absorb formaldehyde, benzene, and carbon monoxide. Not only can some types of plants reduce certain forms of airborne contaminants, but they can also convert carbon dioxide back into oxygen.

Be aware, however, that poorly maintained plants can provide excellent breeding grounds for bugs and nasty little critters so small you can't even see them. If you want plants, be prepared to take care of them.

Change vacuum cleaner bags

Change your vacuum bags often; old ones leak, making a real mess of your air. You may be sucking up crap from the floor, but a leaky or full bag just redistributes it around your home. The best vacuum is a whole-house unit where the filter is located in your garage. Keep in mind, though, that these things are energy pigs, so you need to decide which goal — energy efficiency or clean air — is more important to you.

Chapter 14

Reusing and Recycling: Play It Again, Sam

• •

In This Chapter
▶ Using less of everything
▶ Reusing materials and containers
▶ Recycling when all else fails

• •

Reusing and recycling may not be strictly cost effective because both require extra labor and time on your part, and you don't often get anything in return aside from the knowledge that you've helped the environment. Nevertheless, recycling makes sense for our society as a whole, and that should be enough motivation.

For the most part, your recycling regimen will be dictated by what's available in your community. Some cities have no recycling at all. Some have extensive programs that include free containers (often these are different colors for different materials, like cans, bottles, newspapers, and so on). You'll need to do some research to find out what kind of recycling your utility system offers.

But regardless of your community's standards, you can make an impact on your own, and that's what I get into in this chapter.

Keeping a Record of What You Throw Away

If you haven't already done it, the best way to begin your endeavor is to keep a detailed record of exactly what you throw away. You don't need to do this for more than a week or two, because it's not the details that you're interested in as much as a general idea of how much, and what, you throw away. Most people are surprised and somewhat dismayed at the results.

Get a few sheets of paper or a binder, and keep records in the following categories:

- Aluminum cans

- Glass bottles

- Plastic bottles

- Food and scraps

- Mail

- Newspapers

- Grocery bags and other store bags

- Plastic bags and wrapping materials

- Everything else, including the kitchen sink

You don't need to weigh these items, and you don't need to be precise in terms of quantities. The point is to simply pay critical attention to what you're tossing out. You want the big picture, not the details of each paint color.

After you're done, consider how much of this stuff you really needed to throw out. How much could have been reused or recycled? Even more to the point, why did you buy it in the first place? Do you like garbage?

As you put together your waste-reduction game plan, remember that the most effective solution is three-fold. You want to tackle things in this order:

- ✔ Reduce the amount of "future" trash you bring in or buy.

- ✔ Reuse as much as you possibly can.

- ✔ Recycle whatever is left over.

The following sections examine each of these strategies in more detail.

Using Less of Everything

When you're trying to cut down on waste, the first order of business is simply to use less of everything from the get-go. If you don't buy those popular kids' lunches of prepackaged crackers-bologna-cheese-and-snack, for example, you won't have all that packaging to throw away. The most important way to decrease the amount of trash you throw away is not to bring it into your home in the first place. You can decrease the amount of trash you generate by

- ✔ Being aware of the packaging of the things you buy. Less is more.

- ✔ Stopping trash — read, junk mail — from finding you.

- ✔ Opting for non-paper items when possible.

The following sections offer some practical tips on how to use less of everything around your home.

 When you recycle and reuse, you've already conceded. After all, you have trash you have to get rid of. When you don't use at all, you've won the game.

Avoiding over-packaged products

We live in a world where packaging is, unfortunately, largely dictated by a need to prevent shoplifting. How exasperating when it takes five minutes to remove a simple little gadget from layers and layers of protective wear. You can insist on buying products that are minimally packaged. If enough people did that, market forces would work to convince manufacturers to hold things down.

You can also buy in bulk, and bring your own packaging materials with you. When you go to the grocery store, take along the bags that you took home last time. When you buy vegetables, get them from roadside stands and use your own bags, or don't use any bag at all.

Eliminating junk mail

If you're like most people, nearly every day you receive junk mail: solicitations and flyers for products and services you have no interest in. You toss them into the trash immediately after opening them, if you open them at all. If you want to minimize the junk mail you get, you can stop it by writing a letter to the following address, stating that you don't want to receive any junk mail:

Mail Preference Service
Direct Marketing Association
P.O. Box 643

Carmel, NY 10512
212-768-7277

Or, for a few bucks, you can take care of the matter online at www.the-dma.org.

This service is similar to the "Don't call" registry that prevents phone solicitors from bothering you at home, only it affects junk mailers. After you contact the registry, your mailbox will be much lonelier, and you'll be tossing out a lot less junk.

Here are other ways to reduce the amount of junk mail you receive:

✔ **Don't list your address in the telephone book.** A lot of junk mailers get their data from this source.

✔ **Don't deal with book, DVD, CD, or similar**

Bugzooka

To set the tone for this section and demonstrate how to think outside of the box, here's a curveball for you. The Bugzooka is a humane way to get rid of pesky bugs in your home. It looks and sounds like a kid's toy, but it's very efficient, and fun to boot. You push a big plunger into a plastic tube and a spring is activated. You aim the end of the plastic tube near an insect, and when you pull the trigger, the offending pest is gently sucked (well, okay — I wouldn't want to be sucked into a plastic chamber like this, but I'm not a bug) into an enclosed chamber. You can study his feelers and thousand little eyes once he's in there, although you probably won't want to. Then you free the lucky little bugger outside where he can mingle and breed with like kind. Let this be a metaphor. (Get a Bugzooka from www.realgoods.com.)

clubs. They send way too much junk mail. If you find a particular mailer loading you down, write to them and tell them to stop.

Trimming the paper mountain

Junk mail, discussed in the preceding section, is only a part (albeit a large one) of the paper problem most people have. Newspapers, bills, grocery bags — you can reduce the amount of trash by cutting down on these things, too.

- ✔ **Read the newspaper online.** All you have to do is look at how much newspaper you discard each week to see how much paper waste you can eliminate simply by adapting this habit.

  If you need a paper version of your newspaper (I admit it: I don't want to read my newspaper online; I want to spread it out over the kitchen table in the morning and sip a cup of coffee while I wince at all the bad news), then share it with a like-minded neighbor or two. Whoever gets it last tosses it into the recycle bin.

- ✔ **Pay your bills online.** If your bills still come in the regular mail, pay online to save envelopes and stamps. Even better, request that your bills be sent to you online. Many companies offer this service, and it eliminates the paper waste entirely.

- ✔ **Use only one credit card instead of many.** You'll save paper (think of all the bills and offers you can avoid), and you'll also keep yourself out of trouble.

- ✔ **Use fabric grocery bags and bring them with you to the store.** No more tossed out grocery bags. Look for them at www.realgoods.com, or many grocery stores now sell them at the checkout lanes.

 If you do need to use the bags from the grocery store, ask for paper, because plastic bags take a hundred years to degrade in a landfill. Some communities are banning plastic bags outright for this reason.

✔ **Use a digital camera, store your photos on disk, and view them online.** Save the prints for those that you want to display or put in a scrapbook. (The photo process uses a lot of chemicals, not to mention paper.)

✔ **Don't use disposable diapers.** The number of diapers in landfills is truly amazing. Buy cloth. You can clean and reuse them yourself (parents have been doing it for thousands of years), or you can hire a service that will come to your home to pick up "used" diapers and drop off fresh ones. Either option is cheaper than buying disposables; both are also a lot better for the environment. (And, yes, it's also a lot ickier, but take my word for it: Things are going to get a lot worse when the kids hit 13.)

✔ **Use cloth towels instead of paper ones and durable plastic containers instead of plastic wrap, aluminum foil, or other disposable sealants.** A lot of trash comes from meal prep and storage.

Reusing Saves More Energy than Recycling

Okay, you can't always avoid using something in the first place, so the next best thing is to reuse whatever you can.

If *you* can't reuse it, making it available to others is just as good. The following sections list some helpful guidelines on how to extend the usefulness of items.

Making use of old stuff

Who says something has to be new to be good or useful? A lot of items can be reused, either for the same purpose for which they were originally intended or a slightly (or drastically) different purpose. Here are some examples:

- **Glass jars:** The glass jars you get food in can be reused to store other foods in place of plastic containers. You don't throw the jars away, and you don't have to buy containers at all; it's a twofer deal. Make sure to save the lids.

- **Packing pellets:** You know those really irritating little peanut-shaped packing pellets that you get whenever the UPS truck comes by? Store them somewhere, and then when you send a package, reuse them. They don't weigh much, but they last a million years in a landfill. Whoever invented these things should have to eat some for lunch.

- **Paint:** Nobody ever uses all the paint for a project. When you have four or five odd gallon containers that are half full, mix them together and use the result to paint closets, garages, basements, barns, kids' rooms, and so forth. Paint is a real landfill nightmare, so why not use it up this way instead? Think of it as an adventure.

- **Old towels:** Cut old bath towels into smaller towels for use with messes in the kitchen and elsewhere. These are good for lots of cleaning tasks and dirty jobs: polishing shoes, drying off pets, washing cars, and so on. You can do the same with old T-shirts and old cloth diapers, too.

- ✔ **Table scraps:** By composting the food you didn't eat, you eliminate the need for fertilizers and expensive soil treatments, and you save a lot of unnecessary landfill. You can buy composters which work very well and make the job clean. Or you can compost in a hole in your backyard, which is the best way to go for sheer quality. Dig a hole, and toss your food scraps into the hole (avoid fats, but most everything else is fine). Get some slack lime and toss in a cup once in awhile. Stir occasionally. Within a couple months, you'll have good, loamy potting soil for your landscaping needs.

Finally, one incredibly cost-effective way to reuse most anything is to "borrow" it from your neighbors. This is best done at night, and you should probably wear a mask or something in case they wake up and catch you in the act. Run away, but don't let them see you going back into your own home.

Buying used

You can find a lot of good deals — and a few steals — by shopping for used goods. Consider these things:

- ✔ **Clothing:** Buy your clothes used. You can find a lot of new clothes in used clothing stores. Many people buy clothes that they fully intend to wear, but never do. Eventually these clothes find their way to a charity because the owners simply can't throw away new clothing. And even if the clothes have been worn a few times, so what? In the same vein, donate your obsolete clothes to charities or sell them

365

Composting toilets — for the die-hard composter

Composting toilets don't flush. They use a process called "rapid aerobic decomposition." They feature a "holding" tank where the wastes go to decompose. Around 95 percent of the "material" that goes into a compost toilet ends up venting out as water vapor or gases. That's good to know, isn't it? But relax; these toilets don't smell, or they shouldn't if they're working right.

After the process is complete, you're left with a dry, fluffy, odorless material in the "finishing drawer." You can put this stuff on your fruit trees or ornamental plants (to be perfectly honest, if I found out somebody was using this on their fruit trees, I would politely refuse a dinner invitation, but that's just me).

If you're in an apartment, forget it. If you're squeamish, forget it. In fact, you must be a dedicated advocate of the green philosophy or you can just forget it. For some reason, once I have produced "waste products," I wish for them to exit the premises as quickly as possible. I'm sure I'm not alone in this irrational phobia.

to resale stores so that somebody else can benefit.

✔ **Building materials:** You can reuse a lot of old building materials. Look at places like demolition sites and old dumps. Ask a remodeler for bathtubs, sinks, and such. Some contractors are delighted to have you come and haul this stuff away for them. I once found a guy who was about to pay $500 dollars to have a big, demolished redwood porch hauled away. I took $200, and for the next couple years, I had more wood to build outbuildings than I knew what to do with. I saved thousands of dollars, not to mention some nice, healthy trees.

- ✔ **Sports equipment:** Play It Again Sports has over 300 stores across the country. They've been very successful selling used sports equipment for a lot less than the new stuff, and most people don't even notice the difference. Face it; that new set of golf clubs you paid $1,000 for turned into a used set after your first round of golf. And it didn't even improve your game like you told your wife it would when you were trying to justify the big bucks.

 Great places to find used but useable items are garage sales and swap meets (otherwise known as flea markets, where hundreds of vendors gather to sell used stuff). Many times you can find new stuff that sat on somebody's shelf for years before they decided to sell it for $5. You can find good household appliances, tools that are usually in great shape, clothing, kids' toys, books, and more.

Avoiding disposable products

Many things are manufactured to be disposable: razors, batteries, cleaning brushes, dinnerware, and more. A great way to eliminate all the waste produced by using something only once or a few times before tossing it in the trash is to use things that are meant to be reusable. Many items fall into this category (regular dinnerware, for example, instead of paper plates, and cloth dishrags rather than paper towels), but a few things deserve special mention:

- ✔ **Rechargeable batteries:** They may cost more initially, but they save you (and the environment) in the long run. Here are the economics: Alkaline batteries cost around $1.00 apiece (for good ones) and they produce around 2,000 mAh (milliamp hours) apiece. Then you toss them out. Rechargeable batteries cost around $12 apiece, and a good charger costs around $35, but you can charge a battery 2,000 times. The conclusion: non-rechargeables cost around 22 times as much. And this doesn't even take into account the environmental impact of discarded batteries. The best bet of all is to get a solar recharger, in which case you're getting all your battery power from the sun.

- ✔ **Reusable coffee filters:** You can get reusable coffee filters that are easy to use. (An added bonus? Coffee grinds are perfect for composting.)

- ✔ **Reusable furnace filters:** You simply wash them out when they get filled with dust. They cost more upfront, but they're a lot cheaper in the long run.

- ✔ **Christmas trees:** Here's one of my favorites. Don't kill a tree this holiday season. If you buy a live tree, plant it when the season ends — in your yard, or maybe even in a public park so everybody can benefit. Or buy an artificial tree — no sap, no danger of burning the house down, and no cost (after the first year). They're better than you may think.

Donating to others

If you no longer need something and can't think of a creative way to reuse it, pass it along to someone who can.

Donate old furniture to charities. Most will come to your home and pick it up. You can probably save some tax dollars if you write this stuff off, but get a receipt and don't push it too far, or you'll get audited and indicted (in America, these are often one and the same in the finest tradition of capitalism). Your best bet is to take some digital photos of your donations and store them on your computer, just in case the IRS questions your magnificent sense of benevolence.

Lions Club International collects old prescription glasses and distributes them in third-world countries. Imagine if you didn't have your glasses at all; now imagine how somebody in a third-world country will feel if they're given a pair. Let there be light!

Fixing rather than throwing away

When something goes on the blink, don't toss it and buy new. Instead, fix it whenever possible to cut down on your consumption and reduce waste. Check out *How To Fix Everything For Dummies* by Gary and Pam Hedstrom and Judy Ondrla Tremore (Wiley). If you can't fix it yourself, take it to a repair shop or hire a professional. Better yet, keep your equipment in good shape and you won't have to fix it as often.

Household surfaces that have seen better days can be given a new life, too. You can resurface bathtubs, old stoves, and countertops so that they look brand new.

Recycling the Right Way Saves Everybody Energy

In 2005, over 80 million tons of paper were recycled, but that's only a small fraction of all the paper that gets used. Americans also go through 4 million single-use plastic bottles every hour, yet only one in four gets recycled. So what stops folks from recycling? Mainly inconvenience. Thus, the best way to make recycling a reality is to set up a system that's convenient and easy to use.

For everyday recyclables (paper, plastics, glass, and so on), put bins in the kitchen, if you can. You're more likely to use a handy receptacle than an out-of-the-way one.

Break down boxes and crush aluminum cans so that you don't build up a pile that takes a lot of room. You can get a can crusher that makes the job a lot easier than squashing them under your boots (or on your forehead), although the latter may be more fun.

Aside from the more obvious candidates for recycling, here are some important items to recycle:

- **Laser toner cartridges:** These are full of resins and poisons, plus they take a lot of energy to manufacture. Insist on recharged cartridges when you buy, and hand your old ones in at the same time. Look in the yellow pages under "Computer Supplies" to find a store that sells recycled cartridges and takes in old ones.

- **Appliances:** These can almost always be recycled. Call your trash collectors and they may pick them up right at your door. Or you can donate them when the new equipment is delivered (most appliance stores have active recycling programs — they get some money for the old stuff, but more power to them).

- **Old batteries:** Even the rechargeable ones can be recycled, which makes a lot of sense. For information on recycling batteries, including those from laptops, cellphones, camcorders, and the like, visit Rechargeable Battery Recycling Corporation at www.rbrc.org. A number of large national stores serve as battery drop-off sites, including Lowe's,

Sears, Best Buy, Home Depot, Radio Shack, Office Depot, Target, and Wal-Mart.

✔ **Books:** You can recycle old books, especially the trashy novels without any redeeming literary features (these are the ones that people want, which gives you a good indication of where our society is headed). You can also recycle *For Dummies* books, but in my view, people should always buy brand-new ones. In fact, people should buy five or six, just in case they run out.

For more information on recycling options, check out The Freecycle Network at www.freecycle.org.

Part III

Putting Alternative Energy Sources to Work for You

"I don't know much about alternative energy sources, but I'll bet there's enough solar power being collected on those beach blankets to run my workshop for a month."

In this part . . .

Most people use utility-provided power for their homes. This includes electrical as well as gas (such as propane, natural gas, methane, and so on). Yet there are a lot of alternative energy sources that you can take advantage of. Do it right and you can save money and make your home more comfortable at the same time.

In this part, I show you how to choose a wood stove, help you decide what types of wood to burn, and tell you how to burn them. I tell you all about solar power, which is a very good alternative energy source that's becoming more and more common as the costs come down. Radiant heating systems, biomass heating systems, and geothermal also provide excellent opportunities that you may want to consider. They're covered here, too.

Chapter 15

Burning Desires: Wood and Gas Stoves

Your HVAC system is your home's biggest consumer of energy. Most HVAC systems don't operate very efficiently, even if their workload is minimized. HVACs are big machines, and they take a lot of power. All is not lost, however. By using a stove, you can minimize the HVAC system's "on" time and utilize energy in your home more efficiently. (Because of the energy drain of most HVAC systems, however, remember that a 50 percent efficiency improvement is about the best you can expect.)

Some stoves are better than others, of course, in terms of energy efficiency and/or pollution. In this chapter, I take you through the various stove options and present their pros and cons.

REMEMBER Most of the heat that you generate with a whole-house furnace is wasted on empty rooms and spaces. Which means that heating just the part of your home that you and your family spend the most time in is more efficient than whole-house heating. If you heat without using electric utility power for blowers and air movement, you're operating even more efficiently. Stoves provide for localized heating, and if you design your system the right way and use it properly, a good stove can heat an entire home as well.

Open Fireplaces: The Granddaddy of Them All

When many people think of heating with fireplaces, they picture a fire crackling in an open hearth. They should also be picturing a huge waste of energy and money. Open fireplaces are absolutely *the* worst choice for efficient heating. Why? Because they draw cold air into the home to feed themselves and, due to the chimney effect (refer to Chapter 8), most of the hot air they generate goes right out the chimney. Here's how, in a grim nutshell, these fireplaces work (see Figure 15-1):

1. **You start the fire.** This process usually entails kindling, matches, and some "blowing" to get things going.

2. **You open the damper.** If a cooking vent or bathroom vent is on in your home, or if the HVAC system is on, cold air may rush down the chimney, creating a backdraft and causing smoke to waft out into your living space.

3. **As the chimney effect kicks in, the smoke begins to rise up the chimney, and the fire**

grows hotter and brighter. Orange flames, the norm, mean the wood isn't burning very efficiently. In fact, flames of any kind are inefficient because the wood is not burning very thoroughly. (Efficiency is in direct contradiction to romantic ambient, when it comes to a fireplace.)

4. **Because fire needs fresh oxygen, the fire in your fireplace is now pulling up to 500 cubic feet per minute through windows and air leaks in your home.** If somebody opens a door to the outside, cold air will rush in because the pressure in your home is less than it is outside (if not, the chimney effect wouldn't be working). This air ends up going up the chimney once it's heated in the fire.

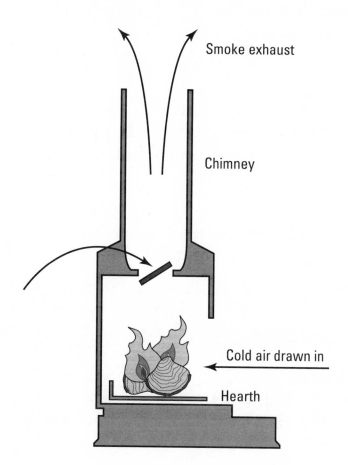

Smoke exhaust

Chimney

Cold air drawn in

Hearth

Figure 15-1:
An open
fireplace.

The end result is that your home is actually getting colder, not hotter. The only part of the home that's getting hotter is right in front of the fire, and this is exactly why people like fires so much. There's no denying the romantic element. But at what price?

If you just can't live without the romantic open flames or you're stuck with what you've got, you can achieve better efficiency with these tips:

- When lighting your fireplace, open a door or window nearby so that the rush of air a fire takes before it settles down to a more static state will only move through a small portion of your home. Once the fire settles down, close the door or window.

- Burn hot, blazing fires because the combustion is more thorough. Don't burn little fires (although at some point your fire will need to burn out, so you'll end up with a little fire anyway).

- Use andirons to lift the logs above the floor so that during the burn cycle the hot cinders fall down onto a bed of coals and burn better and more thoroughly.

- Glass doors limit the amount of air being pulled through the home, but they also limit the amount of heat radiating back into the room, so they're pretty much a wash in terms of efficiency.

- Close the damper as much as possible. When you're not burning a fire, close it completely. This is a hassle, granted, but it makes a big difference. When the damper is open, air will be drawn down the chimney whenever a vent fan or the HVAC system in your home is turned on. Not only does this result in cold air, but it could also mean a big stink and unhealthy air.

Surveying General Categories of Stoves

In this section, I move from open fireplaces to what is referred to as a "stove." These differ by being enclosed in a specially designed burn chamber so that you can achieve much more efficient combustion (by controlling the burn temperature) plus much more efficient dispersion of the heat into your living space. Stoves are made to burn a wide variety of fuels, and the type that homeowners choose depends mostly on availability and cost.

Free-standing stoves simply sit in a corner of your room, without walls or bricks surrounding them. An insert fits into an existing open fireplace slot (a very good way to go from poor efficiency to good efficiency while still using the expensive decorative elements of your existing fireplace).

Before deciding what type of stove you want to install in your home, check with your county building department for requirements, specifications, and so forth. These may make a big difference in your decision on which type is best for your particular application. Also, check with your insurance company; they probably have some dictates you need to follow as well.

Comparing open- and closed-vent systems

There are two important types of venting systems: closed vents and open vents.

With an open-vent system, shown in Figure 15-2, air is drawn from the room and used for combustion, and then the exhaust is vented up the chimney. An open-vent system (see Figure 15-3) is always less efficient than a closed-vent system, because the air used in combustion is inevitably drawn from the great outdoors through cracks and leaks in your home's envelope (thereby making the home colder). In a closed-vent system, air is drawn from the outside and vented back to the outside.

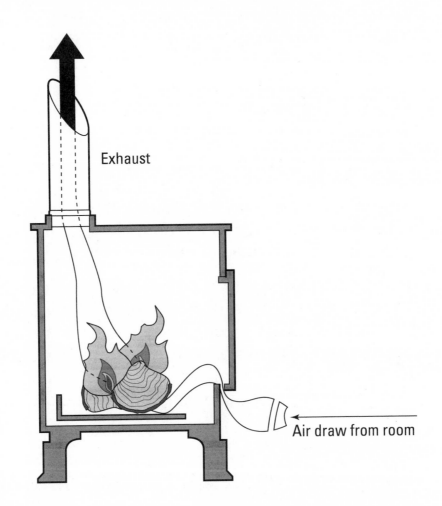

Exhaust

Air draw from room

Figure 15-2:
An open-vent stove system.

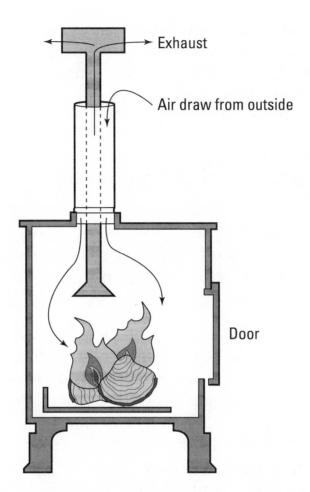

Exhaust

Air draw from outside

Door

Figure 15-3:
A closed-vent
stove system.

Closed-vent systems are safer than open ones. Naturally, you want to seal your home to a high degree in order to make your heating efforts more efficient (see Chapter 7). However, in doing so, you may cause a carbon monoxide or carbon dioxide hazard with an open-vent system. Or you may cause oxygen depletion, because the fire is competing with the human inhabitants for oxygen, and the fire is generally greedier. This problem is particularly dangerous because people don't know when they're being starved of oxygen; they just pass out.

If you have a stove that draws room air for combustion, crack open a window nearby. Instead of having cold air drawn through your entire home, the combustion air will come from that open window. Radiant heat will still work its way throughout the room in which the stove is located.

Looking at free-standing stoves and inserts

Aside from open- and closed-vent systems (see the preceding section), stove types sport another distinction: They can be either free-standing or inserts. A free-standing stove sits in the room proper, whereas an insert is made to fit into an existing fireplace slot.

Free-standing stoves are inherently more efficient than inserts because, all else being equal, more of the generated heat makes it into the living space. Depending on the space they are mounted into, some inserts are completely surrounded by brick and mortar and do a very poor job of getting heat into the living space. Most of it goes up the chimney. Still, an insert is much more efficient than an open fireplace, and if you have an open fireplace, you're not likely to be installing a free-standing stove because then you'll have a big, unused fireplace.

If you're starting from scratch, installing a free-standing stove with a vent system is a lot cheaper than building a fireplace, not to mention the efficiency advantages. On the other hand, free-standing stoves take up more of your home's square footage, are an eyesore, and are more likely to cause burns. In the summer, they're just plain superfluous sitting there looking black and bulky.

Using a Wood-Burning Stove

Wood-burning stoves are the most common stove simply because wood is available virtually everywhere. Because the supply of wood is self-replenishing, it has the further advantage of being renewable. Wood-burning certainly has the most tradition on its side, so more equipment is available, as well as a wider range of raw wood resources to choose from.

Burning wood to heat your home has several pros:

- The operating costs are fairly low if you have a ready source of firewood. In fact, the out-of-pocket expense can be zero, aside from the expense of whatever you use to chop down trees. With little more than an axe and some elbow grease, you're in business.

- A wide variety of heating appliances are available at literally any price you can pay. You can find old stoves for next to nothing, and they work well enough.

- No electricity is required. Fans are an exception, but they're always optional.

- The fuel supply is sustainable. And if burned properly, the impact on the environment is very low.

Trees convert carbon dioxide into oxygen, so a live tree actually mitigates global warming. But a dead tree left to rot on the forest floor releases as much carbon dioxide into the atmosphere as a wood stove that burns the same amount of wood. (The difference is that wood left to rot on the forest floor does so slowly, releasing its carbon over a period of years, and from day to day the outgas level doesn't change much.) The upshot is that if you burn wood from a downed tree, you're not contributing to global warming at all. Still, burning wood does cause a lot of smoke, and some communities ban wood-burning altogether, particularly when pollution levels are high.

If pollution is your concern, insist on burning either dead trees or doomed trees (those that have been removed for building developments or other similar reasons). Don't use trees that have simply been cut down for burning. If you do, insist that a new tree be planted in its place.

Of course, using a wood stove to heat your home has cons as well as pros. On the downside are the following considerations:

- Wood-burning stoves can be very dangerous if they're not installed properly.

- You need a lot of dedicated storage space to store the wood you intend to burn.

- Heavy physical labor is required in chopping, transporting, and stacking wood. And whenever you need wood indoors, you have to tote it in and place it very carefully into the burn chamber.

- Wood stoves create a dirty home environment, with dust and stink. There are a lot of ashes to clean up, and this is a dirty, stinky process that inevitably makes a mess of your home.

- Burning wood properly (to get the most efficiency) requires you to pay attention to the process and continually manipulate the wood stack as well as the damping levels.

- Wood stoves require chimney maintenance. Burning wood creates creosote gunk on your vent or chimney liner, and this can catch on fire if you're not diligent.

Softwoods are much worse in this regard than hardwoods.

✔ The potential for pollution is high if you don't use your wood stove properly (you don't maintain the proper burning temperatures, for example, or you don't keep the stove cleaned out).

✔ Use of a wood stove may increase your fire insurance premiums. You must tell your homeowner's insurance agent that you have a stove (they'll probably ask). In many cases, they'll come to your home to inspect the installation. If things aren't as they should be, your insurance company may refuse you or give you a set amount of time to get it up to code.

 Wood-burning stoves are banned in some areas. In other areas, burning is banned on particularly dirty air days. In these areas, utilities generally offer rebates and subsidies to convert to cleaner systems. Check with your local air resources board.

Types of wood stoves

In producing new clean-burning stoves, manufacturers have taken one of two routes: one that uses a catalytic combustor and one that causes more complete combustion.

Older wood stoves had efficiency ratings of 40 to 50 percent, but today's certified stoves boast efficiencies of 70 to 80 percent. As the efficiency goes up, the pollution a stove creates generally goes down (for one thing, when efficiency is high you burn less fuel; for another, when you burn fuel much more completely, there are fewer pollution byproducts). If you've got a leaky, old stove, it's always a good investment to upgrade.

Check the efficiency ratings of the stoves you're considering, because they may vary quite a bit.

Some wood stoves incorporate a *catalytic converter* (see Figure 15-4), which burns off smoke and fumes that would otherwise exhaust or drift up a chimney. The catalytic converter consists of a honeycomb-shaped substrate coated with a catalyst, usually a precious metal such as platinum or palladium. When the smoke passes through the honeycomb, the catalyst lowers the smoke's burning temperature, causing it to ignite. The result is a more efficient burn, less smoke up the chimney, and less pollution. Most stove manufacturers now offer catalytic models in which the combustor is an integral part of the stove. It is also possible to retrofit some older stoves with converters.

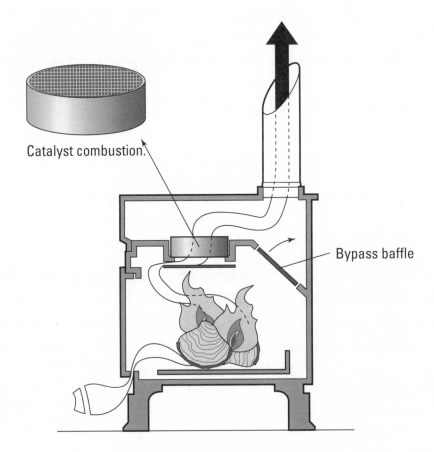

Catalyst combustion.

Bypass baffle

Figure 15-4:
The catalytic stove combustion process.

Starting a fire in a catalytic stove is more involved than doing so with a conventional stove. You have to open a bypass damper when you either start or reload a fire. The damper directs the combustion gases directly up the flue (bypassing the catalytic element) until the temperature is high enough (350°F to 600°F) to get the combustor kicked into gear. This process is referred to as *lighting off*. A catalyst temperature monitor is normally included to let you know when to move the damper.

Catalytic stoves require a lot more maintenance than their conventional counterparts. The catalytic converter needs to be changed periodically. Otherwise, you could actually end up with a very inefficient fire. These types of stoves are more expensive, and probably not worth the cost unless you put a very high premium on pollution.

Burning the right wood

The efficient use of a woodstove is almost always predicated on your source of wood. If you have your own trees that you can cut down and process, great. Or maybe you live in a wooded area and a ready supply of cut firewood is available from local vendors. Very rarely is transporting wood a long distance cost effective, which means you're limited to the types of wood that are indigenous to the area you live in.

Some types of woods are better than others for burning. Two factors determine the suitability of a given wood: whether it burns well and generates heat, and what kind of mess it makes in the process.

Hardwoods are almost always better than softwoods for burning because you get a lot more Btu per unit weight and volume, which means a lot less work on your part per Btu

387

generated. Hardwoods also deposit less creosote in your chimney and vent system, making them safer and cleaner for the environment. Some people are suckers for the fact that softwoods are so much cheaper than hardwoods, but in fact, hardwoods are much more cost effective. Check out www.hearth.com/fuelcalc/woodvalues.html for a calculator on different types of firewood and the Btu you can expect from them.

Any wood you burn must be properly *seasoned,* or dried out (wet wood smokes a lot, won't burn at a hot temperature, hisses and pops and may be dangerous, and puts a lot of crud into your vent system). To season wood, split logs as soon as possible into the size that will fit into your stove and stack them in a dry spot for 6 to 18 months. Pile the wood so that air can circulate. Hardwoods take longer to dry than softwoods do. Humidity and temperature also affect drying times.

Although burning hardwood is better than burning softwood, the latter isn't out of the question. Some things, on the other hand, should *never* be burned in a wood stove:

✔ **Green wood:** Green wood is freshly cut from a live tree. It will smoke like crazy and stink and probably won't burn very thoroughly. Plus, a lot of water will steam out of it, resulting in sparks when you open the door to the burn chamber. How can you tell whether wood is green? See whether it's brittle — if so, it's not green.

Although you shouldn't burn green wood, you can buy green wood in late spring, when prices are very low because demand is down. It will dry over the hot summer months and you'll save money. In fact, if you can, buy a whole gob of green firewood at the same time and you'll get a great discount.

✔ **Garbage, plastic, foil, or any kind of chemically treated or painted wood:** They all produce noxious fumes, which are dangerous and polluting. If you have a catalytic stove, the residue from burning plastics may clog the catalytic combustor.

✔ **Trash (paper or plastic):** Paper wastes tend to make a very hot fire for a short period of time, encouraging the ignition of any creosote deposits in your stovepipe. And synthetic wastes, such as plastic wrappers, produce acids when they burn. Acids make for a very short stove lifetime.

✔ **Manufactured logs (like Duraflame):** This is extremely dangerous. They burn too hot and can cause a fire when you open the door. I am an expert on this warning; one of the most startling things I've ever experienced in my life occurred when I opened a woodstove door while a manufactured log was burning, and the flames literally shot out into the room. I feel lucky to have only paid for this stupidity with my eyebrows.

Burning the wood right

The actual burning process inside your stove represents the biggest factor in safety, efficiency, and convenience.

✔ In the firebox, avoid placing pieces of wood in parallel directions, where they may stack too closely. Always try to get some air movement between pieces of wood.

Adjust the burning embers periodically with a poker to keep your fire burning properly. Unfortunately, there are no rigid guidelines; learning to use your stove optimally takes practice. Just play around with it.

✔ If you're looking for the most heat fast, vary the position of the wood to maximize the exposed surface area of each piece of wood. If you're after a long-term burn (overnight, unattended) minimize the space between the pieces.

✔ Only use wood properly sized for your stove's fire chamber. Smaller pieces burn faster and hotter.

✔ Always keep the door closed when attending to the fire — when the door is open, too much oxygen enters the burn chamber.

 A good technique for producing a relatively clean, long burn (overnight) is to load your stove with a mixture of partially seasoned and well-dried wood about half an hour before bedtime. Leave the damper open to give the fire a good start; then damp the strongly burning blaze down for the night.

Buying wood

If you don't have your own supply of wood, either from your own trees or a friend or relative who's happy to let you have firewood in exchange for clearing the dead trees from their land, you'll need to buy your firewood. Fortunately, you can find it just about anywhere. Unfortunately, you have to watch out for a few things:

✔ Firewood is usually sold in cords. A cord is a nice, even stack 8' high x 4' wide x 4' deep, or a volume of 128 cubic feet. Only thing is, it's never stacked nice and neat so you can rarely tell just how much firewood you're actually getting. You often see filled pickup trucks sitting in grocery store parking lots with a

---

sign advertising the cord price. You agree to buy, they follow you home and dump the wood in your yard, and you stack it and find it's not really a cord at all. So now what? You want to pick a fight with Paul Bunyan? The best bet is to buy from a reputable supplier; get a reference, if possible.

- The length of the wood is important. Many people make the mistake of measuring the opening of their wood stove's door and then ordering the wood cut slightly smaller. This doesn't work because the workers cutting the wood don't measure it (they aren't making a whole lot of money off this deal, and it's hard work, so cut them some slack). You'll get pieces that are too big, and then what are you going to do with those? So allow a margin of about 20 percent when you order the wood.

- Don't buy firewood that's been sitting on the bottom of a huge pile for a couple months or more (especially in bad weather). It'll be covered in mud because the rain washes all the dirt and dust off the wood piled above it. Your burn chamber will then fill with dirt and mud, in addition to the usual ashes. This is heavy, stinky, and inefficient.

Here's a little tip: A good way to save money in what you spend on firewood is to split the logs yourself. Then you can buy about any size logs you want (and save a lot of money to boot). You can get special splitting tools (most tool rental places have them available), or you can work your butt off with an old-fashioned axe.

Maintaining your wood stove

Maintaining a wood stove means having the chimney swept. This entails going up onto the roof (or wherever the vent terminates at the top) and forcing special brushes down that clean away the built up creosote and tar.

A stove that is not damped excessively (and that has a well-designed chimney of factory-built, insulated pipe) may not need a sweep for an entire season. On the other hand, even a comparatively well-installed system could need cleaning as often as every two weeks. Your stove's instruction manual will provide explicit instructions on how to tell when cleaning is needed and the best way to go about it. After installing a new stove, be sure to check the stovepipe for creosoting every two weeks until you become accustomed to the heater's behavior. (Any deposits over 1/4-inch thick indicate that the pipe needs attention.)

You can monitor the accumulation of creosote and other deposits in your stovepipe by tapping on the sections with a metal object. Once you're used to the ringing sound that a clean pipe makes, the dull thud of a dirty one will be distinctive.

It's a good idea to have your stove system inspected by a pro at the beginning of each burn season.

To monitor the operation of your wood stove, check the exhaust coming out of the chimney. You should see the transparent white steam of evaporating water only — darker, opaque smoke will be just slightly visible. The darker the color of the exhaust, the less efficiently your stove is operating.

Heating with a Gas Stove

Many homes have propane or natural gas supplies for cooking and heating both ambient air and domestic water. This is a safe and consistent form of energy, and it's cheaper than electricity, though not nearly as cheap as wood-burning. You can use propane or natural gas to power a stove, and the results can be very rewarding.

For the most part, the safety, installation, and chimney/vent maintenance details are the same as with wood stoves. You don't need to worry about creosote buildup nearly as much, because gas burns more efficiently and consistently than wood. When your gas stove is installed, it will be fine-tuned to burn according to the manufacturer's specifications.

Here are the pros of using natural gas stoves. Many people are switching from wood to gas for all these reasons:

- All you do is flip a switch and you're generating heat. No logs to tote, no fires to start.

- You can maintain temperature with a thermostat-controlled switching system, so you can achieve much better consistency than you can with a wood stove. In addition, gas stoves usually come with very effective blower systems for distributing hot air.

- The gas company (or utility) delivers the gas to your home. In most cases, you contract with a supply company and they come to your home periodically and fill up your tank. You don't worry about a thing (except paying the bill).

- Cleanup is much easier: You don't have any ashes to sweep up and hardly any creosote builds up in the vent system.

- The pollution numbers are very good compared to wood stoves. In regions where wood stoves are banned, gas stoves are almost always acceptable.

- You can get either open flame style units, which look quite a bit like a real fire with the new aesthetic improvements in logs and ashes, or you can get completely enclosed units that offer better efficiencies and more utility.

- ✔ Most units can be used without electricity, which means that, if you lose power, your stove is still good to go.

Of course, as with anything, using a gas stove also has some cons:

- ✔ Some units need electricity. Blowers always do.

- ✔ Gas stoves aren't cheap compared to other alternatives in terms of both fuel expense and installation costs (in fact, they're usually more costly to install), and gas may go way up in price, making this option even more expensive.

- ✔ The flame, although real, doesn't seem as real as that of a wood stove. If you feel a fire just isn't a fire without the smell, sound, and changing flames, then you'll probably be disappointed with a gas.

- ✔ Enclosed units prevent roasting marshmallows.

Looking at Electric Fireplaces

Electric fireplaces and inserts are mostly for show, and they can do a pretty good job of that, if you can buy into the concept and suspend your disbelief. They're inexpensive (no plumbing, no vents, no hassles — just plug and play), and you can get a complete unit that you simply set against a wall, plug in, and voilà. Who's to begrudge a little romance to those in apartments and condos?

Most electric fireplaces come with heaters and a fan so that you can also get them to heat a room for about the same price as an electric space heater. But keep in mind that you're using a lot of electricity to do little more than put on a show, and if your utility is providing you with coal-fired electricity, you're also creating pollution.

Although many people truly like their units, you may get tired of yours long before its lifetime has expired. So before you talk yourself into an electric fireplace as a substitute for the real thing, visit somebody who already has one and check out the way it looks and works.

Electric fireplaces offer the following plusses:

✔ They have zero emissions (at least locally; the power company is still spewing forth to provide your electricity).

✔ They can be installed anywhere.

✔ New technologies make the fire look somewhat real.

✔ They're movable. You can move one from room to room, and take it with you if you move to a new home. You can even sell it in a garage sale.

On the negative side, you have the following:

✔ Fake-looking fires.

✔ No electricity, no bananas; when utility power is out, you're shivering.

✔ Fuel costs are very high — $45 per M/Btu.

Deciding Which Stove Is Right for You

As the earlier sections make clear, when you make the decision to supplement or replace your home's heating with a stove, you have these choices: a wood stove, a gas stove, or an electric fireplace. Each has its advantages and disadvantages. Before you make your decision, however, you should consider what factors determine the efficiency of any stove: things like how the stove generates heat, the amount of space it's capable of heating (and how you can extend that if necessary), and how you can use your existing chimney or vent system, if you have one, with your new stove or, if you don't have an existing chimney, what it would take to build the necessary venting apparatus.

How does the stove burn and heat?

In gas stoves, combustion can be tuned to a high degree, and the stove will always work the same way because it's a closed process that doesn't require intervention (plus the fuel is very consistent). On the opposite extreme are wood stoves, which vary in performance for a number of reasons:

- The wood composition and quality varies quite a bit. Even if you buy the same species, such as oak, and the wood is cut from trees in the same forest, the variations are tremendous.

- Wood is often piled high, and the stuff on the bottom gets muddy. This affects combustion quite a bit, not to mention the mess it makes.

- Stoves vary. The same wood burned in different stoves will combust differently.

- Over the course of the burn cycle, raw wood turns to ashes. Ashes build up and change the dynamics of the combustion process.

- Weather can affect how a stove burns by changing the way the chimney draws. If your home is oriented just right, you may experience severe back drafts on windy days.

Once the heat is generated in the stove, the next issue to contend with is how the stove gets the heat into the room. With some stoves, most of the heat is lost up the chimney. Other types of stoves are very efficient at channeling the heat into a room.

After the heat is in the room, how that heat is utilized makes a big difference in your comfort (Chapter 8 has more details on comfort). Heat rises, so in a large, open room the ceiling will be much warmer than the floor. This is a waste, unless the occupants are living near the ceiling (for instance, if you are living in an inverted gravity zone where things fall up instead of down).

How much area does the stove cover?

In deciding which type of stove is best for your needs, your first order of business is to decide how much of your home you want to heat with a stove. If all you want to heat is a single room, your options are simple because you don't need to move air in a complicated fashion and you can buy a small stove. If you're planning on heating a number of rooms or an entire home, you need to figure out how you're going to move the warm air from the stove to the adjoining rooms. When it comes to moving air, you have several options:

✔ **Ceiling fans:** These are a cost-effective way to reduce fuel bills and even out temperature variations. If your home has high ceilings or an open loft, most of the heat will rise to those areas and eventually migrate out through the roof. A well-placed fan will move this hot air back down into your living spaces (Chapter 13 offers more suggestions on how to move air through your home).

✔ **Ecofans:** Ecofans offer a very efficient and effective way to move the hot air your stove is generating. An Ecofan (check out www.realgoods.com or enter "Ecofan" in your search engine) exploits the simple laws of thermodynamics to move a fan blade without the use of electricity or external power. You set the fan on top of your stove and after it gets hot, the blade spins and moves up to 150 cubic feet/minute (cfm) of air. Ecofans cost over $100, but over the long term they're a lot cheaper than using ceiling fans, and they can make your wood stove up to 30 percent more effective (I said effective, not efficient) by distributing the hot air.

✔ **Your HVAC fan system:** Most HVAC furnaces (the kind that use forced air) have a switch setting that allows the blower to run without having the heat on (Fan Only is a common label). If you run your HVAC system in this mode, it will distribute the heat generated by your stove throughout your entire home.

Smoking out vents and chimneys

You may or may not have a fireplace in your home. If you don't, you'll have to install a chimney or vent system from scratch. If you have an existing fireplace, it may or may not be suitable for the stove option you want to install. The best bet, of course, is to alter the existing infrastructure as little as possible, but this may not be practical or safe.

A properly designed chimney (or vent system) is a prerequisite for any safe stove installation. For example, the flue must be made of a suitable heat-resistant material and it must be separated from combustibles by a specified distance (see county codes and installation specifications for a particular stove).

Rules regarding masonry chimneys used to vent a stove state that they must be lined — usually with clay flue tiles, which should be mortared at the joints with refractory cement and separated from the stone, brick, or block work. The interior surface shouldn't show signs of chipping. Likewise, the exterior masonry and joints should be sound. Unfortunately, the likelihood of an existing chimney meeting all these criteria is not very good (if you're in doubt, have an expert come in and take a look). If the chimney is deficient because it's too large, lacks a liner, or is in poor repair, you have these options:

- **Bring it up to snuff (relining and so forth).** If you choose this option, letting a pro do the job is highly recommended.

- **Abandon it.** For about the same cost as relining, you can install a factory-built, insulated metal chimney. This is a good idea because technology has improved quite a bit, and you'll be getting better performance along with better safety.

- **Install a new stovepipe in an existing chimney.** This is probably the best option of all because not only does it eliminate the problem of the deficient chimney, but it also gives you the option to look into a closed system (a stove, in other words).

  When using a fireplace chimney for stove exhaust, the entry to the fireplace must be sealed, or, if the connector joins the flue above the fireplace, the chimney must be plugged below the point of junction. This precaution not only prevents burning embers from cascading down into your fireplace (and onto your floor), but also maintains the proper draft.

Most county regulations prohibit the passage of stovepipe through any floor, ceiling, or fire wall without special feed-throughs. You may, however, pass your pipe through either a wall or a floor/ceiling if you use a factory-built insulated chimney. If you don't have a suitable masonry chimney, this expensive venting option is your only choice.

Abiding by Safety Guidelines

Stoves obviously pose a lot of dangers. With any type of stove, you can start a fire, create smoke hazards, or get burned badly. To avoid potential danger and the legal liabilities that may come with it:

- ✔ Make sure you know and follow the safety and operation guidelines outlined in your stove's instruction manual. If you don't have an instruction manual, get one online or contact the stove's manufacturer.

- ✔ Contact your county building department to find out what the applicable codes and guidelines are in your area. If you don't follow code and you cause a fire or other danger, you could have an insurance claim denied or even find yourself in legal limbo if there's collateral damage.

- ✔ Call your homeowners insurance company and ask them what type of requirements they have for stoves. Many insurance companies will insist on coming out to your home so they can inspect your stove firsthand. (So many stoves have been installed inadequately that they can't just take your word for it.) Sometimes the insurance company's standards are stricter than the county's, and you may find your insurance canceled or your rates increased if you don't mind your p's and q's.

✔ If you're buying a home with a stove, have it inspected by a pro before you take possession of the home (or before you make an offer). If it's substandard, deal with this problem upfront. Ask the sellers to make things right. They'll have a hard time refusing because they'll take on a lot of liability if they do. Have the chimney inspected as well. It may be coated with creosote, or it may not be up to standards.

✔ Don't install any type of stove yourself. A whole host of details go into the installation of a stove, and failure to pay attention to any one of them can lead to a safety problem. For that reason, I don't include installation instructions for stoves in this chapter, and I strongly recommend that you hire a pro. Although it's true that many novices install stoves themselves, the reality is that if you do have a problem, the consequences could be huge. You may pay big time, or even worse, somebody could die. Nothing is worth that risk. I'm one of the most qualified do-it-yourselfers on the planet, and when I needed a gas stove installed, I had nothing to do with it aside from watching and learning.

✔ Keep in mind that the fuel you burn in your stove is just as combustible while it's in storage as it is when it's in the combustion chamber. If you have a gas tank, it could literally blow up if abused. If you have a wood pile, it'll burn very hot and fast if you're not careful. Always consider fuel storage while you're designing your stove system.

✔ Always make sure to have adequate smoke alarm coverage in your home, and make sure to keep the batteries fresh in every smoke alarm. You should also consider installing a carbon monoxide alarm. It's always better to be safe than sorry.

Chapter 16

Shining a Light on Solar Power for Your Home

From a pollution standpoint, solar power is the most energy-efficient investment you can make, hands down. Sunshine will always be free. Solar power equipment, however, can be expensive and isn't suitable for climates that don't get enough sunshine. Government subsidies play a big role in solar power, but they vary with the political winds. The most definitive factor in determining the viability of solar power is local utility rates; if yours are high, solar energy may be just what you're looking for because the financial efficiency is good. When all the factors are working for you, an investment in solar energy can be much better than an investment in the stock market.

In this chapter, I cover the most popular solar investments, and I present some guidelines on when and where solar

403

power is a worthwhile investment. For more details, consult my book *Solar Power Your Home For Dummies* (Wiley).

Supplementing Your Domestic Hot Water Heater with Solar Energy

Around 20 percent of the typical home's energy budget goes toward heating water. With a solar water heater, you can offset around 70 percent of this cost. You can't offset the entire water heating function, because solar energy is unavailable at night and in bad weather conditions. Thus, a backup source for heat is a necessity.

Over 20 different types of water heating systems are available, but some are just too expensive (high-tech evacuated tube systems work well but cost too much, although that's bound to change because they are the best technology), and others are too cheap — they don't offer enough performance to overcome the sacrifices. The following sections outline the most common types of systems.

 Before you invest in any system, make sure you understand the factors that dictate which type of system is best for use in your home. These factors include

- ✔ **Climate, in particular, freezing weather and exceptionally hot weather.** If you live in a cold climate, you know about water freezing and bursting pipes. But did you know that too much heat can be every bit as damaging as too much cold? Boiled pipes burst just like frozen ones. If you live in a cold climate, make sure the system you get is one that minimizes the potential for freezing pipes. If you live in a very sunny climate, make sure the system you pick can deal with the heat.

- ✔ **Desired water temperature.** How hot is the water you are looking for and what time of day do you need it? Some systems take longer to heat water than others (any system without a secondary reservoir takes longer to heat). Those that include backup heating (electrical or gas powered) will always have hot water on hand, but your utility costs may be more.

- ✔ **Quantity of hot water produced.** How much hot water does your family use, and when do they use it? To calculate how much hot water you need, measure flow and multiply it by the amount of time you and your family spend in the shower. If you also use a lot of hot water for laundry and dishes, add about ten gallons per load. (See Chapter 2 for details on measuring your water flow.)

An ICS batch system

An Integral Collector System (ICS), as shown in Figure 16-1, is the simplest and cheapest, although its suitability is limited to mild climates (with very little freezing and not too much hot weather). This type of system is passive — it doesn't involve any pumps — and is normally plumbed directly between the cold water supply and the water heater, making the plumbing job easy and straightforward. An ICS batch system provides a simple and effective way to preheat water for your existing domestic water heater. Because you're putting hot water into your standard domestic hot water heater, your hot water heater doesn't have to work so hard. (If the water in the ICS system isn't heated, the domestic heater does what it would normally do.)

A 3' x 8' ICS unit holds 30 gallons of water. Collected Btu (the amount of heat that the collector actually captures and converts to heat in the water) are 22,000 for an average day in North America. (The average household uses around 10,000 to 15,000 Btu per person per day.) Larger units are also available: A 4' x 8' unit holds 50 gallons of water and can collect 30,000 Btu per day.

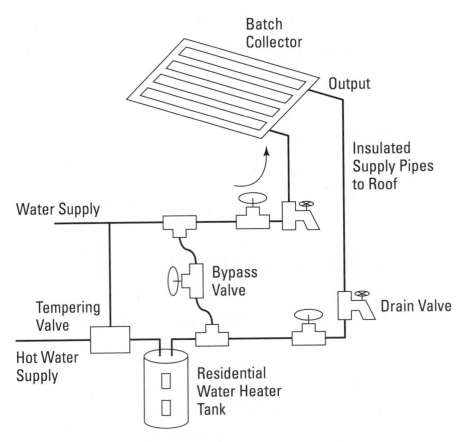

Figure 16-1: *A batch water heater supplementary system.*

For the smaller unit, expect to pay around $1,700 for the collector, plus the cost of pipes, hardware, and labor for installation — around $2,400 is typical. The larger unit costs around $1,900, plus installation. Complete kits are available that include all the valves plus the collector and its associated mounting hardware.

If you're willing to change your habits, the use of an ICS batch system can reduce the energy workload on your conventional water heater to around ten percent. For instance, if each member of the family showers at a different time of day, the batch collector can heat up again between showers. If you take your shower in the afternoon, when the midday sun has heated the water in the tank, your residential heater will have very little work to do. You can run your dishwasher in the late afternoon instead of in the morning, too.

But before you run out and buy an ICS batch system, consider these things:

- ✔ Freezing is a big problem because the collector holds the water being heated (although big batch collectors can withstand longer freezing conditions than less bulky systems). The system has manual drain valves that you can use to drain the water when freezing is a possibility for more than a day or so. You use the bypass valve to bypass the solar collector and revert to normal operation.

- ✔ Too much heat can be a problem. The collector can burst if the water gets too hot. It's best to drain the system when conditions are extremely hot and sunny.

Drain valves need to be located outside (where there is safe drainage), and they may look exactly like hose faucets. You may want to consider some kind of locking valve that requires a key to open. Whatever you do, make sure children can't open them and get scalded.

- ✔ The tempering valve, which prevents scalding water from entering your household plumbing system, is critical. It mixes cold water with the heated water from the collector when the collector water exceeds a certain temperature.

You can always find out how hot the water in the collector is by sampling from the downstream drain valve. Another good idea is to install an in-line thermometer.

✔ A full collector can weigh upwards of 500 pounds. Even empty, it weighs a lot. So give some serious consideration to how you will lift the collector up onto your roof or wherever you plan on mounting it. (Roofing companies have cranes for lifting heavy weights; you may need to hire one for an hour.) And make sure your roof can support the weight when the collector is full. You don't want to find out the hard way that it can't.

A drainback system

A drainback system is an indirect, active, closed-loop system. It's indirect in that the liquid being heated in the collector is not the water that you actually use in your home; the heat is transferred via a heat exchanger that moves the heat from the collector liquid to the household water supply. It's active in that it includes an in-line pump. Figure 16-2 illustrates this type of system.

Although much more expensive to install than ICS systems, drainback systems are an excellent choice for most climates, except those that receive a lot of snow and get very cold. They're the best choice in hot climates. The advantage is that the danger of freezing is minimal.

Drainback systems are designed so that the fluid drains by force of gravity. Sometimes pipes sag and the low points retain some water, which can burst the pipes during freezing weather. To avoid such a scenario, make sure to adhere to the installation guidelines.

In a drainback system, a controller reads the two temperature sensors and then determines when fluid should be pumped through the collector. When the pump is turned off, the fluid in the collector and feeder pipes drains back into the drainback tank (such a clever name).

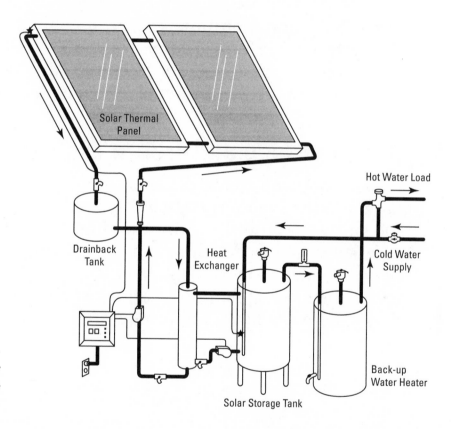

Figure 16-2:
A drainback-style solar water heater system.

Most manufacturers offer complete kits that tell you everything you need to know about these systems and that work very well — if you stick with the plan. Following are a few facts worth knowing about drainback systems:

- You can use fluids other than water in the closed-loop heat exchanger circuit, but water is best because it's cheap and doesn't degrade when it gets hot.

✔ To eliminate the risk of freezing pipes, you must mount the pipes so that they all have a slope and mount the collector so that it drains completely, too.

✔ Copper pipe with a minimum diameter of ¾" works best.

✔ The pumps consume energy, thereby decreasing efficiency. However, if you use a PV cell (see the later section "Solar PV Systems: King of the Energy-Efficiency Hill" for details), this isn't an issue.

A closed-loop anti-freeze system

Closed-loop anti-freeze systems, shown in Figure 16-3, are far and away the most widely distributed type of system in the world because they work in almost any climate. Most new solar homes feature closed-loop anti-freeze systems because they're low risk and very effective. I would recommend them for most applications. Keep in mind, though, that they're expensive and not entirely problem-free.

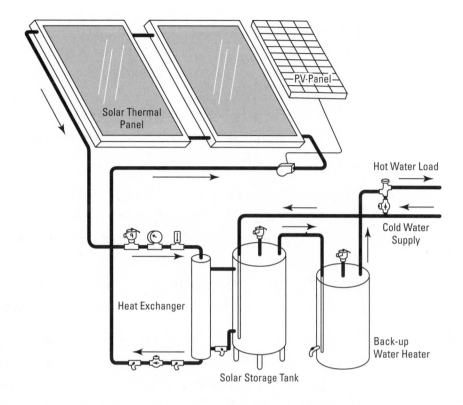

Figure 16-3:
A closed-loop anti-freeze solar water heating system.

Labels in figure: PV-Panel; Solar Thermal Panel; Hot Water Load; Cold Water Supply; Heat Exchanger; Back-up Water Heater; Solar Storage Tank

A special water heater tank incorporating a heat exchanger is used with one or more flat plate, roof-mounted collectors. Glycol, or some equivalent anti-freeze fluid, fills the collector and routing pipes. A controller measures the temperature in the collector fluid, as well as the temperature in the hot water tank. When heat is available for transfer, pumps are activated to move the collector fluid.

A typical system costs around $5,500 installed (see Chapter 4 for details on the type of tax breaks and rebates you may qualify for), and complete kits are available. Although installation of the parts is no more difficult than for other systems, charging the closed loop can be tricky. If you don't do it right, you can damage the system and get inefficient performance.

If you're considering a closed-loop system, keep these things in mind:

411

- You can mount the flat plate collectors in almost any configuration. The closed loop is always full of fluid, so the pump pressure requirements are much less finicky than those of a drainback system (explained in the preceding section). In addition, the collector can be mounted at a great distance from the exchanger.

- The pump can be very small, with very little head pressure, translating to lower power and better efficiency. Running these types of pumps off a PV panel increases efficiency even more. (At night, when there's no sunlight to power the PV panel, there's no hot water to be pumped anyway.)

- The major limitation is the tendency of the anti-freeze fluid to degrade over time, resulting in inefficiency and the buildup of deposits on the interior walls of the pipes and collector. Periodic servicing of the fluid is a must. Because injecting new fluid into the system has to be done just right, it usually needs to be done by a qualified serviceperson.

- The best way to prevent the fluid from overheating is to make sure the closed loop is circulating at all times when it's sunny out. You can get scalding hot water in your domestic tank, and a tempering valve is critical.

- You need to use copper pipe because it's the only material that can withstand very high temperatures.

Make sure the copper pipe is well insulated if there's a chance that children might touch it. The pipe can get extremely hot.

Solar PV Systems: King of the Energy-Efficiency Hill

In one fell swoop you can completely offset your electric utility bill and generate zero pollution. Millions of photovoltaic (PV) systems are being installed all over the world, and the costs are decreasing due to economies of scale. But PV systems are not for everybody because they require a considerable upfront investment.

There are two basic types of systems: intertie, which work in conjunction with the utility grid, and stand-alone, which require batteries and other special support hardware. Here, I focus on the intertie systems because they comprise the vast majority of installations.

Seeing the advantages of a PV system

The two biggest advantages of having a PV system are reducing pollution — you can literally erase over 40,000 pounds of carbon dioxide a year by going with a solar PV system — and saving money.

Net metering and why it's sooo good

Net metering means that you can sell your excess power back to the utility company. Under most net-metering laws, utility companies must pay you the same retail rate they charge their own customers for power.

Net metering is great for PV system economics because every solar system, whether PV, water heating, or another type, has a certain maximum capacity. Maximum capacity depends on a number of things: the size of the system, the orientation and location of the solar collectors, and how much sunlight is available. On a cloudy day, system capacity is much less than on a sunny day. On a hot summer day, the capacity can be very large. The point is, solar systems don't put out consistent power from minute to minute, day to day, or season to season. Some days you get way more than you need; other days, not so much.

With a PV system tied in to the grid (as opposed to a stand-alone system), you can use as much power as you need, and your PV system merely contributes whenever it can. Picture it like a bank. You put money in during the day, when the sun is shining, and then later on you can make withdrawals. What you don't use is all sold back to the utility.

In some regions, solar PV is even more advantageous because the utilities have what's called time-of-use (TOU) rate scheduling, where electricity rates are highest during peak usage time (from noon until 6 p.m.). The rate during this period can be over three times the rate at off-peak times. The timing is perfect for solar PV systems because they generate a majority of their power during peak time (remember, by law, the utilities must pay you the same rate they charge for power, so at peak time they must pay you peak rates).

 Solar PV is an investment tool, but you must change your power usage habits in order to capitalize on the advantage. The harder you work your investment, the better it pays off.

Government subsidies

Government has a vested interest in promoting solar power because of its overwhelmingly positive environmental impact, as well as the desirable political impact of energy in-

414

dependence. The best way to promote solar power is to get more people to invest in it, and the best way to do that is to subsidize it. Subsidies, rebates, and tax breaks are wide-spread and becoming more prevalent with each passing day. In some parts of the country, the total discount on a system can be over 50 percent.

Protecting yourself against future rate increases

All investments require you to predict the future. If you think energy costs are going to rise quite a bit, solar energy is a very wise option. Your power bills won't increase no matter how much energy costs rise. This is a very powerful form of portfolio management called hedging, where you not only get a good return on your investment but also ensure that regardless of what happens in the future, your investment will still pay off. In fact, the more energy costs rise, the better your original investment in solar will turn out to be.

When energy costs rise, those with solar power will still be able to use the same amount of energy. Those without will be scrambling to conserve or to buy solar equipment (which makes yours more valuable). You ensure not only financial security but also lifestyle security when you invest in solar energy.

Increasing property values

Your property value can increase by more than the cost of your original solar PV investment. Not only will you save on monthly power bills, but you'll see an almost immedi-ate appreciation in your home, in many cases, equal to or greater than the cost of your equipment.

Understanding the basic parts of every solar PV system

An intertie solar PV system, shown in Figure 16-4, is actually very simple, despite its high cost. The collectors collect sunlight and convert it into a raw electrical signal. Wires transmit this signal down to the inverter, which converts (why it isn't called a converter is beyond me) the power to 110VAC that is useable in your home. The meter is used so the power company can ding you, of course. And switches are there for safety purposes. The following sections explain the important parts of a solar PV system.

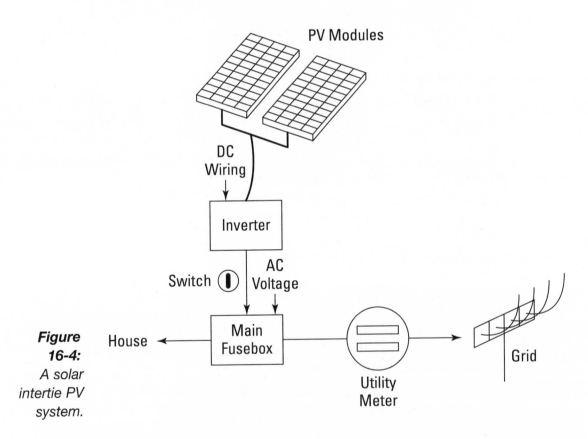

Figure 16-4:
A solar intertie PV system.

Ground-mounted systems are more expensive than roof-mounted systems because they require concrete posts and special frames. On the other hand, you can orient the panels any way you want, so the extra cost may be offset by increased production.

 Install a smaller system than you think you need, and allow for the possibility of future expansion by buying an inverter big enough to accommodate the panels you may add in the future.

PV panels

PV panels, which comprise about 60 percent of the system's cost, are the single biggest expense. They take up the most space as well. For most users, finding the space for the panels is the hardest part of the investment because it's critical that they get a lot of sunshine. This depends quite a bit on the orientation of your roof.

Different types of panels are finding their way onto the market. The technologies aren't important to you, but the configurations may be. Some panels are flexible, and some can be mounted directly over tiled roofs. Some panels are being made into roofing shingles. Most of the new technologies are going to need some maturation to compete with the tried-and-true flat panels. It's best to avoid new technologies until they've proven themselves.

Be sure to check the warranty and the manufacturer's reputation and longevity. Most PV panel warranties are for 20 years, but beware: Panels degrade over time. System warranties specify a percentage of original power output over time, say, 80 percent after 20 years. Inevitably, your system will put out less and less energy.

Inverters

Inverters are the next biggest expense. Inverters take the low-voltage, high-current signals from the PV panels and invert them into 120VAC, which is directly compatible with grid power. Inverters cost around 50 cents per watt, or around $2,500 for a typical installation. Options include monitoring functions, safety features, expandability ports, and so on. The most popular feature is a digital display that tells you exactly how much power your system is producing.

Disconnect switches and more

Disconnect switches are of critical importance and need to be mounted within easy reach. Every member of your family should know exactly how to turn the PV system off for safety reasons. Power meters are usually provided by the utility company when they come to your house to inspect your system and connect it to the grid. Wiring, conduit, and connections to your household's main fuse box are minor expenses, but comprise a big chunk of the labor for installation. You want the installers to hide the conduits, if they can.

Getting the PV system installed

The installation of a PV system involves the following steps:

1. **Perform an energy audit.**

   Some states require an energy audit before you can buy a solar system. California is making this a requirement if you want to collect their sizable rebate. Why? It's not really in the interest of your contractor to help you reduce your power consumption before you buy a PV system because that means they'll be selling you a smaller system. But the payback is much better if you save money by conserving prior to buying a big PV system. The cheapest energy is that which you never use. Plus, using as little power as possible is in society's best interest.

2. **Decide on a PV system and how to finance it.**

You must collect cost and performance estimates for PV systems, including the following:

- PV system costs, lifetimes, expansion potentials, warranty, and so on. The best bet is to call contractors and have a preliminary conversation about these issues. They're familiar with all the rebates, subsidies, and tax credits available because they help them sell systems.

- The physical setup. How much roof space will a system take up? Do you have a suitable roof, facing approximately south? What condition is your roof in? Will any work need to be done before you install the system?

- Rate structures. Find out which structures you qualify for *once the equipment is in place.* Your current structure may not be applicable anymore, and you may have options to choose from. Can you change structures later, if you don't like the one you're in? Can your utility company change structures on you later? You could find yourself in a real bind if you install a system under a certain rate structure, only to get a nice letter from your utility informing you that they're changing your status.

- What is the payment schedule for the investment? You usually have to make a down payment (typically $1,000) at contract signing.

Then you pay approximately half the remaining balance at the beginning of the installation, and the other half after the system is in place.

- What are your financing options and costs?

3. Choose a contractor.

Talk to as many contractors as you can. Get them to come to your home and look at your situation in some detail (they can't give you an accurate quote until they do; any phone quotes are only approximations).

4. Review the contract.

After you choose the contractor, a contract will be written up. Be sure to pay attention to the following:

- What guarantees are included in the contract?

- Exactly what are you buying? A pile of installed hardware, or a system guarantee?

- Under what conditions is the contract voided?

- Can you pull out? You usually have three days to change your mind — if they don't tell you this, ask.

5. Wait for approvals from the county building department and any subsidizing agencies to begin installation.

Expect this to take up to six weeks or more.

6. Have the system installed (and inspected).

Installations typically take a couple of days. The county inspectors will look at your system and certify it. The utility company is very concerned with your system because you will be feeding potentially dangerous power back into their grid. If utility employees are working on the grid nearby and your system isn't working properly, they could get a nasty shock.

7. **Have the utility company come out with a meter and connect you to the grid.**

When everything is ready, the utility company will install a new power meter and officially hook you up. Now you're in the power-generating business, and you can brag to all your friends.

8. **Bone up on how to operate your system.**

Your contractor needs to walk you through the entire system and explain the hazards and proper operation. You should be aware of potential problems and how to identify them. At this point, you can watch the display on your inverter cranking out numbers. Your contractor should explain exactly what the numbers mean.

9. **Submit paperwork for final rebate payments, if necessary.**

Rebates are not payable until the system is in place and working properly. If your contractor is receiving the rebate directly, you don't need to do anything. If you're receiving it, you will want to get it as fast as you can.

Powering Pumps and Motors Directly

PV panels can be used to directly power DC electrical motors (no batteries required). If you don't have access to electricity, this can be very useful. If you simply want to cut back on pollution, this is a good way to make a contribution.

Supplying water with a solar pump

Solar water pumps can be located anywhere sunshine is available. All water pumping systems include a few basic components (see Figure 16-5):

- ✔ **A reservoir:** If you want to run water to your house, the storage reservoir should be located above the house so that when a tap is opened, gravity provides the water pressure to the faucets.

- ✔ **A faucet:** Crank the handle, get water.

- ✔ **A switch:** To turn the system off and on. If there is no water to be pumped, you don't want to run the pump dry or it will burn up.

- ✔ **A submersible DC pump:** A submersible pump goes down into the water supply and has the advantage that it is always *primed,* that is full of water. (Without the water, the pump would burn out.)

- ✔ **A water supply:** The water supply can be a well or a creek/river, lake, or other body of water.

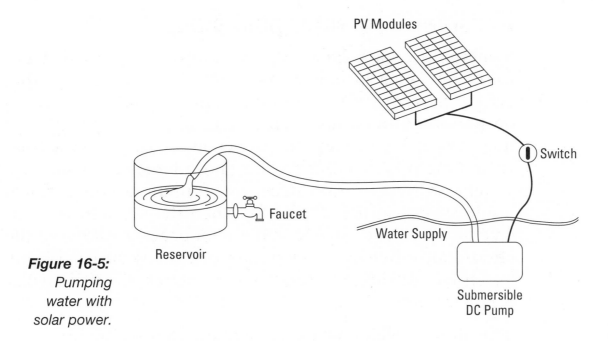

Figure 16-5:
Pumping
water with
solar power.

PV Modules

Switch

Faucet

Reservoir

Water Supply

Submersible
DC Pump

In order to specify system size, you need to make the following calculations:

- **Daily water usage, in gallons.** Calculate both average and maximum usage.

- **Available sunshine, in average hours per day.** If having water available at all times isn't critical (that is, if you can tolerate a few days of drought), the reservoir may be smaller. If you need water all the time and sunshine is inconsistent, you need a larger reservoir, along with larger PV modules so you can fill the reservoir on sunny days.

- **Difference in vertical height between the top level of the water source and the output end of the pump hose.** This number is called the pump's *head pressure.*

Considering a solar pool pump

Swimming pool solar-powered pumps are expensive upfront, but once installed, you never have to pay another cent to power your pool pump. Conventional pool pumps, on the other hand, are relatively inexpensive upfront, but they cost a lot to run. In particular, if you have a solar swimming pool heating system and a large-scale solar PV system on a TOU rate structure, running a conventional pump system in the afternoon, when the sunlight is available for heat (you have to run a pool heating system in the afternoon; otherwise, it won't provide any heat), is very expensive. In the long term, you're better off with a solar pump system.

The more sunshine you get, the more the pool pump runs. This works nicely because pool utilization hours are usually determined by the amount of sunshine as well.

Using Wind and Water for Solar Power

Like solar collectors, windmills and hydropower generators are powered by the sun, but in an indirect manner. Windmills and hydropower generators both generate voltages with spinning turbines. The concept is very simple. When you apply a power source to an electric motor, the shaft spins. If you manually spin the shaft of an electric motor, on the other hand, its two wires will output power. The physics work in either direction. Turbines are simply electric motors run backwards. Inverters are required (just as with solar PV panels) to convert the raw voltages from the rotors into usable power.

Wind and water may be available at any time of day or night. Wind, however, can come and go from minute to minute. Water resources generally don't vary much over the course of a day but they can vary over seasons. They're also subject to droughts when no power may be available at all for extended periods. The good news is that you can get rebates and subsidies for wind and water power just as you can for PV systems and water heating systems. They're all solar power and are grouped together in this regard.

Blowing with the wind

A wind turbine, shown in Figure 16-6, looks like a small airplane with a huge propeller, which is basically what it is.

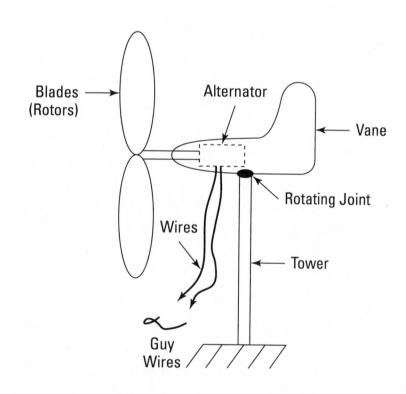

Figure 16-6:
A wind
turbine.

The pros and cons of wind power

Wind power has several advantages. It can be generated anytime, day or night. Wind is available almost everywhere, in all climates. In many of the worst climates, it's very powerful. In some locations, wind is virtually a constant (magnitudes may vary, but output is always available). Because wind speeds vary over terrain, you can find locations on your property that provide maximum potential. Ridge lines, coastlines, and the tops of barren hills are the best candidates.

Wind power has its disadvantages, too:

- Extremely high wind conditions may destroy or damage a unit (turbines need a minimum amount of wind to begin working, but they don't need a tornado).

- Obstructions like trees, houses, barns, and so on all affect wind speed. And because wind direction varies, obstructions in one direction may or may not be important in other directions. The best bet is to stay well away from all obstructions, although this may not be possible. And finally, precisely because wind is variable, you definitely need batteries.

- Mounting is a bear. In general, the higher the unit, the more capacity it will output. A height of 100' is considered optimum, and that's a long way up there. The mounting must have a tremendous amount of integrity because of the torques that need to be withstood.

    The installation is the tricky part. Hire a pro. If you don't know what you're doing, you could literally be killed trying to install a wind turbine.

- Rotors are noisy and obtrusive when they're spinning. The bigger the blades, the more power they generate and the noisier they are. They also attract a lot of visual attention and may clutter up a placid environment.

Available sizes and cost

The smallest turbines (6' rotors) sell for around $1,000, not including installation (tower building and raising, wiring, and so on). They output 400 watts of power at 28 mph (this is a pretty good wind) and can withstand winds up to 110 mph. You can use these numbers to get an idea of how many kWh per day you can expect, on average; then you can devise a battery bank accordingly. A turbine with a 15' rotor produces 3.2 kW at 28 mph for around $8,000, including installation.

Tower costs vary depending on height, but a typical tower kit for a small turbine with a height of 50' runs around $700. The higher up, the more effective; but the higher up, the more expensive as well.

Using water for your power needs

A hydropower system is basically the same as a wind system, except the turbine is spun by water pressure instead of air movement. There are two basic kinds of hydropower systems; submersible systems, which are inserted down into moving water such as a river or a creek, and stationary systems, which use water pressure. (Hydropower dams are all stationary systems; the deeper the dam, the higher the pressure and the more power available.)

Consider these things if you're interested in water power:

- You don't need batteries (although they do make the system work better). You can assume your hydro generator output will be pretty constant, at least from hour to hour. Over the course of a year, you may have major variations.

- You can install a water system of virtually any size

427

power output if your water source is big enough. If your water source is small, power outputs will fluctuate quite a bit and may be zero for extended periods or during droughts.

✔ You can generate power day or night, in any weather (freezing may cause problems, but the right design can usually prevent this).

✔ Hydro systems have very long lives, are relatively trouble-free, and require very little maintenance. But the upfront costs are expensive, particularly for stationary water systems.

✔ Complex electrical system designs and mounting schemes are difficult with water pressures pushing all the time. This is not a trivial system design to tackle, although do-it-yourselfers can safely do it if they're patient and willing to make multiple adjustments until the best arrangement is finalized.

Heating Your Swimming Pool with a Solar System

Swimming pool heating is one of the most common uses of solar energy. The idea is simple: A solar collector is set out in the sunshine and the swimming pool filter pump system is used to move water through the collector and into the swimming pool. A minimal system can cost less than a few hundred dollars and works reasonably well. The cost for an average full-up system (roof-mounted) runs around $4,000. That's a lot of money, but compared to using electricity or gas it's a good investment because the energy is free, not to mention environmentally friendly.

Getting started with a simple setup

The simplest system for heating your swimming pool uses a single solar panel (see Figure 16-7). If you use a pool cover in conjunction with the solar panel, you can raise the pool temperature up to 15 degrees.

Your pool system already includes the pump, controller, and filter, along with PVC pipes that route the water flow. You simply break into the PVC line after the filter (never before), and run a couple of flex hoses (or PVC, if you prefer) to the solar collector panel, which can be laid out on the ground or set against a hill (or other support) to achieve some angular tilt toward the sun.

Solar collector panels are sold at most pool supply stores. You can get a 4' x 20' panel for around $200. Flex hoses cost around $15 apiece. Adaptors are sometimes necessary.

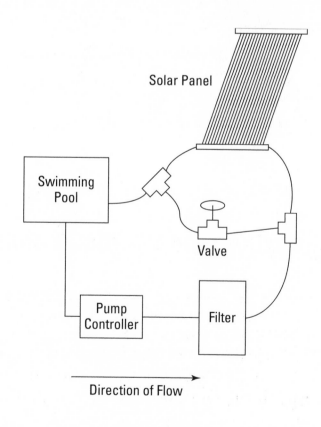

Figure 16-7:
A simple swimming pool solar heating system.

Here are some tips to run the system for best results:

- ✔ Place the solar panel where it will get the most sunlight when the pool pump is running. The more sunshine, the more heat into the pool.

- ✔ Adjust the pump run time to match maximum sunlight conditions. Running the pump longer will result in more heat in the pool.

- ✔ You can use two or more solar panels. The best bet is to configure them in parallel, as shown in Figure 16-8. This configuration offers the water multiple channels, reducing the overall water pressure while heating the same amount of water.

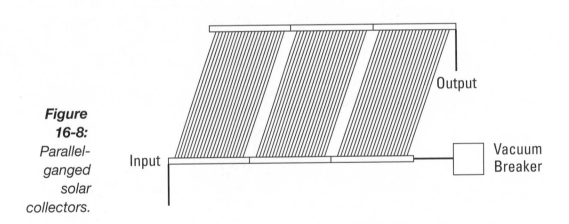

Figure 16-8: *Parallel-ganged solar collectors.*

Going the whole nine yards: A complete system

The entire system for a typical swimming pool solar system, shown in Figure 16-9, includes quite a bit more than the simple starter system described in the preceding section. In addition to the parts that come standard with traditional pools (pump, filter, the pool itself, a bunch of screaming kids, and so on), it also has collectors to collect sunlight and convert it into heat, valves to control the flow of water and determine whether the pool system is using the solar heating components or is simply in bypass mode, and a motor valve that measures the temperature of the pool water and determines whether heat is needed or not (if the day is cloudy and cold, or it's raining, it's hardly worth expending the extra energy it takes to run the solar heater).

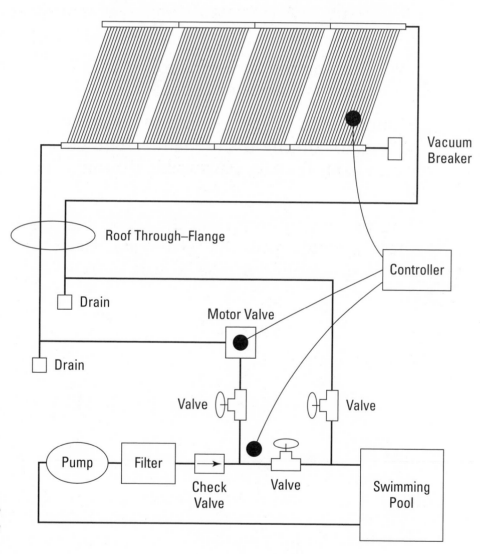

Figure 16-9:
A complete swimming pool system.

431

For these systems, the solar collectors are almost always mounted on your roof. A slight downward tilt is necessary to facilitate draining during the purge cycle. When the controller deactivates the motor valve, the vacuum breaker allows the system to purge itself of liquid. This is important for two reasons:

- ✔ You don't want water in the collectors at night because it will cool down, and when you first activate the collectors the next day, you'll dump cool water into your pool. This is obviously at odds with your goal.

- ✔ Purging the water ensures it won't freeze up and burst the pipes or collector.

Manual drain valves are used to deactivate the system in off seasons or during maintenance. The check valve prevents water from flowing backwards through the pump and filter.

You can buy a complete kit if you want to install one of these systems yourself. (Kits are always highly recommended, even if they cost a little more.)

Chapter 17

Radiant Heating Systems

Radiant heating can be much more efficient than conventional heating means, like forced air and stoves. Radiant implies not so much a method of generating heat as distributing that heat. You can use an electric heater, a gas heater, or geothermal or solar methods to equal effect with radiant heat systems. In this chapter, I go through the basics of radiant heating methods.

The most prevalent way to use radiant heating is through coils embedded into the floor. These can be either electric heating coils or narrow diameter tubes for the transmission of water or other liquids. The upfront costs of these systems are higher than conventional heating means, but the operating efficiency pays back in both increased comfort levels and lower energy costs.

Masonry heaters, which are very similar to stoves, have very high thermal masses, and their combustion chambers (usually for wood fuels) are very carefully controlled to achieve up to 90 percent efficiency. They work on the radiant heating premise, and I touch briefly on the pros and cons of heating your home with these heaters in this chapter as well.

Radiating Heat with Radiant Heat Systems

Radiant heat works by warming the surfaces in your home, as opposed to simply warming the air (as conventional heating systems do). The result is a much more stable and comfortable ambient:

- ✔ **Radiant heat doesn't use moving air, which has a cooling effect (see Chapter 8), to warm things up.** For that reason, you feel warmer in a radiant heated room at the same temperature as a forced air heated room. Radiant heat is also more efficient because it doesn't use big blowers (motors always take a lot of energy to run).

- ✔ **Radiant heat doesn't dry out the air.** In fact, it doesn't change the humidity of a home's air. (Humid air feels warmer; dry air feels cooler.)

- ✔ **The chimney effect isn't as pronounced with radiant heat as it is with other forms of heat.** A radiant heater generally releases heat near the floor (most new systems are actually installed in the floor), so the heat naturally rises up to the people in the room.

- ✔ **Radiant heaters tend to heat everything in a room.** When they're installed in a floor, you can literally walk barefoot on a tile floor in the middle of the coldest winter day and still feel perfectly comfortable. Radiant heating is much more comfortable in general. People who have lived with radiant heat never want to go back, and they notice the difference in comfort quite a bit when they visit hotels or other people's homes where forced air systems are operating.

✔ **Radiant heat systems can achieve a greater warming effect with less energy than forced air heaters because the thermostat can be set lower.** If you have a forced air heater, you have to offset the cooling effect of moving air by setting your thermostat a few degrees higher. This effect is real, not just a matter of perceived comfort. A radiant room can actually be a few degrees cooler and feel better at the same time. Obviously, this means you use less energy.

✔ **With a radiant heat system, each room can have its own separate temperature controller.** You can shut entire portions of your home off from heat or turn unused rooms way down for big savings. And the temperatures that you set in individual rooms will be very well maintained, in spite of weather conditions or any other variations.

✔ **Radiant systems provide cleaner air quality, and they don't use filters.** They don't blow air around and stir up dust.

The drawback of a radiant system is that it takes much more time to heat a room (by the same token, once the room is warmed it takes a lot longer to cool off). By contrast, when you come into a cold house and turn on your forced air system, you get immediate hot air. If you want, you can stand over the vent and warm yourself very quickly. Not so with radiant heat.

Old-Style Radiators

Many old buildings use radiators set up in the corner of each room. These are big, bulky, heavy metal grids through which hot water or steam is pumped. They get very hot, and they're very noisy (clicking, sighing, groaning, sizzling, and spitting). A big water boiler is located in the basement, and tons of pipes and plumbing components are required. Old time radiators are vestiges of the past and inefficient to boot because pipes always leak heat into the surrounding air.

Thermal mass in the sunshine

You can effect radiant heat with solar power by building a sunroom or greenhouse. See Chapter 16 for more information, or check out *Solar Power Your Home For Dummies* (another Wiley book authored by yours truly) for a lot more details.

The idea is simple: Let the sun heat a thermal mass (like a concrete floor or a heavy barrel filled with water) during the day, and then at night let that heat radiate out into your living space. The effect can be very dramatic, and if you combine this with the fact that you also get some aesthetics, it's worth looking into.

Overhangs (structures built over windows to control the amount of sunshine that enters at different times of the year) are particularly useful for modulating this effect. See Chapter 12 for more details about overhangs and other solar exposure controls.

A number of outdoor boiler systems are very popular in remote areas that work well with these types of radiators, and they're a cinch to install. I merely point out here that these systems are still available, and if you want to use them, you can get the equipment very cheaply (used, especially) and they work well. Note that I didn't say great. If you're really serious about using radiant heat, radiant heat floor systems are much better.

Radiant Heat Floor Systems

Radiant heat floor systems are probably the most common form of radiant heat used nowadays, for a number of good reasons. The idea is very simple. You heat your floor with a grid of coils installed underneath the floor (see Figure 17-1).

Types of radiant floor heaters: Electric or hydronic

Radiant heat floor systems can use either electric or hydronic (liquid) heating elements:

✔ **Electric systems:** Electric systems are not as efficient as hydronic ones, but they're still more efficient than forced air electrical systems. Plus, a radiant heat electric system is much easier to install and maintain.

✔ **Hydronic systems:** With a hydronic system, you can use any number of sources for the heat. The most common source is a water heater that's essentially the same as a domestic water heater. But solar heaters are also common, as are geothermal ones.

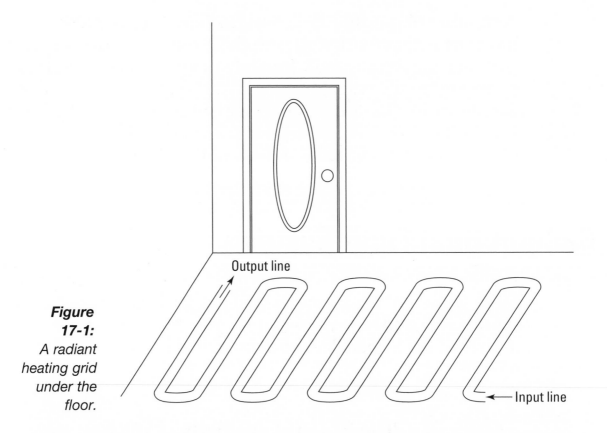

Output line

Input line

Figure 17-1:
A radiant heating grid under the floor.

The more thermal mass in the floor, the better these systems work. So tile (or a similar product) is the best floor covering material. You can also use vinyl (make sure it's rated for the application) and laminates. If you use wood, you need to be careful how it's installed because the heating and cooling cycles will make the wood expand and contract. Float floors are the best bet for wood. Carpet also works, but it's not as efficient at transferring the heat into the room, and you need to make sure that the carpet is rated for the application (be sure to get the proper backing material).

Installation tips

Basically, a radiant heat floor system goes beneath the floor surface. You can build one up on an existing floor and then

438

add a new layer of floor above the radiant elements, or you can remove the existing floor surface and start at the sub-floor level.

Not all floor surfaces are conducive to radiant heating, so make sure to check at your floor dealer. Tile works the best, and vinyl is a no-no. Wood floors are alright, but they tend to expand and contract over time and this may cause warping. Most manufacturers will specify whether their floor surface works with radiant heating.

If you're a do-it-yourselfer, installing an electric system is much easier than installing a hydronic one. Not a lot can go wrong with an electric system, and if something does go wrong, it's pretty easy to fix. With a hydronic system, a lot more can go wrong, and it's often a bear to repair. Also, with a hydronic system, if you put the floor covering in place and something goes wrong, you've got a potential disaster on your hand when the liquid seeps out. This can be a real mess. Not so with an electric system.

If you're remodeling and need a heater in a basement or an add-on room, using electric radiant heat in the floor can be very inexpensive compared to other options. When you're adding space to your home's interior that needs to be heated, you generally can't just tap into the existing whole-house HVAC system because it was designed with a specific capacity in mind, namely the size of your existing home. Tapping in could render the whole-house system incapable of doing the job adequately. Your HVAC system may not be able to keep up on the coldest winter days, despite being perpetually on. You can install a radiant floor system without tapping into your existing HVAC and have a more comfortable, efficient room to boot.

Heating Up the Joint with Masonry Heaters

Masonry heaters are designed for very hot fires in their combustion chambers (typically over 1,300°F). The heat passes through a series of baffled chambers called *heat exchangers,* which draw the heat from the air and transfer it into a dense, solid material. The heat is then radiated slowly and passively into the living space of your home. The heat is just as slowly absorbed into the walls, floors, ceiling, furniture, and, eventually, into the people in the room. The ambience is very comfortable, and nearly everybody who has ever experienced a masonry heater's effects swears by them.

Masonry heaters have a tremendous amount of mass, which in practical terms translates into very consistent, even performance. Even when doors are momentarily opened to the outdoors on a cold day, the home does not feel much different because it's not so much the air that's warm, but the entire home.

Although the initial costs of masonry heaters are high — expect a minimum of around $8,000, not including what it takes to beef up your foundation or chimney work — they're very efficient. Efficiencies of masonry heaters can be up to 90 percent, which is truly impressive.

The following sections explain what you need to know about masonry heaters.

Like a conventional wood stove — but not

In some ways, masonry heaters are like wood stoves in that they burn wood and radiate heat. But there are important differences:

- Masonry heaters need to have their combustion cycle more carefully controlled than wood stoves do because the fire is so much hotter. Opening and closing doors is more critical. Except during fueling, the doors remain closed with most units. Some allow for the door to be open, but then the fire is more like a conventional fireplace and the efficiency is diminished.

- The amount of heat a masonry heater generates is controlled by the amount of wood burned (not the amount of oxygen added to the burn chamber, as with conventional stoves). The burn temperature needs to be highly controlled, and varying the oxygen varies the temperature.

- You can use most any wood to good benefit — and less of it than you'd use in conventional stoves — because masonry heaters extract Btu extremely efficiently from the wood. (The fuel used in masonry heaters is thinner in diameter because more air circulation is needed between the pieces of wood.)

- A masonry heater takes a long time to heat up to its steady state operating temperature. With conventional stoves, the heating effects take hold in just 15 minutes. But with a masonry heater, you need to plan ahead. If you come home from a few days away, your home won't heat up for hours. On the other hand, you can go to bed at night when your masonry heater is working full bore, and when you wake up in the morning your home will be nearly the same temperature.

- Masonry heaters can be used in many locales where other types of stoves are banned due to air pollution. Because they burn wood so thoroughly, the pollution impact is minimal.

Despite all the ways masonry stoves differ from conventional stoves, they do share a few of the more irksome characteristics:

✔ You need a source of firewood (although some masonry heaters are coming onto the market now that use other fuel sources).

✔ Burning wood is labor intensive, regardless of how efficiently you do it.

✔ They tend to be dirty to operate. Around the unit you may notice a coating of soot (true with all wood stoves!).

Installing masonry heaters

The biggest issue with masonry heater installation is the weight. These heaters are too heavy for a single person to move into place. In fact, the larger units may take a forklift, which is why they should be installed while the home is being built. Some units come disassembled, which makes installation much easier (if you know how to assemble things, that is). In general, installing masonry heaters is similar to installing a heavy wood stove. Refer to Chapter 15 for more details on installing wood stoves, in particular, the chimney and venting requirements.

The biggest factor in terms of a masonry heater's effectiveness is its location. It should be in the center of your home, preferably in a large room. If it's not, you're sacrificing potential efficiency. Masonry heaters work best in homes with open floor plans, where the heat can spread throughout the entire living space, slowly and evenly. In fact, most masonry heaters are installed in new home construction, where the home design is centered on the masonry heater.

You can't put one on a floor unless it's built to support a lot of weight. Masonry heaters have a tremendous amount of thermal mass, which translates into a lot of mass, period. Your existing fireplace pad may not be suitable for a masonry heater. Although you can install a masonry heater yourself, I wouldn't advise it. Better to hire a contractor who knows all the ins and outs.

For more information about masonry heaters, go to the Masonry Heater Association's Web site at www.mha-net. org. You can get kits, or you can find contractors who will do the whole job for you.

Chapter 18

Heating with Biomass Stoves

Biomass is a generic term for many different types of materials provided by Mother Nature. Strictly speaking, wood is biomass, and if you really want to get nitpicky, oil is probably biomass. For our purposes, I restrict the discussion to corn, wood pellets, leaves, and poop. These are the most common biomass products simply because the supply of raw materials are the most prevalent. You may find local biomass products that are cost effective in your own area, and not in others. Don't despair, however. You can still get a good idea of the basic pros and cons of using biomass fuel by reading this chapter.

Using Biomass for Fuel

In a nutshell, biomass is organic material (plants and animal waste) used for fuel. Examples of commonly used biomass fuels are corn, wood pellets, straw, certain types of grasses, and autumn leaves. And, not to put too fine a point on it, poop is biomass, too.

Strictly speaking, wood is biomass. But in this book, I separate wood from other biomass products because most other sources treat wood and biomass as distinct entities, even though they aren't. To help you avoid any confusion, I'm going to stick to that convention.

Here's what you need to know about burning biomass:

✔ Biomass can be a very clean-burning fuel or a very dirty-burning fuel. Knowing what you're doing is the key to success. Do it right, and you can burn biomass more cleanly than you can burn wood and most other options as well. Do it wrong, and

Compost piles: Biomass at work

A compost pile is an example of biomass at work. You throw garbage and any old organics you have lying around into a special hopper, and the decomposition process creates heat by breaking down the materials. You can use the final product any number of ways, including fertilizing your landscaping and burning in a stove. For that matter, burning autumn leaves is a biomass combustion process (although it's probably best to just call it "burning leaves" if you don't want people to think you're a nerd).

burning biomass can create a lot more pollution than most other options.

✔ The market for biomass is completely different than the market for firewood. The decision on whether to burn wood or not is predicated largely on whether you have access to firewood (and on which types of wood supplies are in your area mainly because wood is expensive to transport across large distances). Many biomass products, on the other hand, are commonly transported long distances, so this same restriction doesn't apply. Wood pellets, for example, come in compact bags that can be stacked on pallets and moved easily. Also, because the energy density is high, you get more bang for the buck.

✔ Biomass products, like wood pellets, are processed and bagged, and you generally take delivery of pallets with a forklift setting them down neatly into your storage area (unlike wood, which is usually quite a tangled mess; see Chapter 15). As a result of the processing and bagging, the energy density of most biomass products is much greater than wood, so you need less storage space.

Biomass is generally easier to work with than wood in terms of carrying the fuel from storage to the stove and loading your stove's combustion chamber. Wood is usually very dirty to deal with, but biomass rarely is (unless you're dealing with poop, which goes into a dimension beyond dirty).

Getting the Lowdown on Biomass Stoves

Biomass stoves and furnaces are designed to burn biomass fuels. In appearance, biomass stoves are similar to wood stoves, and they transfer heat the same way. But biomass stoves are set up to burn at different temperatures and may require more or less oxygen in order to gain the highest efficiencies. Biomass stoves also come with hoppers that feed the raw materials into the fire; you can't simply stack a pile of wood pellets and burn it the way you'd stack wood in a wood stove.

Biomass stoves are generally more efficient than wood-burning stoves because they take much less labor, and biomass combustion processes are well-controlled (like masonry heaters — see Chapter 17). Very little babysitting is involved. These stoves have automatic augers that feed the fuel into the burn chamber. You simply load a very big hopper, and the fuel feeds down into the fire only as needed. You can control the feed rate by means of a thermostatically-controlled switch, and you can mount the thermostat either by the stove or in a remote location.

 Just as with wood stoves, there are a large variety of biomass stove types, too many to cover in a single chapter, in fact. Your best bet is to research your local area to see what works best for your particular needs. Ask at stove shops, and if possible, find somebody who has a stove and ask about it (you'll probably get a more honest answer this way than at the stove store).

Your decision on which type of biomass to use is generally dependent upon which types of biomass are available in your area. The Midwest favorite seems to be corn stoves. In the Northwest, you find a lot of pellet stoves (pellets are made of byproducts of lumber processing, like bark, sawdust, twigs, and so forth). Economics of both equipment and fuel cost are the deciding factors. If you're concerned with the environment, keep in mind that biomass is sustainable and less polluting than both electric power and fossil fuel power, so it's a wise choice even if the cost is the same.

 At some point, there will be more biomass stoves than wood stoves simply because the supply of good wood is going to dwindle, whereas biomass (especially poop) is literally everywhere. Processed biomass products can be made of so many different raw products, in virtually any state of quality, that they will overtake wood as the number one means of stove combustion.

You can buy a very cheap biomass-burning stove and get inefficient performance, or you can spend a lot and get excellent convenience and efficiency. Regardless, burning biomass is almost always safer than burning firewood.

You can heat your entire home with a biomass furnace installed in your basement. Or you can heat a single room. How you plan to use your stove determines the size and operation of your equipment. Well before you buy any stove, ask at the stove shop what your options are and then go home and consider the details, as well as how you'll implement them once you get going.

Burning Up with Pellet Stoves

The main operational advantage of pellet stoves is that they're very easy to use. You fill the hopper with manufactured pellets and the rest of the process is largely automatic. A thermostat keeps the temperature at a preset point, and an auger feeds material into the combustion chamber so that you don't have to worry about it. You can fill the hopper once a day or even less often if it's not too cold out, and your home will stay at the set temperature. Pellet stoves can usually burn different types of materials as well, such as corn, coir fiber (from coconut husks), and

Outdoor boilers: The next worst thing

Outdoor boilers are a species of combustor appliances. As their name implies, these are positioned outside of your home and, as such, are exempt from Environmental Protection Agency (EPA) emission standards. When used properly, they work well. They're inherently safer than stoves and other heating appliances that are located inside because if something goes wrong (either a fire or smoke hazard), it's outdoors where it won't matter (okay, maybe it will, but not as much, and maybe it will be the neighbor's problem, not yours).

Outdoor boilers are advertised as capable of burning nearly any kind of fuel, and that's true. You can even toss in some poop and it'll burn, although you can only imagine what the smoke might smell like. But the real question is how efficient outdoor boilers are and how much they pollute. The simple fact that they work doesn't mean they're a good idea.

The efficiency and cleanliness of any combustion process is a function of temperature and other controlled parameters, such as oxygen supply. Although an outdoor boiler may burn just about anything, as advertised, a jack of all trades is always a master of none. These devices rarely offer any kind of precision combustion, so they take up far more fuel than they're worth. You may save some money on upfront costs, but in the long run you'll pay.

nutshells. With very little work, you can get an even, consistent heat source.

Many types of pellets are made from byproducts of other lumber processing ventures, like sawdust and ground wood chips. Some pellets are even made from corn stalks (usually wasted since they have no nutritive value) and nut hulls, or from other crops like switchgrass. (Too bad they can't make pellets out of politicians, other purportedly organic entities with little or no intrinsic value.) Pellets are like recycled products, and even better for the environment because of it.

In a nutshell, here are the advantages of burning pellets for heat:

- ✔ **The operating costs are low.** Pellets have a high energy density, and the stoves take very little power to run.

- ✔ **Pellets are renewable and produce the lowest emissions of any solid fuel.** Wood pellets, like wood (see Chapter 15), are neutral in terms of their effect on global warming because wood left to rot on the forest floor creates as much carbon dioxide as wood burned in a stove. And pellet combustion in

Growing trees the fast and furious way

Certain species of trees grow very fast, such as poplars and mulberries. In the future, there will be large farms and cooperatives that plant nothing but these types of trees and other fast-growing biomass sources for use in heating.

This is an interesting environmental issue because Mother Nature doesn't often favor the fastest-growing plants. They are not the strongest or heartiest, so there's a certain anti-Darwinian undertone in all this. Of course, the same may be said for the hyper-expansion of human presence enabled by vaccines and other technological advances. Perhaps when Mother Nature decides to eradicate the pesky human infestation she'll also get rid of our bio-engineered monstrosities as well.

a biomass stove is controlled much more accurately than wood combustion in a wood stove, so the combustion is more thorough and the efficiencies are much better. In addition, most of the industrial companies that manufacture pellets replenish the trees they cut down to make pellets.

- ✔ **If burned properly, pellets can be very clean and efficient.** Smoke is minimal, and the burn is clean enough with pellet stoves that you often don't need to vent the exhaust all the way up the chimney, so installation is easier and cheaper. There is also less creosote, which is safer for the home and cleaner for the environment. (No matter how cleanly pellets burn, though, cleaning out the ashes is a filthy job.)

- ✔ **Pellets are easy to store and handle.** Pellet storage requires only around a third of the space that wood requires, so if your space is limited you may want to consider this option. Bags come in 40-pound sizes (and up, but you need to be burly enough to lift them). Another plus is stored pellets don't attract the spiders that firewood does.

- ✔ **Venting is easier with a pellet stove than with most other stove types.** You need only a stainless steel vent pipe run to the great outdoors.

Of course, pellet stoves also have a few disadvantages:

- ✔ **Most stoves require electricity,** although you can get battery-operated versions.

- ✔ **Combustion gases pose a danger,** as is the case with any burning process.

- ✔ **Your insurance rates may increase when you install a stove of any kind in a preexisting**

home. Make sure to call and find out.

Burning, Not Popping, Corn

Corn is the second most popular biomass fuel because it's so readily available in many parts of the country. To be effective in combustion, corn must be very dry (unlike the stuff you eat). Corn can also be very cheap and clean, if you have a ready supply of quality product.

Prices fluctuate across the country, and, as you would expect, corn is cheapest in the Midwest where it's grown the most. (I grew up in the middle of Illinois, and corn was not only a fact of life, but in the late summer it was pretty much all of life.) You can buy dried corn directly from a farmer, or you can buy processed sacks of it that are easier and cleaner to handle (and a lot more expensive as well). If you're a corn farmer, you can heat your home for nothing at all. And if you like to eat small rodents, you can get plenty of free meat in the deal.

Other grains also work in essentially the same fashion as corn. Wheat, barley, rye, sorghum, and soybeans can be dried and burned at low cost and with low environmental impact. As with corn, this is really a question of access. People in cities don't burn soybeans simply because they can't store soybeans and don't have a ready supply.

The bright side of burning corn

Like other types of fuel burned in biomass stoves, corn can be a very consistent heating source because the stoves use automatic feeds and large hoppers. It's also very clean burning and low on the pollution scale. Burning corn and other grains offers these advantages as well:

- It's the cheapest renewable fuel (at least for the time being). However, with the price of ethanol (which is made of corn) increasing, the cost of raw corn also increases.

- Its environmental impact is very minimal. Corn grows fast and furious and is perhaps the best renewable energy source on the planet.

- Simple venting requirements allow for inexpensive installations. A short stainless steel pipe run is sufficient, and this makes corn burning possible in many applications where wood burning is impossible.

- You can make whiskey out of the same corn that heats your home, and *that* has warming properties all its own.

The downside of burning corn

Burning corn creates some unique problems that non-corn burning homeowners don't face. If corn weren't so cheap, not nearly as many homes would use it for heating, all things considered:

- Storing corn takes up more room than storing wood pellets because the energy content of corn isn't quite as good as that of wood pellets. In other words, you have to burn more corn to get the same amount of heat that you'd get from pellets.

- Corn has a limited lifetime, unlike other fuels. It may rot, or rats may eat it before you can burn it — a problem you have to address proactively or risk being overrun. Talk to somebody who has a corn stove or burns corn before you decide to take the leap. What you'll hear is that, although you may be able to control the problem, you can never really eliminate it.

✔ Your home will have a sweet smell, not unlike popcorn. Whether this sounds like a good thing or a bad thing to you, people with corn stoves get used to the smell and seem to like it. (An alternative that avoids this olfactory dilemma is a big furnace in the basement, rather than a stove in the living space.)

✔ You have to buy a stove entirely dedicated to burning corn. In some regions, these stoves are very rare, and servicing can be hard to find.

Other Biomass Uses You Probably Aren't Interested In (For Good Reason)

Horses and cows each produce from 10 to 16 metric tons of manure per year, depending upon pasture conditions and the amount of organic litter used for bedding. That's a lot of manure. You can stack it clear up to the sky, if you're so inclined. Compost a delectable stew by tossing in some garbage, waste straw, cane stalks, and pretty much any other organic material you can find, and what do you have? A rich mixture of dense fuel. In other words: Poop is biomass fuel. If you burn it right, you can get a lot of heat (this is not too different from the way English burn peat).

I do not include details on burning manure in this book, but I will tell you that you need a special burn chamber, and it needs to be stationed outside. You need heat exchangers and other equipment to bring the heat (and not the potential smell) into your home.

The joy of cooking: Making your own methane

You can convert cow manure into a very energy-dense gas by building a special fermentation processor. The malodorous raw material is pumped into a *digester silo* where it is heated to 95°F, at which point fermentation is activated. Anaerobic microorganisms break down the organic matter to produce a gas that's two-thirds methane and one-third carbon dioxide. The odor is similar to rotten eggs. The gas inflates a large plastic storage bellows. Methane is drawn off into a combustion-powered generator to produce electricity, which can be used to power nearly anything. All you need is a big pile of cow poop, but that's not hard if you have a bunch of cows. In fact, it's unavoidable.

You also need processed poop (although, if push comes to shove, you can just toss some poop into an open fireplace and it'll burn pretty well).

Chapter 19

Geothermal Energy: Straight from Mother Nature

One of the cleanest and most efficient heating and cooling solutions comes straight from good old Mother Earth herself. You can use air, ground, and water as sources of heat rather than burning fuels or using electricity (which almost always derives from burning fossil fuels). Electricity is, in fact, dirtier than other energy sources because it's so inefficient.

In this chapter, I give you a lowdown on how heat exchangers and heat pumps work; then I take you on a brief tour of how and why you may want to exploit geothermal sources of energy. In a nutshell, they're one of the more expensive energy options in terms of initial investment, but in the long run, they're cheaper because their operating costs are so low. At the very least, they pollute less compared to other options.

The (Very) Basics of Geothermal Heating and Cooling

The majority of heating in the modern world is done by means of combustion. Gas heaters are combustion-driven, as are stoves of all kinds. Electrical power is used to drive a lot of HVAC systems, but ultimately that power is usually derived from fossil fuel combustion (although some electric power is nuclear, some is hydro, and so on, a majority is derived from combustion). Geothermal energy, on the other hand, uses pumps and compressors to move heat from here to there. No combustion takes place, and no internal components get really hot, as opposed to electric furnaces, in which very hot grids transfer heat to the air moving over the grids. In addition, geothermal systems can save you between 30 and 70 percent on your monthly utility bills.

Seeing how geothermal energy works

Here's how a geothermal system works: The temperatures three to four feet below ground stay pretty much the same all year long, unlike outdoor air temperatures, which can fluctuate a great deal. The temperature remains stable at this depth for a couple of reasons: First, the earth absorbs nearly half of all the heat energy that hits it from the sun. Second, heat from the earth's core works its way toward the surface. The good news for you is that you can take advantage of this phenomenon with a geothermal ground-based system.

Geothermal ground-based systems circulate a water-based solution through a loop system that's buried underground. With one piece of equipment (admittedly complex) you can heat and cool your home and provide some or all your home's hot water, too.

A geothermal air system, on the other hand, takes advantages of the fact that air, regardless of its temperature, still contains some heat. A "heat pump" simply moves heat from the outside environment into your home, or vice versa. This works in both directions; you can both heat and cool a home, using a geothermal system.

- ✔ **During a heating cycle:** In either ground- or air-based systems, the fluid circulates through the loop, extracting heat from the ground or air. Then this heat is sent to the geothermal unit, where it's compressed and delivered to your home via your normal duct work or through a radiant heating system.

- ✔ **During a cooling cycle:** In a ground-based system, the heating process (explained in the preceding bulleted paragraph) is simply reversed: The unit removes heat from the home, circulates it through the ground where it's cooled by the ground temperatures. For an air-based geothermal system, the unit exchanges the heat in your home for the lack of heat in the air, thus cooling things down. The air expelled from an air-based heat pump can be much hotter than the ambient, outside air.

Don't worry about where the heat comes from in the first place. The answer to the question "How do you get heat and cold where there is apparently none?" is pretty complicated, and to understand it, you need to know quite a bit about thermodynamics, a branch of physics that deals with the interaction between energy and work, and the laws associated with them. Even people who are really smart in physics and study it in the best colleges in the country don't completely understand it, so don't feel bad that you don't either.

Looking at heat pumps

At the heart of geothermal processes are heat pumps, which basically move heat from one location to another. When you use a heat pump to generate heat, you move heat into the region where you want it (namely your home). When you use a heat pump to cool your home, you're basically just moving the heat out of your home, into the great outdoors. Moving heat out is the same as cooling.

There are two distinct types of heat pumps: air-source and ground-source. They use the same basic equipment, but have different means of effecting the heat exchange. As a result, their practical operations are markedly different:

- ✔ **Air-source heat pumps** are the kind you see in stand-alone HVAC systems. They use ambient air to heat or cool a refrigerant contained in a compressor system. They are especially suitable in moderate climates, as they perform both heating and cooling functions with reasonably good efficiency.

- ✔ **Ground-source heat pumps** are very similar to air-source heat pumps, except they use the earth as their heat exchange medium. They are more efficient than air-source pumps because the earth is much more consistent in terms of temperature. *Note: Geo-exchange* is the common name for ground-source heat pumps. It's just a matter of terminology, but you'll see both terms (*geo-exchange* and *ground-source* heat pumps) in use. Look at the GeoExchange Web site: www.geoexchange.org for installers, equipment, and so on.

Water (lakes, streams, and so forth) can also be used as the exchange medium, but this is rare because water temperature changes more and water is harder to access than earth (plus very few people have a ready access to a suitable supply). Therefore, I don't bother including information on water-source heat pumps here.

The beauty of both air- and ground-source heat pumps is that they can work in reverse. They are capable of both heating and cooling because the process is essentially the same, except backwards. This makes for a more financially efficient investment in equipment.

Advantages of heat pumps

Heat pumps have their share of pros and cons. On the plus side, heat pumps tout the following characteristics:

- ✔ **They offer steady, even heat and cooling.** Fluctuations in temperature are fewer compared to traditional combustion equipment, and this increases comfort.

- ✔ **They take up less space than traditional combustion equipment** because of their two-for-one advantage (they can both heat and cool). Plus, there's no need for a chimney or venting system because there's no combustion (they still may use ductwork to distribute the heat, but radiant systems are more common because they are a natural partner). There aren't any fuel storage requirements, either.

- ✔ **They're safer and cleaner than other options.** They don't create on-site air pollutants like smoke, carbon monoxide, and so forth. Nor do they create ashes or creosote. No combustion occurs, and none of the components become extremely hot.

Disadvantages of heat pumps

On the downside, the following cons apply to heat pumps:

- ✓ **They require more maintenance than some other options.** Systems require a number of parts, and heat pumps are more complex that combustion systems. If you look inside an air-source heat pump, you'll see what looks like the space shuttle.

- ✓ **They require electricity — sometimes a lot.** This not only affects energy efficiency, depending on how you're getting your electricity (nuclear source, combustion source, and so on) but it also means that in a power outage, you're stuck.

- ✓ **They're slow to respond.** They work best in steady-state conditions. If you come into a cold home and turn a heat pump on, it will take awhile for the house to heat up.

- ✓ **Absolutely no romantic element is involved.** Unless, of course, you love the high-tech complexity of the space shuttle.

Considering cost and payback

Heat pumps offer lower operating costs than most other options, and they can operate at efficiencies greater than 400 percent. This simply means that for each Btu of energy expended on moving heat from either land or air, four times more heat energy is extracted. This does not mean that the heat is free, however, and cost efficiency is the real question. Nor does it mean that pollution efficiency is better than it is with most other options.

461

After running the compressors and pumps and accounting for all the other inefficiencies that heat pumps entail, the overall efficiency is better than most heating processes, and this is why heat pumps are attractive. But the equipment is very expensive. Heat pumps are complex pieces of equipment with many more options for Murphy to exploit (unlike, say, fireplaces).

Deciding Whether an Air-Source Heat Pump Is Right for You

Air-source heat pumps are widely used in mild climates where the units don't have to work inordinately hard. In very cold climates, you probably want a combustion heater that can crank out hordes of Btu in a short time. But if you're in a mild climate, an air-source heat pump is probably one of your best choices. They connect to the existing ductwork, like any other heater or air-conditioner, and they accomplish both heating and cooling in the same package (refer to the earlier section "The (Very) Basics of Geothermal Heating and Cooling" for details). It's rarely the case that an air-source heat pump is used with a radiant heating system, but it can be done if you decide it's worth the extra cost (which it may very well be; see Chapter 17 for more details on radiant systems).

As you consider an air-source heat pump, keep these things in mind:

- The heat source, which is air, is free and limitless. No increase in energy costs will ever raise the price of air.

- Although air-source heat pumps require an expensive upfront investment in equipment, they're the least expensive type of heat pump to install. And because installation is relatively easy, you can get a wider variety of qualified installers to give you a bid. Competition is always a good thing.

Air-source heat pumps for a residential home cost more than other options for heating and cooling. The payback comes in terms of lower power bills.

✔ The technology is mature and getting better all the time. You can rest assured that if you get new equipment, the quality will be good in terms of both design and implementation.

✔ Air-source heat pumps are better for some climates than for others. If you live in a climate that requires heating and cooling in approximately equal amounts, an air-source heat pump is a viable option. If you need a lot more heating than cooling, a stove system is a better bet (with portable air conditioners, if need be). In moist, cold weather, air-source heat pumps don't do very well and the efficiency suffers. You may need some backup heating means if the temperature is less than 10°F for more than eight hours.

The best bet is to use a gas stove in conjunction with an air-source heat pump. The heating cycle of a heat pump is less efficient than the cooling cycle, and a gas stove (or other type of stove) has the advantage of allowing you to heat locally. This is inherently more efficient than a heat pump that powers your entire home.

✔ Air-source heat pumps can be very noisy — fans make noise with most HVAC systems, but when you add the compressor you get some real rock 'n' roll.

✔ Air-source heat pumps need abundant electricity. If your power goes off, you're not heating or cooling.

Deciding Whether a Ground-Source Heat Pump Is Right for You

The effects of the seasons are nonexistent about six feet underground (I suppose this has some interesting implications for cemeteries). In northern states the ground stays at a consistent temperature of around 50°F, which is a lot warmer than the air aboveground in the winter months. In hotter climates, the ground can be as warm as 70°F year-round.

Ground-source heat pumps take advantage of the constant temperature within the earth to heat and cool your home. But the capability comes at a price: Expect your system to cost $8,000 to $15,000, and a lot more if your ground situation isn't conducive. (By comparison, a conventional forced-air system costs around $7,000 for a typical home.)

Ground-source heat pumps are very expensive because they require extensive piping systems. These systems allow maximum contact with the earth that's used for the heat exchange. You need some land to work with, and you need to be able to dig some complex wells or trenches.

The most common options are open- and closed-loop piping systems and vertical and horizontal piping systems:

✔ **Open- and closed-loop piping systems:** An open-loop system, shown in Figure 19-1, uses existing ground water, while a closed-loop system has its own dedicated fluids and the heat is moved via exchange.

Your contractor can tell you which system is best for your area. In many areas, the ground water is pretty crummy (because of mud, minerals, salt, and other reasons) and therefore unsuitable for open-loop systems.

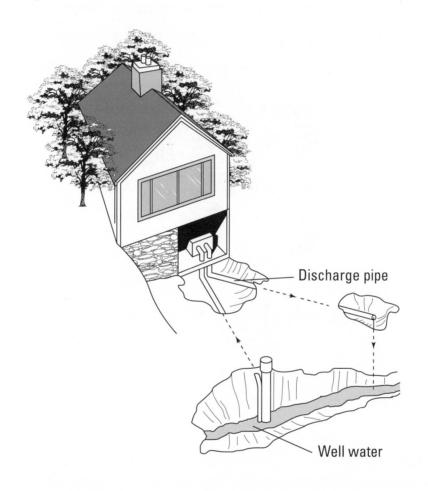

Discharge pipe

Well water

✔ **Vertical and horizontal piping loop systems (shown in Figures 19-2 and 19-3):** Horizontal systems are easier to install but don't work as well as vertical systems, which require deep holes very similar to those used for water wells. Horizontal systems also require a lot more land; if you're pinched for space, you need to go vertical.

In general, the economics of using a ground-source heat pump are not good unless you use a lot of heating and cooling. If you're in a climate that requires a lot of heating in the winter and a lot of cooling in the summer, then the amount you'll save on your power bills will eventually pay back the very high initial cost of installing a system.

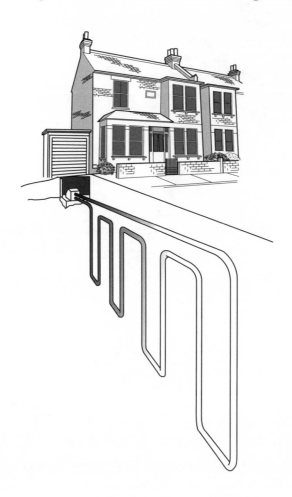

Figure 19-2:
Vertical-loop piping system.

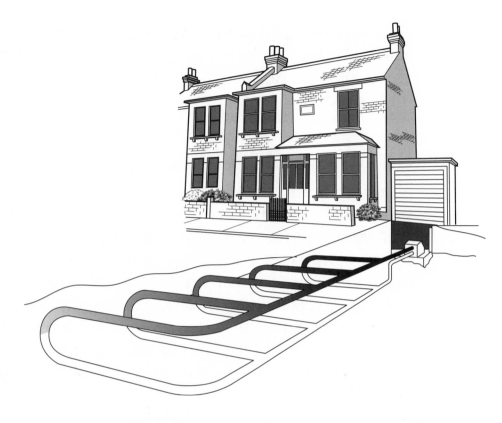

Figure 19-3:
*Horizontal
piping loop
system.*

Choosing a design

The design and installation of the ground-source heat pump are very important. The ground has to be suitable and the system itself has to conform to the availability of heat — you may need a much bigger system if your ground is not at the optimum temperature. Your main criterion for selecting a manufacturer and specific type of system should be performance. Look for the Energy Star seal, in particular. Also look for the Air-Conditioning and Refrigeration Institute (ARI) seal of approval.

Shy away from a new system that has not proven itself over time. It may sound great in theory, but then so did New Coke. There are already too many risks inherent in the proposition to bite into another that you don't have to.

Ground-source heat pumps are better for new homes than existing homes. The systems are so extensive that retrofits are difficult, and you may end up making compromises that you don't want to make.

Hiring a qualified installer

Not very many contractors are capable of installing these systems. So when it comes to hiring a contractor, make sure your contractor knows exactly what he or she is doing. If you can, use a contractor certified by the International Ground Source Heat Pump Association (IGSHPA — www.igshpa.okstate.edu). And get references. Let me state this in stronger terms: If you have a problem with an air-source heat pump, it's right there where you can get to it to work on; it can be worked on or even exchanged if things go really awry. The same can't be said of a ground-source heat pump. With a ground-source system, once it's in the ground, it's nearly impossible to get to. If something goes wrong with your piping and the contractor who installed it has vamoosed, you're in for a world of hurt.

If you don't have some competition in your area, watch out because you may end up paying not just a lot (the normal amount) but a whole heck of a lot. You may also end up with an unreliable source of servicing and maintenance. Many ground-source heat pump customers complain that they can't get prompt service. If you don't have a backup system for heating, this could be very problematic.

If your climate is very cold in the winter and mild in the summer, using a ground-sourced heat pump with a radiant heating system in your floor is a great combination because you can simply heat water directly, and this heated water is then pumped through the floor grid of the radiant system. You can also use that hot water generated by the ground-

468

source heat pump in your domestic supply, thereby killing two birds with one stone (although killing birds is probably not strictly in sync with the green mantra). Radiant heat is very quiet, and in combination with the quiet ground-source heat pump, your home will be virtually silent and without moving air. (**Note:** If you use a forced-air duct system, you need extra equipment — which costs more — to convert the hot water into hot air, as well as to move the hot air through the ducts.) Be aware, however, that using radiant heat in your floor doesn't work very well for cooling in the summer.

Getting a rundown of pros and cons

While ground-source heat pumps offer some advantages, there are also quite a few disadvantages. Keep both in mind as you decide whether investing in one is right for you:

✔ The ground is always available as a heat source. It's even more consistent than air. But — and this is a biggie — ground-source heat pumps require specific ground characteristics, including water content, mineral content, iron content, and so on. A neighbor may have a ground-source heat pump in operation, but that doesn't automatically mean you can do the same.

✔ Ground-source heat pumps are just as good at providing you with domestic hot water as providing you with heating and cooling. Most installations are a combination of functions, and this is smart efficiency planning.

✔ A ground-source heat pump is very expensive upfront, but once the system is installed and running, the operating costs are extremely low. In fact, ground-source heat pumps offer the lowest life-cycle cost of any heating system options, and this includes the expensive upfront investment.

✔ Pollution is extremely low, as is environmental impact. An added bonus is that ground-source systems make hardly any noise at all.

✔ If you want to completely ignore your system (a viable sentiment, so don't deny it if you feel that way), you may want to look elsewhere. A ground-source heat pump needs routine maintenance, and you need to keep an eye on how your system is working because problems are usually subtle rather than catastrophic, at least initially. If you totally ignore your foundering system, it'll get to the catastrophic point, and then you may as well just sign over your firstborn.

If something goes wrong with your piping system after it's in place, finding the problem will be very difficult and very expensive to fix. And at the end of its life, the underground piping system basically needs to be torn out and redone in its entirety. This ain't cheap.

✔ Ground-source heat pumps need electricity to operate. No electricity, no heating or cooling.

Part IV

Considering Efficiency When You Buy, Build, or Sell a Home

The 5th Wave   By Rich Tennant

"Look, once and for all you two have to decide on where you want the house site so we can finish putting in this driveway."

In this part . . .

If you don't live in an energy efficient home already but want to, you have three options: buy one, build one, or convert one. Any of these options requires you to make wise decisions because you can't rely on anybody else to make them for you. This is especially true when many energy efficiency technologies are unproven.

In this part, I show you how to decide between buying an existing energy efficiency home or buying a conventional home to convert into an efficient home. For those of you inclined to build an energy efficient home from the ground up, I show you what to look for in potential home sites and tell you what you need to know about energy efficient design and orientation.

Chapter 20

Looking at Community Solutions to Energy Efficiency

D ifferent types of communities have different attributes that can make becoming energy efficient more or less accessible. With the interest in green living on the upsurge, many cities and states have taken steps to make themselves havens for environmentally conscious citizens. But maybe you don't want to live in a community at all. Perhaps you want to join a commune or you're interested in going *off-grid,* or back to nature. Each situation has its pros and cons, though more cons are associated with going it completely alone.

The best communities are those that dedicate their fundamental philosophies to going green, and more and more of these are cropping up all the time. In this chapter, I review the ways that you can benefit from different types of community structures.

Checking Out the Characteristics of Green Communities

Green cities promote environmental policies geared toward making it easier for their citizens to be kind to Mother Nature. Public transportation is readily available, in order to reduce pollution, for example. In addition, subsidies and tax advantages are easy to get from cooperative city councils, and building departments demand certain energy efficiency features to be built into new homes and retrofits.

So how can you distinguish between truly green cities and posers? The characteristics outlined in the following sections are indicators of municipalities that take energy efficiency and pollution reduction seriously.

 Most newspapers are now available on the Internet. You can quickly check out a community by reviewing the real estate ads in its newspapers. If you find no mention whatsoever of parks, rivers, energy efficiency, and the like, you can conclude that the community in question doesn't place much emphasis on green living. You can also get a good feel for how much homes are going for and how much you'll have to pay each month to live in the community. Find out whether a good number of solar and/or energy-efficient homes exist in the community, and check out the difference in prices between these homes and conventional ones.

Air quality

In an effort to improve air quality, over 250 cities have

committed to conforming to the Climate Protection Agreement, which encourages cities to reduce their greenhouse gas emissions by 7 percent from 1990 levels. (For some cities, the reduction would be a lot more than 7 percent from current levels because the levels have been rising since 1990.) Some of the best cities include the following:

- ✔ **San Francisco, California:** California is one of the best states, with more conservation measures and actual mandated environmental standards than any other state in the country. San Francisco epitomizes how these measures can be implemented in a community.

- ✔ **Portland, Oregon:** Portland is very green. The city has a tremendous number of trees and supports energy-efficiency efforts at the household level. Community spirit is active, which helps a lot.

- ✔ **Austin, Texas:** The capitol city of Texas, Austin supports heightened awareness of green initiatives.

- ✔ **Boulder, Colorado:** Boulder has long been a leader in the green movement, and the city's historically environment-friendly infrastructure gives it a head start over most cities. Public transportation is very easy to access.

- ✔ **Cincinnati, Ohio:** Cincinnati has significant property tax abatements for all LEED certified buildings (Leadership in Energy and Environmental Design, a very important licensing agency for building design). This encourages sustainable development.

Other cities that have outstanding records for encouraging clean air and water and widely available public parks and open areas are Eugene, Oregon; Chicago, Illinois; Minneapolis, Minnesota; and Honolulu, Hawaii.

 A list of the top 10 green cities is put out annually by National Geographic's *The Green Guide,* which affords consumers information about a wide range of green issues. Check out www.thegreenguide.com.

The EPA maintains an Air Quality Index (www.airnow.gov) that assigns relative scores for ozone and particulate matter. Take these scores with a grain of salt, not because they don't matter, but because they don't give the whole story. Some cities with poor scores are endeavoring to improve their air quality with widespread public programs; focusing only on the score and not the direction the city is going can give you an incomplete picture. In fact, cities with poor air scores have more incentive to fund and sponsor improvements, so you may find that they offer more subsidies and support.

My hometown of Sacramento, California, has some of the worst air quality scores in the nation, yet California is the best state (at this writing) for promoting and funding energy-efficiency investments, and Sacramento is home to an impressive number of energy-efficiency and solar companies.

Air quality is more important to some people than it is to others, and it varies over the course of a year. So use your judgment when reading the Air Quality Index numbers.

Public transportation

Commuting is a big factor in finding an energy-efficient community. An automobile driven 12,000 miles can easily emit more carbon dioxide per year than a comfortable home. In general, cities that take green living seriously provide good public transportation, which enables citizens to save a lot of energy on transport costs. Public transportation is also much less polluting than having thousands of cars on the road, so everybody's air quality benefits.

Some cities, like Chicago, make public transportation easy and convenient across the board. You can literally go anywhere in Chicago by way of bus, train, or subway. But cities like Los Angeles have relatively nonexistent public transportation networks (aside from their world-famous cacophony of crowded freeways). You may or may not want to use public transportation, but the fact that it exists in a workable state says a lot about a city's general attitude. Check a city's public transportation by using it — or trying to, as the case may be.

Utility structures

When you check a city's utility structures, take the following into consideration:

- ✔ **Where does the city get its energy?** Is it nuclear? Derived from coal plants? Driven by hydropower?

- ✔ **How much pollution per kWh does the city's utility generate?** The average number of pounds of carbon dioxide per kWh is 2. Anything less is good. Any community that gets power from a nuclear reactor will be way below the average.

- ✔ **How much does power cost?** The fact that power is expensive may be a good thing, even though it costs more. Expensive power means that efficiency investments are more cost-effective, and efficient homes are worth more because they're cheaper to live in. And when power rates are high, the community is likely to be cleaner because less power is used.

✔ **Is a tiered rate structure utilized?** Tiered rate structures allow residents to use as much or as little power as they want, but the rates penalize profligacy.

At any rate, power rates are going to be rising for everybody, and there's no telling how much. It's impossible to get information on how utility rates may move in the future, but you can find out how much rates have risen in the past. If they've been consistently going up 10 percent per year, you can safely bet that they'll keep moving the same way. On the other hand, if they haven't risen at all, a massive increase may be in store.

 Check out a community's utility rates by going online to the Web sites of the various utilities. You can check the online yellow pages under "utilities" to find the names — and sometimes even the Web addresses — of a community's utilities. You can also check out www.sustainlane.us and www.eere.energy.gov/greenpower for lists of cities that promote and subsidize the use of alternative energy.

Recycling programs

Check out a community's recycling programs. Recycling is possible for any household, but it helps if your community has set up a formal regimen whereby recycling is centralized and encouraged. When this is the case, the costs of transportation and processing are borne equally by all citizens through utility bills. Recycling that makes financial sense is a much better bet.

The better communities provide recycling containers that you set out on the street with your regular trash. The best provide different containers for different types of recycled materials — for instance, aluminum and metal, plastics, newspapers, and boxes. Some communities even remove lawn clippings and organic refuse.

Water supply

A city's water supply is critically important for a number of reasons. First, it must be pristine and clean. Otherwise, you'll have to buy drinking water or a filter system. Some cities have grungy-tasting water, and even though it may not be harmful to your health, it still makes you feel grungy.

Second, some cities simply don't have enough water. You can conserve, but if too many hands are reaching into the pie, costs are likely to rise, as is the amount of pressure to reduce usage even more. Consider whether a city is a candidate for severe droughts (most western cities are). Find out what happens when a drought occurs. If the city forbids watering lawns, for instance, you may have an expensive problem on your hands.

Find out whether the community has installed water meters. If so, homeowners are a lot more likely to use less water. In communities where water meters don't exist, the people have absolutely no incentive to use less water.

Unfortunately, politics can enter into the equation. In California's central valley, there is a constant tug of war between farmers and cities over who gets water rights. These water wars affect development, and the cost of homes rises because supply can't meet demand.

Housing designs

Home designs in green communities are ultra-efficient, with solar exposures and strategically planted deciduous trees. Homes feature thick insulation, double-pane windows, window coverings, automatic awnings for hot summer days, solar attic vent systems to purge hot air from attic spaces, whole-house fans, and solar light tubes in all kitchens. Skylights are used as much as possible, along with passive solar heating and cooling arrangements.

Some communities specifically demand sustainable housing designs. The U.S. Green Building Council (USGBD) runs a program called Leadership in Energy and Environmental Design (LEED) that sets criteria for what constitutes green building. These criteria include things like

- Insulation properties in the walls and ceilings.

- The design and placement of windows in a building (called *fenestration*), which affects not only the insulation properties but also the availability of solar lighting and heating.

- The type and operation of any HVAC systems.

- Use of water resources and on-site means for conserving water.

- Installation of any solar energy systems.

Visit www.energystar.gov (the ubiquitous Energy Star!) for a list of builders familiar with the LEED tenets.

Miscellaneous factors

Check out a city's parks by visiting them. Are they well maintained, indicating a laudable degree of civic pride? Or are they crime-ridden and dirty? Parks may very well be a metaphor for a city's civic stance.

In Chapter 4, I address government incentives for energy-efficiency investments, which include rebates, subsidies, and tax deductions. Check state and local government's Web sites for information regarding energy-efficiency is-

This old house

One of the best ways to practice efficiency is to buy an old home and refurbish it. This takes far fewer resources than building a new home from scratch, and it saves a lot of infrastructure costs as well. Many cities are experiencing a renaissance in their older neighborhoods as younger families move into dilapidated homes and invest both time and money in refurbishing. Older architecture seems to offer a lot more character and charm than the newer, mass-produced style of buildings. Nothing is as cool as an old brick wall in your living room.

The problem with a lot of older homes is that they have poor insulation (most have single-pane glass windows) and failing plumbing and electrical systems. You may need to completely gut an old home in order to make it more energy-efficient. On the other hand, most older homes have open fireplaces, and you can install a newer, energy-efficient insert cheaply and easily. See *Green Building & Remodeling For Dummies* by Eric Corey Freed (Wiley) for more details.

sues. Most municipalities at least pay lip service to environmental issues, and some of them actually mean what they say.

Roughing It by Going Off-Grid

Being *off-grid* means not being connected to a public utility for your electrical power. This also usually means that you're not connected to gas, water, and sewer utilities. If you're thinking about going off-grid, keep these things in mind:

✔ **The cost of bringing utility power in is prohibitive.** If you're off the beaten path, you can usually get the utility company to bring power in, but you have to pay for the long line lengths and poles, trenches, and so on. This can sometimes cost over $100,000.

✔ **You don't have any utility power available, period.** Going off-grid seems to be a romantic notion, but it's not necessarily the most efficient

482

way to go. If you don't get much sunshine or have enough wind or water to make alternative energy sources viable, being efficient and pollution-wise off-grid is very difficult.

Understanding your off-grid options

You have choices when you go off-grid. If you want to rough it, you can use propane. It works well for heating, cooking, and refrigeration. Wood stoves are popular for remote houses and cabins because a supply of firewood is usually readily available. But at some point you're going to want to plug in your television, and then your choices are more limited.

Gasoline- or natural gas-powered generators

Gasoline- or natural gas-powered generators are inexpensive and can put out a lot of power, when needed. But they're noisy, cumbersome, and smelly, and they pollute quite a bit. If you're out in the middle of nowhere, a gas generator is inherently contradictory to the peaceful coexistence you have chosen.

Off-grid solar power systems

Off-grid solar power systems (including hydropower, wind power, and PV systems) provide electrical power, but it's relatively expensive. Using PV electrical generating systems connected to the grid (intertie) enables you to sell your excess generating capacity back to the utility and therefore use 100 percent of your system's productive capacity (Chapter 16 has the details). Conversely, when you install an off-grid solar PV system, you don't get anywhere near 100 percent utilization, plus you need batteries, charge controllers, and more. All this extra equipment is expensive

483

and maintenance intensive.

From a pollution standpoint, using an intertie PV system does the world more good because more usable power is generated. Each kWh of energy you generate with an intertie system offsets that much energy from the grid — it's a one-to-one relationship. This is not true of an off-grid system. A lot of the potential energy generation is wasted because it's not used (if you're on vacation, generating capacity is completely wasted). And batteries are inefficient, so you waste energy in that regard as well.

 Stand-alone systems are generally subject to rebates and subsidies, just like intertie PV systems and hot water systems. See Chapter 4 for details on how to research this subject.

Realizing the ramifications of going off-grid

Going off-grid takes commitment and knowledge. You need to understand what you're doing with an off-grid system; you can't just plug and play. So before you sign on, give careful consideration to the following facts:

- **Going off-grid takes work.** It means you have to take care of batteries, monitor system performance, and adjust your habits on a daily basis, depending on how much power your system is generating.

- **Going off-grid is expensive.** In general, off-grid PV systems cost at least twice as much per kWh as intertie systems and take ten times more attention on your part.

- **You have to deal with the spent batteries.** No big deal, you think? Think again. Batteries are disposable waste nightmares because they're so full of nasty chemicals. Carbon dioxide is an important pollution culprit these days, but it's not the only one. Ground water pollution is a growing problem. Waste management is expensive and increases everybody's tax burden. If you aren't very savvy with your batteries, their lifetimes can be atrocious. So the pollution problem is increased not only by the mere use of batteries, but even more so by ignorant use of batteries.

✔ **Conservation measures are required with off-grid systems.** Although conservation is integral to the beginning of any efficient lifestyle, it's even more important with off-grid systems because the economics dictate it. The best way to start is by building an energy-conserving house, with maximization of solar potential (see Chapter 21). Efficient appliances and personal habits are also a must.

✔ **Most banks will not touch an off-grid home.** You may not be able to get a first mortgage, and second mortgages are even more prohibitive. If you ever want to sell your house, being off-grid will drive away 99 percent of potential buyers, and the higher cost of a mortgage, if one is even available, will be reflected in a lower selling price. If you have a choice, being off-grid is not an investment at all — it's a discretionary luxury.

Chapter 21

Building an Energy-Efficient Home from the Ground Up

· ·

In This Chapter

▶ Finding the right lot for your energy-efficient home
▶ Drumming up your new home's design
▶ Getting into the specifics of materials
▶ Biting the bullet and getting started

· ·

Ⅰf you can do it, starting from scratch is the best possible way to go with an energy-efficient home. You have the world at your fingertips, and you can design your new home to your heart's content. You can buy energy-efficient appliances and light fixtures, and you can install an energy-efficient HVAC system, including geothermal or solar power.

If you think you can't afford it, keep in mind that building an energy-efficient home costs no more than building a conventional home. Add the fact that your energy bills will be dramatically lower, and a "green" home can actually cost less on a monthly cash-flow basis.

But building from scratch is also a demanding process, full of unanticipated surprises — some good, some bad. (To get an idea of the difficulties as well as the rewards, read *Building Your Own Home For Dummies,* by Kevin Daum, Janice Brewster and Peter Economy [Wiley].) This chapter gives you the basic information about building an energy-efficient home from the ground up so that you know what to look for, what to think about, and what to expect.

Picking a Spot for Your New Home

Perhaps the most fun part of building your own home is choosing a building lot. You probably already know the region or city you're going to be building in. You may even have narrowed it down to a particular neighborhood. As you scope out possible home sites for your energy-efficient home, remember that location means more than just a nice neighborhood. All the things you'd consider if you were building a traditional home still apply — neighborhood, landscaping, size of lot, and so on — but you need to be aware of a few other factors, too, as the following sections explain.

Evaluating local building codes and regulations

As you consider various locations for building an energy-efficient home, you need to find out whether the local building codes support such a project in the first place. Unfortunately, some communities are behind the times and don't have laws and codes that are accommodating. Here's how to get the information you need.

Contacting the local building department

Contact the local building department at the county headquarters and discuss your plans with a representative to find out exactly where this community stands. Some go out of their way to be supportive and charge smaller fees for energy-efficient homes; some can supply you with the names of local builders that can help you out; and some even subsidize energy-efficient homes.

While you're at it, get a feel for how onerous and expensive the building process is going to be:

- Ask whether energy-efficient homes have been built in your area and in your particular neighborhood.

- Ask how much fees and permits will cost — you may be shocked to hear the answer. Some communities want to restrict growth, and one of the ways they do this is by charging astronomical fees for new homes. If this is the case, you may want to consider another community or consider buying an existing home and converting it into an energy-efficient home.

Contacting the local homeowners' association

Contact the local homeowners' association or read through its charter. Many local association bylaws contain bans against solar panels because they're ugly. Even though these restrictions are probably illegal, you may want to abide by rules against having solar panels in public view by orienting your house so that the panels face south but are not visible from the street. This requires the front of your home to face north.

I know of one installation where the homeowners decided to put the solar panels off to the side of their house so that they wouldn't be able to see them, but their neighbors could. A neighbor sued and was joined by the homeowners' association on the general grounds of violating the "visual appearance" clause. The association won because the judge found that the homeowner himself was declaring the panels visual blights by the mere fact that he didn't want to look at them. Everybody lost a lot of money — even the winners — and that's the bottom line. When it comes to rules, work within them, and don't be stubborn.

Talking to experienced local contractors and other homeowners

Find local contractors with experience building energy-efficient homes. They'll be able to answer a lot of your questions very accurately and may be able to show you energy-efficient homes that they've built, giving you good ideas for your own home. You may also be able to talk to the homeowners. Real-life experience is ten times better than anybody's theory.

Measuring the energy-efficiency potential of a lot

A key characteristic of energy-efficient homes is that they use solar power (which also encompasses water power, wind power, breezes, landscaping, thermal mass, and so on) as much as possible, particularly the passive components like lighting and ventilation. You have to be a lot fussier about your lot when you build a solar home, not only because you may use domestic hot water supplements (refer to Chapter 16), but also because the solar philosophy relies heavily on *natural* lighting and heating capacities. (See my book *Solar Power Your Home For Dummies*, published by Wiley, for more details.)

With solar power, orientation becomes a critical factor. You want to choose a building site that lets you orient your house with a good southern exposure for PV panels and water heating collectors, as well as for windows, sunrooms, and living spaces. On some lots, this is very difficult because of the street orientation and the location of trees and other shade-makers.

As you scope out building sites, ask yourself the questions posed in the following sections. The answers let you get to the heart of just how appropriate a particular lot is for your energy-efficient building plans.

 Keep notes on how each possible building site stacks up. For each site you evaluate, jot down the answers to the questions outlined in the following sections. If you keep your comparative analyses of the various location options consistent, you'll have an easy reference to help you make your final decision.

What are your solar exposures?

Solar exposure is key to energy-efficient construction. What latitude are you in? What is the sun's path over the course of a year at that latitude?

For each site, stand in the middle of the lot and plot the sun's course. (You may have to do some guesswork about what the situation will be from a rooftop or a porch that hasn't been built yet.) Different spots on a lot have different solar exposures and different shading issues. Look for deciduous trees and try to envision your house with those trees on the southern exposure, but not shading solar collectors on the roof. Try to avoid cutting down trees. Although you can plant trees, they won't rival natural, healthy, indigenous trees for a long time.

What are the prevailing winds like?

Prevailing winds are critical (see Chapter 13 for ventilation and cooling issues). Natural breezes are absolutely free and can make a major difference in the comfort of a home. Look for locations where breezes are magnified in the summer by hills and terrain. In the winter, you want natural brush and landscaping to diminish cold winds from the north.

What's the water situation?

Water rights and drainage are important. Try to find out whether any water problems exist; check with the county building department or the local water utility. The last thing you need is to move into your home and discover that the water supply is foundering. If city water isn't available, do you need a well? If your neighbors have wells, are they producing? A well can be good or bad: You won't have a water bill, but you'll need expensive equipment, and you may need to filter the water.

You also need to determine the natural drainage of the property. Some locations for a home simply won't work unless you radically alter the property's contour (which goes against the green mantra). How much water will your property require? Are you going to landscape? How much water will that require, and will it affect drainage?

 Pay attention to the landscaping of the neighbors. If you scrimp on water-devouring landscaping, your neighbors may frown upon your maverick ways. Better to know now than to find out too late.

What are the future plans for the area?

Don't forget to determine what may happen in the future. Is a shopping mall planned next door five years hence? How about a freeway? Or an airport? To find out about these kinds of things, ask your realtor and your county building department. For that matter, hang around the local coffee shop and see what's what. Make friends with the waitress by giving a nice big tip. Next time you go in, ask for some local gossip. It could save you a lot of money and aggravation in the long run.

Designing Your Home

When most people build their own homes, they follow these two steps: First, they look through books of home designs and find one they like. Second, they go out and find a lot. When you build an energy-efficient home, you reverse these two steps, finding a lot first and then designing your house. Why? Because each lot will support a different style house, with a layout that maximizes views, breezes, landscaping, and so on. So your house design should be a function of the lot. Don't commit to a particular house design and then insist on finding a lot that will bear it out.

Design your home on a twelve-month basis. Consider all the different seasons.

Size matters: The littler, the better

The smaller the home, the better the potential for energy efficiency. A smaller house uses less building materials, is cheaper to maintain, requires less HVAC capacity, and uses less energy.

When you build an efficient house, keep it small and appoint it well. If you think bigger is always better, remember that large houses can seem small, and small houses can seem large. The key is the design. You can make a small

492

house every bit as spacious as a large house by doing the following:

- ✔ Avoid long, wide hallways.

- ✔ Combine utility functions like laundry and storage.

- ✔ Put in less bathroom space (make bathrooms tall rather than wide for a spacious effect).

- ✔ Combine the living room and family room into one central great room.

- ✔ Add a nice sunroom off the living area.

- ✔ Place windows where you can get good, unimpeded views to the outdoors.

Orienting the house on the lot

When it comes to plotting out where and how your house will sit on the lot, keep these points in mind:

- ✔ **Make sure the long axis of the house runs east to west.** This creates the greatest southern exposure. The front of the house can face either south or north. Up to 20 degrees off true south works well enough.

- ✔ **Ensure that the roof has maximum sun exposure.** Roof exposure is critical for locating solar collectors, although you can plan on ground mounting if you have enough room. Mounting on the roof is usually best because it gives you better immunity from shadows. Plus, the panels can be hidden more easily by means of clever design. Ground mounting requires *wire runs* (trenches dug where long lengths of thick gauge wire will be buried — an expensive component), and hiding the panels usually entails shading issues, making the process more difficult. You do not need to locate all your solar panels on one expanse of roof, although visually this is usually more tenable.

✔ **Deciduous trees work well on the western and southern exposures.** A house often feels much nicer in the morning with direct sunshine, so try to keep eastern shading to a minimum. Eastern kitchens are more congenial because you avoid hot afternoon exposures, while ensuring a bright morning wake-up call. A southeastern breakfast nook is ideal.

✔ **Hillsides work very well for providing insulation via earth berms and half basements.** Hillsides facing south are the best bet because you can get two floors' worth of good sun exposure while enjoying northern insulation.

Figuring out a floor plan

The floor plan of a home can impact its energy-efficiency capabilities. Whether you build a large or a small house, a few general design principles apply:

✔ **Go with a central design.** Central designs, in which the home is oriented around a central nucleus, work much better than houses with wings, which are difficult to heat and cool and require more maintenance.

✔ **Design your house with heat movement in mind.** Open airways, for example, make a house seem more spacious, as well as ensuring natural air movement. Avoid long, meandering hallways and rooms with odd angles and high, unventilated ceilings. Basically, you want to exploit the chimney and greenhouse effects, and optimize the movement of natural breezes by venting appropriately (all of which are explained in detail in Chapter 13).

✔ **Place rooms in such a way as to maximize the positives and camouflage the negatives.** For example, a western exposure is typically hot and uncomfortable in the late afternoons and evenings, so putting the garage on that side of the house creates a buffer. Or perhaps the view from one side of the house is unattractive, in which case the garage should go there. You can also achieve a buffer from cold winter winds by placing the garage on the windward side of the house. Likewise, family rooms generally work best on a southern exposure because that's where your family is likely to spend the most time and get the most benefit from solar potential. Use screened-in porches to shade windows on the east and west sides of the house.

 Consider time of day versus room usage in your layout. Are you in a home office all day? Do you want to wake up in the sunshine? A kitchen on the eastern front is nice. A master bedroom on the northern front stays cooler, quieter, and darker.

✔ **Arrange your windows strategically.** Sunrooms and windows are always best on the south side, where they can take advantage of the sun exposure. By contrast, the light on the northern side of the structure is cold and dull; windows on that side don't allow any heat from the sun in but do let heat escape out. So put closets, bathrooms, laundry rooms, and other such rooms, which can tolerate poor lighting and smaller windows, on the

495

north side. By reducing windows on the northern exposure, you can increase insulation.

✔ **Use overhangs deliberately.** Energy-efficient houses always have well-designed overhangs over the windows, porches, and doorways, particularly in the family room.

Incorporating energy-efficient technology

When you build a home from the ground up, you have the perfect opportunity to incorporate not only building designs that increase your energy efficiency, but you can also include energy efficient appliances and other add-ons:

✔ **Non-electrical lighting:** Use solar tubes, reflectors, orientations of windows to maximize sunlight entry, and so on. *Celestories* (windows located high up in a room, generally facing southward) can provide both heating and lighting over the course of the year.

✔ **PV panels and solar water heaters:** Go to Chapter 16 for details on solar panels and Chapter 11 for info on solar water heaters.

✔ **A gas, wood, or other type of stove:** Put it in the family room where you can use it to provide the vast majority of your heating needs (particularly if your home is centrally designed). Most of the time you don't need to heat your entire house. In the same vein, portable room heaters and air conditioners are much cheaper to operate than a whole-house HVAC system.

✔ **Features with more thermal mass:** The more thermal mass, the more consistent the temperatures in the house. Slab floors are best for this reason.

Going beyond conventional styles

You can use nontraditional home construction methods. Check out *Green Building & Remodeling For Dummies* by Eric Corey Freed (Wiley) for a range of home building styles that can offer far greater energy efficiency than conventional styles. Here are some of the options you may want to consider:

- **Straw bales:** Just like it sounds, a house made of straw bales (like that of the three little pigs, although I'm not trying to imply anything here). Features excellent insulation properties and inexpensive construction. You'll probably have a tough time finding a contractor who knows the ins and outs.

- **Adobe:** Sun-dried bricks; inexpensive, low energy to make.

- **Rammed earth:** A technique that uses earth, or dirt, to create incredible insulation levels. You will probably have a tough time finding a contractor; look on the Internet.

- **Cob:** A method by which you can create odd shapes and contours with natural elements. Good insulation, inexpensive, kind of zany.

- **Pneumatically impacted stabilized earth:** A method that uses good old Mother Earth for insulation and stability.

- **Structural insulated panels:** Prefab panels made of Styrofoam sandwiched between plywood. You can build a very solid, well-insulated home from these panels at low cost. Look to see a lot more of these in the future because they take less *invested energy,* which is the amount of energy consumed in the manufacturing process.

- **Insulated concrete forms:** Thick walls with incredible insulation levels. The home stays very comfortable in both hot and cold weather, and the utility bills are low. But the cost of construction is high because the method is so new.

Solar rooms with concrete floors and masonry walls work well. Big stone fireplaces with winter exposures to sunlight also work well in conjunction with overhangs.

Choosing Your Materials

After you define the general design of your house, it's time to specify particular materials and equipment. When choosing equipment, always pay attention to the lifetime of the product, not just the initial cost and energy consumption. Having to replace the equipment in a few years is hardly efficient.

Construction materials

In this book, the context of energy efficiency is geared predominantly toward the consumption end of things — in other words, the energy it takes to make your home work. But energy is also required in the building process and in the manufacture of the building materials that go into your home. Consider the following ways of minimizing your energy usage:

- ✔ **Use recycled building materials whenever possible.** Many, especially recycled wood products, are available.

- ✔ **Use products manufactured near your construction site.** Doing so minimizes transportation costs.

- ✔ **Don't use solid woods.** Laminates and veneers save rain forests and look like solid woods. The synthetics are made of recycled plastic containers (like milk containers) and last much longer than real

Making your own lumber

Just like your distant forebears, you can cut down your own trees and make your own lumber. Fortunately, the process has drastically improved since the Paul Bunyan axe technique. Now you can buy special rack and rail systems that let you fell a tree, set up your equipment right there on the ground next to the tree, and cut precise depths and widths of lumber. You need to dry the wood properly in a kiln, but that's not difficult.

A neighbor of mine cut some oaks down and hand-carved them with a chain saw. He used them to construct the big frame members for a barn. Talk about character! He built not only a functional barn but also a lasting legacy.

An alternative is to hire somebody to turn your trees into lumber at a cost that's competitive with commodity lumber. If you have a number of trees on your lot that you need to fell, this may be a very cool option. Imagine living in your home knowing that the lumber came from that very spot. If you've got an old maple or oak tree that needs to come down anyway, you can have it turned into lumber and make some really classy furniture out of it.

wood. Plus, you don't need to paint them with nasty chemicals, and they won't warp or chip.

✔ **Use indigenous materials whenever possible.** This includes using rocks from your own property for landscaping purposes, if feasible.

✔ **Use roofing shingles that are reflective and provide good insulation.** Unless, of course, you're looking for a hot attic in the winter more than cooling in the summer. In either case, consider how you're going to vent your attic in both the summer and winter. Radiant barriers in the attic space, for example, are much easier to put up during a home's construction than after the fact. And the material is relatively inexpensive considering the potential benefit. (For details on these barriers and other ways to insulate your attic, head to Chapter 7.)

✔ **Avoid aluminum framed windows, which conduct too much heat, and, at the very least, specify double-pane windows.** You can get triple-pane windows, as well as special windows with gas insulation between the panes, but the cost goes up markedly.

The aesthetic quality of your windows determines the value of your house to a large degree. Spend some extra money for nice-looking frames, grids, and special functional features. At the very least, you want windows that are easy to operate because you'll be opening and closing them a lot.

Energy-efficient systems and appliances

Obviously, an energy-efficient home is tricked out with energy-efficient appliances and systems. Following are the highlights of interior appointments of an energy-efficient home. You can find out more about these by going to the respective chapters within this book:

✔ **Window blinds, awnings, and sunscreens:** These provide visual appeal while providing insulation and preventing sunshine when you don't want it. After all you've been through, don't skimp here because these have a huge impact on how efficient your home is. They can literally make or break the ambience of a house. See Chapter 12 for the lowdown.

✔ **Flooring:** Tiles have more thermal mass than wood, which means they hold much more heat energy (if left in the sun, they will stay warm long after the sunlight is gone). They also cost less, last longer, and require less maintenance. Both tile and wood are infinitely better than carpeting for a variety of reasons, as explained in Chapter 6.

✔ **Insulation:** A well-insulated house is a more energy-efficient house. That's why your insulation should be as thick as you can afford.

✔ **Heating and cooling:** To make your HVAC as efficient as possible, use the smallest HVAC system you can and, if necessary, supplement or replace it with energy-efficient alternatives. Chapter 8 discusses ways to maximize an existing HVAC system; Part III has a whole host of ways to supplement it.

✔ **Ventilation options:** How well air moves through a house has a lot to do with how comfortable that home is. Think about installing ceiling fans, an attic vent fan controlled by a thermostat switch, and/or a whole-house fan. You can find information on all of these in Chapter 13.

✔ **Appliances:** If you're building a home, chances are you're buying heating and cooling equipment, lighting, and at least some new appliances. Always opt for the most energy-efficient models you can afford. See Chapter 11 for more info.

✔ **Plumbing:** Use as few sinks as possible, and keep the piping runs as short as you can. (Head to Chapter 10 for ways to decrease your water consumption.)

- ✔ **Swimming pool pump:** If you're building a swimming pool, consider a solar-powered pump. It's expensive upfront, but you'll never have to pay a cent for pump power. A solar pump can provide even greater efficiency if your house is in a region with time of use (TOU) metering. See Chapter 16 for the lowdown on solar systems for swimming pools.

A word about installing PV systems

When you decide to use a PV system, you have to determine whether to install it during construction or after.

Your initial thought may be to install it during construction, but that may not be the smartest move. Why? You can't know how much energy your house requires until you've lived in it for a year or so because your energy consumption will depend on your personal habits and how the house interacts with weather patterns.

- ✔ **Installing it during construction:** If you install a PV system during construction, you run the risk of getting more power than you use. If your system is intertie (connected to the grid, which the vast majority of systems are), which it definitely should be if you have the option, you won't get anything back from the utility if you provide them more power than you use (see Chapter 16 for more details on intertie systems). In other words, you'll be spending more than you need to and getting no benefits for the additional expense.

- ✔ **Installing it later:** The problem with waiting is that it prevents you from financing the PV system as part of your new house. You may be able to get an equity

502

loan, but the terms won't be as favorable as if you simply wrap the PV financing into the original home loan.

Your best bet is to wait a year or so before you install your PV system. Design the layout so that you can install your system easily when it's time: Leave room near the fuse box for an inverter and switches. Make the roof pitch and construction optimum for PV panels.

 If you decide to install the system during construction, estimate your energy needs and install a system that's *smaller* than you think you will ultimately need. You can buy an oversized inverter (the part that changes the raw electrical signals from the panels on your roof into useable household power) so that, after a year or two when you know more precisely how much energy you need, you can simply put in a few more solar panels. (Chapter 16 has more details on PV systems.)

Pounding Nails: What to Know When Construction Begins

So construction is set to begin. You'll be happy to know that building an energy-efficient house isn't much different from building a conventional one. You don't need a contractor who has built energy-efficient homes before. The passive aspects of good energy-efficient design are part of the architectural plans, so any contractor should be able to do the job properly. The construction process is the same, too. Installing energy-efficient equipment isn't any different from installing other equipment. Any competent contractor can do it.

As you watch your home grow from the ground up, keep

these general points in mind:

- ✔ **Be patient.** Building a home is a major project, probably the biggest one you'll ever undertake. Expect the whole project to take at least a couple years.

  Don't count on your home being completed by a certain date because it probably won't be. It will take on a life of its own, just like your kids. You think you can program them the way you want, but they outgrow your controls and become their own beings.

- ✔ **Be prepared to compromise.** Insisting on perfection is impractical and unnecessary. You can make design adjustments to accommodate inevitable compromises.

- ✔ **Hire a good general contractor.** In most states you can be your own general contractor without a license, but going this route isn't a good idea, even if you know what you're doing and have the time and organizational skills to pull it off. (Many people who have decided to go it alone have regretted it simply because the project takes so much time and energy.)

  Building homes is the livelihood of contractors and, as a result, they're very conservative about committing to big jobs. They have all, unfortunately, seen potential jobs go away at the drop of a hat, and they've been left in a lurch. So never treat your new home project casually. Your decisions can have major consequences for others, and you have a responsibility to proceed with respect for the magnitude of how you are influencing other people's lives.

Chapter 22

Buying and Selling an Energy-Efficient Home

The bulk of this book is dedicated to defining energy-efficiency projects you can do in or around your home. But perhaps you're interested in moving into an existing efficient home where everything has already been done for you. Or perhaps you want to move into a conventional home suitable for energy-efficiency updates that you plan on either installing yourself or contracting out for. Maybe you're looking to sell your energy-efficient home.

Whether buying or selling, your goal is always to get the best deal you can. With conventional homes, maneuvering for the best deal is a well-defined game played by the buyer, the seller, and both agents. But things gets a little trickier with an energy-efficient home because the market is relatively untested, and things are changing fast. You need to understand how energy-efficiency technology, like solar technology, the price of homes in your area and how different stoves and heating and cooling systems play with the market in general. If you're selling an energy-efficient home, your tasks include educating potential sellers. Finally, because energy-efficient homes generally cost more than conventional homes, you need to understand how to put a number on this difference. In this chapter, I give you all the information you need.

Buying an Existing Efficient Home

If you want an energy-efficient home, you can build your own (Chapter 21 explains how), but that's a long, arduous task. An easier and generally less time-consuming solution is to buy an existing efficient home.

Unfortunately, not a lot of energy-efficient homes are out there — at least not today. This situation will change quite a bit in the coming years, but for now, if you want an efficient home, you're going to have to look hard for one, and you may be disappointed with what you find. Restricting yourself to buying an existing efficient home will probably mean making some big compromises on the type and style of home you want.

When looking for existing energy-efficient homes, heed the maxim "Let the buyer beware." If you find an energy-efficient home that you're interested in, you need to make sure the equipment is sound and does what it's supposed to do. The following sections tell you how to evaluate an energy-efficient home.

If you live in an area where solar communities are springing up, count your lucky stars and head there to take a look. These communities are designed for energy efficiency and environmental friendliness. All the homes, designed by professionals who know how to make solar systems work to their fullest potential, feature both passive and active solar power. Energy-efficient equipment like HVAC, water heating, and so on is standard fare. In addition, most of these communities include special recycling centers to ensure minimal environmental impact.

In most states, real estate law clearly states that if a piece of equipment is attached to a house, it's part of the house. Doors are part of a house, whereas refrigerators are not. In theory, all solar equipment is part of the house, but this is often misunderstood, particularly with regard to swimming pool systems, which sometimes end up going with the seller to his new house. If you buy a home with energy-efficient equipment already installed, make sure to get in writing exactly what equipment is staying or going. Otherwise, you may be in for a nasty surprise on moving day.

Evaluating just how energy efficient a home is (or isn't)

In addition to the usual pest, roof, and other inspections normally done for a real estate transaction, you need to have energy audits and solar potential inspections if you're thinking about buying an already existing energy-efficient home. Specifically, you need to evaluate how energy-efficient the home is, identify the kind of energy-efficiency (especially solar) equipment it has, and determine the condition of that equipment.

Energy-efficiency equipment increases the maintenance responsibility of any house. You need to know what you're doing and how to use the equipment, even if it's all in perfect working order. Unfortunately, because energy-efficiency concepts are relatively new, most realtors and market professionals don't thoroughly understand the ins and outs. So it's up to you to arm yourself with the information you need to understand exactly what you're getting into.

Taking a quick look

A relatively quick look-see can tell you quite a bit about how effective the energy-efficiency features of a home are:

- **Look at the home's orientation and landscaping.** Is it situated in such a way as to maximize the solar exposure? Are deciduous trees in the right spots? Refer to Chapter 21 for information on the importance of orientation and landscaping.

- **Check out the home's electrical, HVAC, and water heating systems.** What type of HVAC does it have and how old is it? (If it's old, over fifteen years, you'll probably have to replace it.)

- **Check the major appliances.** A central vacuum (in which the vacuum is located in the garage and special PVC pipes run through the house so that all you have to do is plug in the wand to vacuum wherever you are in the house) is a plus.

- **Evaluate the home's layout.** Some designs are more conducive to energy efficiency than others (refer to Chapter 21 for details).

- **Pay attention to the windows.** Check for overhangs and awnings over windows. Are the blinds strictly decorative, or do they also have functionality?

✔ **Check for thermal masses.** Thermal masses are things like concrete floors and walls, tile floors — any mass that holds a lot of heat. Are they arranged so that they catch sunlight during the day, which results in better heating efficiency at night? Are they being used effectively both inside and outside the house?

In addition to your quick look-through, you also may want to conduct an energy-efficiency audit — not just for the energy-efficient equipment, but for the entire house. (Chapter 3 gives more details on energy audits.) You can have this done as part of the usual due diligence, or you may want to pay for it upfront before you start getting serious about the house.

Perusing the power bills

Ask to see the power bills for the past year. If the seller doesn't have them, he can easily get them from the utility company. If you can't get any power bills, something is wrong. The vast majority of efficient home owners are proud to show off their power bills.

 If, in examining the bills, you notice that some monthly bills are unusually high, it could mean that the efficiency equipment was broken at that time. Ask why the bill blipped, and take warning if the answer doesn't jibe with the seller's claims of how often the equipment went down.

Looking closely at the efficiency equipment

Look for energy-efficient technology. For example, are solar tubes showing on the roof? Skylights? Solar panels? Do they look new or old? Once you know the type of equipment, get the following information:

- ✔ **Where the equipment was purchased and who installed it:** Are these companies still in business, and if not, why not? If it's a do-it-yourself job, have it checked out by a pro, or, if you're a do-it-yourselfer and know what to look for, check it yourself.

- ✔ **Whether local building department permits were obtained for the equipment:** If not, why not? A permit implies that a building inspection was performed, which ensures that the work was done to code. Without a permit, the work may be substandard, although not necessarily. The point is, the risk becomes yours. You may want to insist on the seller getting the necessary permits, although they're going to balk because it's a big hassle.

- ✔ **Warranty information and records regarding system performance and maintenance:** How much time is left on the warranty? Ask whether the warranty is transferable (this is important). Have any warranty repairs been done? If so, pay attention to what went wrong. If several warranty repairs have been done, beware — especially if the warranty is about to expire.

- ✔ **Manuals:** You want the original manuals that came with the equipment. You may be able to get these on the Internet, but a conscientious owner (the kind you want) should have them. Read through the manuals, and you'll understand the equipment and what it's going to need by way of maintenance and repair.

- ✔ **System use vs. system capacity:** Determine how

much equipment is being used versus its maximum capacity. If there's a solar water heater, how much of its capacity is being used to offset the current power bill? If the solar water heater is capable of outputting twice as much energy as it currently is, is this important to you? If your family is bigger, you'll use more hot water, and you'll probably use more energy in general. This may or may not be reflected in higher energy bills.

Personal habits enter into these calculations, so temper what you find with a consideration of how the seller's energy usage may differ from your own.

You can easily check a PV system by looking at the power output on a sunny day near solar noon. First, check the panels and see how far off the optimum angle they are. Then simply read the digital meter on the face of the inverter. This will be the maximum amount of power you can expect to get out of the system.

Anticipating changes and repairs

Before you reject or accept an existing energy-efficient home, you need to determine what kinds of changes you'd want to make to improve the home's energy efficiency and what kinds of repairs may be just around the corner. Then you can decide whether these tasks are ones you're willing to take on. Some questions to ask include:

- **Can the systems be expanded?** For instance, is the inverter larger than its current output power? If so, PV panels can be added. A hot water system can usually be expanded by adding more collectors.

- **Could you get more out of the equipment by making a few changes?** Are there trees shading the collectors that you could cut down to get more productivity? Are the collectors dirty and unkept? Are vicious little creatures like raccoons nested somewhere, jealously guarding their domicile?

✔ **Does the roof need to be replaced?** You'll get a roof inspection as a matter of routine. If the roof needs to be replaced and it contains solar equipment, you'll have to pay to get the equipment dismantled first, and then reassembled after the new roof is in place. Solar power won't be produced during this period, either.

✔ **If there's a net metering agreement, does it carry over?** What is the rate structure going to be? If it's not going to be the same as the one in place the last few years, the utility bills that you get are going to be different. Can you change the rate structure if you want?

Determining the value of an existing efficient home

If you like the home and everything seems to be on the up and up, you're ready to make an offer. An energy-efficient home costs more than a comparable conventional home, most of the time. To determine what's reasonable, you need to know what a comparable conventional home would cost and then add the value associated with the energy-efficiency equipment.

You should be able to get an accurate estimate on how much a conventional home is worth from your realtor. The tricky part is determining the value of the efficiency equipment. Why? Because to do so, you really have to determine two values: the value to you (what you're willing to offer for the house) and what a bank will value the property at. Some banks are completely ignorant of energy efficiency and may not add any value at all for efficiency equipment, while others understand its value (see Chapter 4 for more on financial issues).

Here are some things to do and consider as you try to determine the value of an energy-efficient home:

✔ **Try to get what realtors call "comps" — the recent sales prices of comparable homes in the same local area.** Gauging a home's value this way may not be completely accurate, but it's the best place to start. At the very least, you'll find out how buyers are operating. If no value seems to be placed on energy-efficiency equipment, you're in luck as a buyer (though this is bad when you're selling).

✔ **Figure out how much it would cost to have a contractor come in and install all the energy-efficiency equipment that is already in place.** Be sure to include not only the equipment but the installation labor and any other costs as well. A solar home's equipment should never be worth more than this amount, although buzz can sometimes send values higher. Plus, do-it-yourself projects are more difficult and a lot of people simply don't want to do them, so they'll pay more for equipment that's already in place.

✔ **Compare energy bills for the efficient home versus a comparable conventional home.** How much less are the energy bills? View this as a monthly payment on a second mortgage, and then determine the loan balance that would result in that monthly payment. Realize that you can buy more house when you don't have a monthly utility bill.

The key to an energy-efficient home is having more money each month to do things other than pay utility bills.

If you think power rates are going to go through the roof in the future, an efficient home is worth more. Keep in mind that past records are fine and dandy, but it's the future that counts. Energy-efficient homes not only cost you less in energy bills, but they will also see less increase when rates go up. When you buy into energy efficiency, you're insuring your future against severe cost jolts. This is worth something, although it's very hard to enumerate.

- ✔ **Determine how much it's worth to you to mitigate pollution.** See Chapter 5 for a method of enumerating this rather intangible issue. The bottom line is that we're all going to be paying to accomplish this laudable goal.

- ✔ **Call your homeowner's insurance agent and ask about solar equipment and how it might affect your insurance rates and terms.** If the equipment has not been inspected and permitted by the local building department, bring this up. Ask about any odd construction techniques, like rammed earth. Some insurance companies won't insure this kind of dwelling because state law mandates them to build an identical house in the event of a claim. It may be impossible to get an identical house if the one you're looking at is an oddball (geodesic domes, watch out!).

- ✔ **As you would with any house, think about how long you anticipate living there.** If you're going to be staying for a long time, you don't need to worry about selling a home, only about buying it. If you're going to be living in the area for a short time, you should be as concerned about selling as you are about buying.

Maybe the most important question to ask yourself is whether you would buy this house if it were exactly the same structure, but without any efficiency equipment. How much you would pay for it then? How much you're willing to pay comes down to how much you want the house. That's the bottom line. Your realtor is going to have to help you come up with a competitive offer, which is far beyond the scope of this book.

Buying an Existing Home to Upgrade

There are good reasons for buying an existing conventional home and installing energy-efficiency equipment yourself, as opposed to buying a completed efficient home:

✔ **You have a lot more options.** In some areas, efficient homes are a real rarity and you may not even be able to find one that's for sale.

✔ **Your equipment will be brand new with a full warranty.** Because homeowners rarely install expensive equipment right before they sell, the equipment on existing efficient homes is usually older, which can mean more maintenance and less efficiency.

New equipment is always better than old because technology is always improving. Plus, your improvements may qualify for subsidies or tax incentives; see Chapter 4 for details.

✔ **If you're a do-it-yourselfer, you can install equipment for much less than a professional**

515

contractor. That means the value you place on some types of efficiency equipment will be less than what a seller is probably going to demand for a completed home. You will know the equipment better, and you won't have to trust a seller's claims of performance. Keep in mind, though, that you may be able to get a guarantee of performance when you buy an efficient home. When you do the installs yourself, there are no guarantees of any kind, or at the very least, they are hazy.

✔ **You can install equipment as the need arises, timing your efficiency improvements in ways that most benefit you.** This is especially important if you finance the purchase of your home with a first mortgage, which won't include your equipment improvements. This means you'll have to find another way to pay for your upgrades. Doing them a little at a time is one option. Another is getting an equity loan, but ultimately this will cost you more (in monthly payments) than simply buying a completed energy-efficient home and wrapping all the extra value into one first mortgage.

 You may be able to demand that some improvements be done before you buy an existing home. Perhaps you can get a seller to install some solar or other energy-efficiency equipment as a condition of sale. If a water heater is shot, perhaps you can demand a solar water heating system be put in its place, for example.

If you're going to buy an existing conventional home and install your own efficiency equipment, you need to carefully and accurately evaluate its suitability. Here's a checklist:

✔ **Read Chapter 21 on designing and building an efficient home from scratch.** When you're looking at a prospective home, compare its features with the ideals expressed in Chapter 21.

✔ **Make a list of all the efficiency investments that will work in your new home; then estimate the costs for doing each project, based on the construction and layout of the house.** This is relatively easy for active solar energy, like PV and hot water, and for installing things like fireplaces and stoves, where you can get a good idea of the cost by simply talking to a local retailer. But it's going to be tougher for passive features, those built right into the home's design, such as skylights and window orientation. You'll probably find that moving walls and cutting into ceilings isn't really worth the cost, given the potential savings on your power bills. Passive solar is much easier to design and build into a home than it is to modify a home for.

To figure out where the most egregious energy sinks are so that you know what you're facing and can prioritize your improvements, get a professional energy audit, if possible. A seller may let you do one, but it's a tough request to make before an offer is on the table. Inspections are normally done once an offer is made and accepted.

✔ **Evaluate existing energy equipment for potential improvements.** Is the HVAC old? Perhaps you can demand that a new one be installed. How about wood stoves or gas stoves? Attic vents?

Installing energy-efficient equipment on any home usually entails tearing out some existing equipment and forking over the money for new equipment. You should have a good idea of what you want to do in your new home, and some idea of the price of the upgrades.

Selling Your Efficient Home for Big Bucks

You want the most you can get for your efficient home, of course. To get top dollar, you need to know what buyers look for when they're in the market for an existing energy-efficient home. The first section in this chapter, "Buying an Existing Efficient Home," goes into detail on what buyers should look for. As a seller, here's what you need to know:

- **Keep good records of everything.** If you can't validate your energy-efficiency claims, your systems may be worthless. Or even more detrimental to your cause, you may cast yourself as untrustworthy in general — why else would you be making claims that you can't back up?

- **Find a realtor who knows efficient houses, and how best to offer them for sale to the market.** You want to capitalize on "buzz" — in this regard, some market strategies work and some don't. The right realtor will let the right buyers know you've got an efficient home for sale.

- **Target the right market.** At present, most people have no clear idea what energy efficiency means, beyond the fact that utility bills will (or should) be lower. These people are not likely to pay you more for your energy-efficient home than they would pay for a conventional home. As energy rates rise, this will change, out of necessity. But one thing is always true of marketing: You need to reach the right buyers to get the best price. Shotgun approaches (blasting at the whole world and hoping you'll hit something) is almost always unproductive.

✔ **Price the house correctly.** You're going to price your energy-efficient home higher than a conventional home, and rightly so. But if you don't reach the right market, your home won't sell, and then you'll have a reputation in local Realtor circles for trying to sell an overpriced home.

Realtors see overpriced homes as a waste of time, and they don't bother showing them. The initial entry of a home onto a market is the most important time because Realtors lose interest in a house that doesn't sell. Even if you subsequently lower your price, they still won't get as enthused as they will with a house that's new on the market and priced correctly.

The bottom line: Always be square with everybody all the time. People know when you're playing games.

Part V
The Part of Tens

The 5th Wave   By Rich Tennant

"Dual-flush toilets, recycled-content tile, flow-
reduced faucets...Where's it all end, Stan?"

In this part . . .

Every handy, good looking, information-packed *For Dummies* book ends with quick reference lists to help you along. The lists here are packed with information on some of the best and easiest ways to become more energy efficient.

And because this is the last part of the book, I've allowed myself the liberty of letting loose — a tendency my editor did her darnedest to keep in check. If you don't find this part as entertaining as I do, blame her: She ruined all my jokes.

Chapter 23

Ten Best Energy-Efficient Investments

● ●

In This Chapter

▶ Getting the greatest effect for the least moolah
▶ Creating a more comfortable home environment

● ●

I don't like work, even when somebody else does it.

— Mark Twain

A penny saved is a penny earned.

— Benjamin Franklin

These twin sentiments pretty much sum up this chapter. The best energy-efficiency tips are those that are easy to do and give you the best payback. The crème de la crème is achieving both.

Installing a Programmable Thermostat

For $40 to $150, you can install a programmable thermostat to automatically control the temperature of your home. (Some thermostats can also control the humidity — a good option if you want to ensure a comfortable environment.) The trick with a programmable thermostat is to minimize the amount of time the system is turned on when you're not home. If you're at work all day, you can turn off your HVAC system, or at least raise the temperature in the summer and lower it in the winter, while you're away and then program it to turn back on a short time before you're due home.

 If you're on a peak rate schedule, a programmable thermostat can save you even more because you can avoid using your HVAC during peak hours.

Payback of your original investment only takes six months to two years. You would be hard-pressed to find any other type of energy-efficient investment that works so well.

Chapter 8 has lots more information on what you can do to save money on your HVAC system.

Sealing Your Home's Envelope

Most leaks in ductwork and heating and cooling vents are very easy to fix and take little more than a few twists of your wrists. Some, like the ones in your attic or basement, are very difficult to get at. The worst culprits are leaks around windows. But every leak costs a lot because it allows cold air to enter your home in the winter and hot air to enter in the summer.

To fix leaks, you generally need nothing more than caulk and weatherstripping, two of the least expensive fix-it products made. Some window leaks may require that you buy special seals, but these are generally harder to find than they are expensive.

If you spend less than $100 on materials like caulk and

weatherstripping, you can easily save this much in one year's time. Plus your home will be more comfortable, with fewer drafts and temperature fluctuations from room to room.

Another way to seal your home's envelope is fill in the gaps in your insulation. This investment takes an initial cash outlay, but you'll unquestionably save on heating and cooling bills, and your home will be more comfortable to boot. Most insulation investments pay back in around two years. Your home will also be worth more because you can show a prospective buyer your smaller utility bills, and they'll factor this into their offering price. Go to Chapter 7 for more on insulating your home against drafts.

Sealing the Ducts in Your HVAC System

If the ducts in your HVAC system aren't properly sealed, you're wasting a lot of hot or cold air that could be better spent warming or cooling your home. Although sealing these ducts can be a hassle — you may have to climb into the attic, crawl around underneath your ground floor, climb ladders, or twist yourself into the shape of a pretzel — you won't spend much money, and you'll get an incredible return on the money you do have to spend.

The first thing to do is survey what needs to be done. Inspect all the ductwork: Turn your HVAC on first because a lot of the leaks will be very obvious with a simple glance. Check for smaller leaks by using the wet hand technique described in Chapter 7.

To fix leaks in the ductwork, tape them where you can. If insulation is falling off (a very common problem), tape it back up. Given how cheap and effective this fix is, the payback can be less than a month.

Always wear a dust mask when working with ducts (say that fast, five times).

Installing a Flow Constrictor Shower Head

A flow constrictor is very simple: It's just a washer with a hole of a preset size that you install inside the shower head. The smaller the hole, the lower the flow, and bigger the hole, the greater the flow. For a measly $15 and up, you can easily save that much in a couple months just by installing a low-flow showerhead (or as it's so fashionable to say these days, a Lo Flo showerhead). You don't need to sacrifice the quality of your showers, either. You save tons of water, but even better, you save tons of heat energy, and that costs a lot more than water these days.

Lo Flo heads are simple to install:

1. **Unscrew the old head.**

    You may actually need pliers for this, but go ahead and give it a try before you trudge all the way down to the garage.

2. **Take the old head with you to the hardware store and buy a good-quality, Lo Flo head that you like the looks of.**

    Take the old head because there are different sizes of mounting threads, or different types of mounting schemes. Also, get one that can be adjusted.

     If you have problems with mineral deposits in your water, buy a cheap head because it won't be long before it gets all gummed up with crud.

3. **Screw the new head on.**

You don't have to trudge all the way down to the garage for pliers because if you use the rubber gasket that's provided, you don't have to screw the darn thing on very tight in order to get a good seal.

Note: If you have a solar water heater, you don't have much incentive to save hot water. You're better off watching an old movie on the telly.

For more ways you can reduce your water consumption, go to Chapter 10.

Insulating Your Water Heater

Feel your water heater. If it feels warm to the touch, that means heat is leaching out, and instead of warming your water, it's warming the air — uselessly. So wrap an insulating blanket around your water heater. The payback will be around two years.

Insulating blankets, which cost around $20 to $30, are easy to install (just read the instructions that come with the blanket) and easy to find (they're about as common as thumbtacks). Measure the dimensions (diameter and height) before you go to the hardware store. (You may want to call before you go and make sure they have them.)

 Wear gloves and a long-sleeved shirt because insulation can make you itch a lot, and that takes more energy than you want to expend.

Head to Chapter 11 for other things you can do to increase the efficiency of your water heater and a plethora of other home appliances.

Plugging In Fluorescents

Traditional incandescent bulbs give off a lot of heat as well as light. In the summer, or when it's warm, you don't want the heat because it just makes your air-conditioner work harder. So in warm climates fluorescents are more efficient than incandescents. Installing a fluorescent bulb in place of any light bulb in your home that's on for more than a couple hours a day will pay back in around one year.

Unless the light fixture is on a high ceiling, screwing in a fluorescent light bulb should be easy. Plugging in fluorescents is also a good idea for fixtures that are hard to reach. You'll save labor and aggravation in the long run because fluorescents last a lot longer than incandescent light bulbs, so you won't have to climb that ladder nearly as often.

Go to Chapter 9 for more on lighting your home more efficiently.

Installing Motion Sensors

Install motion sensors (described in Chapter 9) in your garage or in closets and basements. You won't have to reach your arm up and flip the switch (which saves a lot of effort, especially if your arm is very large). And when you leave the space, the light will go off by itself. It's always good when things happen by themselves — that way not only do you not have to expend energy, but you don't have to think about it, either.

Motion sensors are also a great idea for outdoor security lights, which otherwise tend to be on all night long. With a motion sensor, the light comes on when something trips the sensor and goes off again automatically.

Putting Insulating Sleeves on Hot Water Pipes

You may have to reach over your head or go down into your basement or crawl space, but fitting elongated sleeves of foam insulation over hot water pipes makes a big difference.

First, measure the diameter of your pipes, then approximate the length you will need. At the hardware store, they'll fix you up for cheap. Fitting this stuff around the pipes is actually kind of fun because nothing can go wrong. You don't even have to cover the entire pipe; any little bit will help. There are very few things you can do in this life where nothing can go wrong, but this is one of them. Well, I guess you could put the insulation on cold water pipes. But it's still fun.

Changing HVAC Filters on a Routine Basis

If your HVAC filters are dirty, the machinery has to work much harder, and your utility bill goes up very quickly. So change the filter whenever it gets clogged with dust. How can you tell? Most of the time all you have to do is listen. A dirty filter sounds like it's whistling.

If you buy filters in bulk, you can get them for less than $5 apiece. Also, when you buy them in bulk, you'll have them handy and you'll be more apt to change them when it's time.

 The expensive filters, usually advertised as electrostatic, aren't worth the extra money you pay unless you've got some health issues that require you to buy these more expensive filters.

Tuning Up Your HVAC System Regularly

Properly maintained mechanical systems work better and more efficiently than systems that haven't been maintained. So tune up your HVAC system every few years. You can pay a pro to do this — it's worth the hundred dollars or so it costs because a pro knows how to get things working as efficiently as possible. (Be wary, however, of being sold something you don't need, in which case the payback will be dubious.) Alternatively, you can tune up your system yourself if you have an instruction manual.

If you've got a combustion system, I don't recommend tackling this task yourself unless you're an experienced do-it-yourselfer. Combustion systems are tricky to adjust, and they carry the potential of explosion if you do something drastically wrong. If you've got an electric system, the job is a lot easier and safer.

Chapter 24

Ten Ridiculously Easy Energy-Saving Tips

Some energy-saving solutions are ridiculously easy — so easy, in fact, that you may not have thought of them. Or if you did think of them, you may have thought that easy is the equivalent of ineffective. *Au contraire.* This chapter offers ways you can become more energy-efficient with very little work and little, if any, cost.

Turn Down the Thermostat

Lower the temperature in your home in the winter and raise it in the summer. Consider that most humans who have lived on Earth throughout the course of history have not even had access to air-conditioning, and heating was spotty at best. They survived just fine. So can you.

Close Doors and Dampers

Close the fireplace damper when the fireplace is not in use. If you don't, the warm air (which you've paid for in your heating bills) just gets sucked out the chimney. It's amazing how many people don't do this, and it's easy. Just make it a habit.

You can also close off unused rooms and unused ducts. At a minimum, close the doors — even better, close the register.

Lower the Temp on Your Water Heater

You can save a lot of money by simply lowering the temperature on your domestic water heater. Most homes have the temperature set too high; 113°F is hot enough. See Chapter 10 for more details.

Use Your Microwave

If you need hot water, use your microwave oven instead of using the stove or letting the water run from the tap until it's hot enough to satisfy you. The microwave uses a lot less energy than the stove, and filling the water pipes with hot water from heater to tap just to get a cup doesn't make much sense.

The microwave is a more efficient alternative for most cooking chores, too. Steaming vegetables, warming leftovers — even boiling water — takes less energy in a microwave than it does on a stove top or in an oven. Using the microwave also reduces the amount of heat that gets released into the room — definitely a consideration during the hot months when you're trying to stay cool.

Clear Kids' Toys Out of Radiator Vents

Many radiator vents have obstructions on the inside. Kids drop their toys; animals drop their toys; that remote controller you can't find has fallen down in there. Or maybe a chunk of carpet fell in when you were remodeling. All you have to do is pull the vent cover off, get a flashlight, bend over, and look down inside. Removing obstructions makes a huge difference in the efficiency of the HVAC operation, and makes the room much more comfortable to boot.

Use Warm or Cold Water instead of Hot

By simply using warm or cold water instead of hot, you can increase your energy efficiency and save money:

- ✔ **Wash clothes in cold water.** Using warm or cold water in your washing machine can save quite a bit of energy. About 75 percent of the time you don't need hot water. Although this may not work for the dirtiest loads, it works just fine for most. Detergents especially made for cold-water washing help, too. So give it a try, and see what comes of it. The worst that can happen is you have to run the clothes through again on a hotter cycle. But you'll probably find that most of the time it doesn't matter.

- ✔ **Flush the garbage disposer with cold rather than hot water.** The problem here is that most of the time when you turn your hot water on, you have to wait awhile for the hot water to arrive from the water heater. During this time, hot water is actually filling up the pipes between the heater and your disposer. This heat is then wasted. Even worse, in the summertime it ends up warming your home. If your air conditioner is on, it has to work harder. You lose in every way.

Lock Closed Windows

Leaks in your home's envelope are one of the biggest causes of inefficiencies, and can cost quite a bit of money in terms of energy bills. If you simply lock your windows and doors when you close them, you'll improve the seal. Granted, this isn't a real big deal, but every little bit helps.

Do All Your Laundry at Once

Never do a partial load of laundry; it wastes energy. Fill up the machine. Even if the machine has a switch that adjusts for smaller loads, it isn't nearly as energy-efficient as washing a full load.

Always dry loads consecutively in your clothes dryer to take advantage of residual heat. When your dryer is cold, it takes a considerable amount of heat just to warm the machine up.

 Clean the dryer filter before every load. Doing so is easy and makes a huge difference in terms of energy consumption.

Skip the Dishwasher Drying Cycle

Believe it or not, you don't have to use the drying cycle on your dishwasher. Your clean dishes will dry very nicely, thank you, if you simply open the machine up, especially in the summer.

When it's very hot, use a fan to exhaust the humidity out of a nearby open window. Aim the fan out the window so that the humidity is sucked right out as soon as possible.

Plant a Tree Where It Counts

For around $30, you can buy a small deciduous tree in healthy, vigorous condition. Plant it in front of your big picture window so that it shades the summertime sun and allows for sunshine in the winter.

Depending on how fast the tree grows, payback is between five and ten years, which may not be rapid but *is* one of the best ways to increase your energy efficiency. You can't do any better than planting a tree in your yard.

Chapter 25

Ten Best Solar Investments

....

In This Chapter

▶ Identifying the best money-making propositions in solar power
▶ Making your house look a lot better
▶ Creating a more comfortable home environment

....

I n my estimation, solar power is the best way to invest in energy efficiency. Your personal situation dictates the type of solar investment that's best for your own home, but there are some projects that stand out for being sensible and practical, in both monetary and aesthetic terms. In this chapter, I give you my list of the ten best solar investments, based on my own personal experience, as well as feedback from many others who have worked with solar energy.

 Using solar energy to increase efficiency doesn't always require solar technology or equipment. Many times, it just requires that you take advantage of the sunshine that comes naturally into your home and yard.

PV Systems

Photovoltaic (PV) systems are the grande dame of solar investments and are going to experience hyper growth over the coming years. You can get a feel for just how much humans impact the environment when you realize that, on average, economically active Americans are responsible for nearly 40,000 pounds of carbon dioxide per capita. You don't need to be a politically active environmentalist to come to the conclusion that we need to do a lot better. Nor do you need to believe in global warming.

PV systems offset the most carbon pollution because so much inefficiency is inherent in our electrical power grid. For each kWh of energy you create with a PV system, you are saving five or six times that much utility-generated power, most of which comes from coal-fired plants in North America. PV systems allow for tremendous environmental leverage, and that will never change.

Strictly from a monetary standpoint, PV systems are becoming increasingly competitive, and as energy rates rise, they will eventually become extremely good investments. For more information on PV systems, head to Chapter 16.

Solar Swimming Pool Heaters

The average swimming pool costs around $20,000 to install. It takes up a big chunk of your back yard, and requires a lot of maintenance. Swimming pool chemicals are expensive, and you have to measure the water all the time for chemical balances. Chlorine and sunshine tend to eat pool equipment, particularly the plastics that are so common, so equipment lifetimes are limited. You need to clean the filter periodically, and occasionally you need to empty the pool out and start over, which makes a big impact on your water bill. The bottom line is, a swimming pool is quite a luxury item, probably the most expensive luxury you will ever purchase.

If you're going to put this much time and energy into a pool, one of your goals is likely to be extending the swim season as much as you can, and that means using a pool heater. When you install a heating system on your swimming pool, simply put, you can use your pool three or four times more than without a heater. The water will be much more comfortable, and you'll be able to swim over a longer season.

Of the kinds of heaters available — propane, electric, and solar — go for the solar heater. From a pollution standpoint, a solar heater is ideal (zero pollution) compared to the sinful alternatives (propane and electric). After the initial investment, solar heaters are also less costly to operate: Try nothing compared to what you have to pay to power a propane or electric heater. And although you can extend your swim season with a non-solar heater, keep in mind that the cost of heating the water will rise as the temperature falls.

Solar Water Heaters

Solar water heaters, when properly designed and installed, are great investments. Most people can afford a few thousand dollars for a solar water heater system without taking out loans. You can find do-it-yourself kits that work with existing water heaters, so you can keep your investment down in that way as well.

You can install a very simple batch-type system. Kits are

available that allow you not only to do the installation yourself, but also to build the collector yourself. Alternatively, you can find designs for nominal fees and build the entire system completely from scratch for less than a few hundred dollars.

A big benefit of a solar water heater is that you never need to conserve on hot water, regardless of how high energy rates go. From a pollution standpoint, water heating typically comprises around 18 percent of your power bill, so you can save exactly that much from your carbon footprint.

If you are on a tiered rate structure, a solar water heater cuts into the most expensive part of your power bill first. For example, if you save 18 percent of the electrical energy you use, you may be able to save closer to 30 percent of your total power bill (see Chapter 5 for more details).

PV systems are more popular than solar water heaters, but new plastics have been developed that are going to change this. Look for new technologies, and you'll find one that is ideal for your own application.

Solar Yard Lights

For very little cost, you can put a whole range of fun and interesting lights around your yard. They charge during the daylight hours, and they come on at night. You'll be surprised at how little sunlight they need, given the amount of light they put out.

Unlike low-voltage systems, which require very thick gauge wires that you need to run around your yard, solar lighting is as simple as one, two, three. And if you don't like the way things look, changing the layout is as simple as four, five, six.

Try both the static lights and the little, changing-color decorative lights. You can get a whole range of different mounting schemes, so you can put them anywhere.

My experience is that solar yard lights don't need to be in any direct sunlight at all. Put them under a tree and they'll work. And you can get a light that has a PV panel connected to the light itself by means of a wire, so you can put the PV panel in direct sunlight, and the light under your porch roof.

Window Blinds

Windows are a major source of heat transfer. In the summer, windows let in too much heat energy. In the winter, windows allow a lot of heat to escape. Your house would be much more energy efficient if there were no windows at all. But this is absurd. After all, windows attract a lot of attention (they break up walls, which are monotonous) and they're a source of natural sunlight. The eye is naturally drawn to a window, particularly a big window in your family room or living room. The solution? Put in window blinds that have good insulation.

Window blinds make a big difference in the overall tone of your home. With the right blinds, you can significantly reduce heat transfer as well as reflect most incident sunlight. The functional effect is dramatic. The aesthetic effect is even more so, if you choose the right ones.

 The best candidates for window blinds are large windows in family rooms and living rooms. They'll give you the most bang for the buck. Go to Chapter 12 for details on how to use blinds and other window covering for energy efficiency.

Overhangs

By judiciously using overhangs, described in Chapter 12, you can make your home more comfortable and save on your power bill at the same time. By shading your southern windows appropriately, you can increase the natural lighting in your home in the winter, when you want as much light as possible, and decrease it in the summer (lots of light makes you feel warmer).

A well-designed overhang over a porch or sunroom minimizes temperature variations. Nobody likes a home where the temperature swings wildly over the course of a day. And temperature variations tend to make materials swell and shrink, which causes cracking and premature wear.

Overhangs are very reasonable do-it-yourself projects. You don't need electrical or plumbing experience. Rarely do extraordinary weight requirements entail the use of a professional engineer. And if you keep things modest, you don't need to get a county building permit or permission from a neighborhood association design committee (who would probably love your proposed project anyway).

Sunrooms

Sunrooms let you increase the usable square footage of your house cheaply, with maximum functional effect. They also allow you to use the natural heat from the sun to heat your home, which is very energy efficient. A sunroom can be added onto an existing home for far less cost than a conventional room. You can put in nearly any size room you want, and do-it-yourself kits are straightforward and well-designed. You can build one out of aluminum, wood, or even plastic corrugated materials that cost very little. You can also put in any number of windows you want. You can install a wall of windows, or just a few. You can incorporate a concrete floor (for maximum thermal mass) or you can use an existing wooden or synthetic deck.

If you do it right, you can build a sunroom without getting a building permit (forego electric power and don't connect it rigidly to your house). If you insulate it well, you'll have a family room for about one-fifth the cost of adding a conventional room to your house. Go to Chapter 12 for details.

Swimming Pool Covers

Okay, I can hear the howls of indignation over this one. Swimming pool covers are a big hassle. But for the amount they cost compared to what they can save, they're actually a great deal. Swimming pool covers basically accomplish the same thing that solar pool heaters do (see the earlier section "Solar Swimming Pool Heaters") but cost about 3 percent as much.

If you're in a climate where you don't need a pool heater over the course of the summer, you can extend your swimming season a month or so at both the beginning and end of the season by using a cover then and only then.

Retracting mechanisms are available that work well enough to prevent you from hating your cover because you have to fold it up by hand every time you want to use the pool. The cheapest manual retractors cost around $300. You can install an electric retractor, but then you're starting to talk about the kind of money you spend on solar water heaters, so you may as well put in a solar water heater instead.

Solar Attic Vent Fans

Solar attic vent fans are an easy do-it-yourself project with potentially big results. If you've ever gone into your attic space on a hot summer day, you know what real heat is all about. It can get so hot that it's dangerous. Temperatures over 160°F are not uncommon.

All that heat stays up there all night, and it tries to go through the insulation in your ceiling, down into your house. Most homes have passive, natural venting schemes designed into the attic space, but older homes didn't really give it much thought, and newer homes tend to solve the problem with increased R-values of insulation. Imagine getting that heat out of the attic.

A properly designed solar attic vent fan can move a lot of air (see Chapter 13) over the course of a day. The system works hardest when you want it to, when there's a lot of hot sunshine. You don't need to run expensive household electrical power up to the fan's location (the electricity comes from a low voltage PV panel instead), which means you can install one just about anywhere you want, and without worrying about codes or inspections or building permits.

As a do-it-yourself solar project, installing a solar attic vent fan is ideal because you get to use some PV panels, which is fun (if your definition of fun is cool hardware). You won't get any electrical shocks from the low voltages that PV panels provide (compared to the high voltages used in conventional house wiring), and the tools required are minimal. You can do a project in a single day, and you can learn a lot about your house by studying the layout and functionality of your attic.

For a few hundred bucks, you can do something really nifty and make a big difference.

Landscaping

Okay, landscaping isn't strictly solar, if what you're looking for is technology that grabs sunlight and makes it go to work in a constructive way. But we don't always need to grab photons and train them to get the most benefit out of the sun. Landscaping is the hands-down winner as the best solar project because you get so much in return:

- ✔ Planting hearty, healthy, happy, deciduous trees in the right locations around your house gives you cooler summers and warmer winters, but most of all, you can look out your windows and be reminded of why you care so much about the planet Earth.

- ✔ Planting bushes, shrubs, and trees as windbreaks allows you to enjoy natural breezes in your home, without the sound of whirring fan blades to remind you of technology.

- ✔ Plants create oxygen out of carbon dioxide, the modern bugaboo of environmentalism. If there were enough trees in this world, global warming would not be such an imposing issue.

- ✔ Putting in landscaping yourself gets you outdoors and exercising. There's a certain simplicity to digging a hole. It's about as close to nature as you can get, and that in itself is justification.

Index

D

loose joints, checking for, 207
loose fill insulation, 186–87
low-flow showerheads, 526–27
lumber, making your own, 499

M

maintenance
    costs, 87, 129
    pools and spas, 280–81, 284–85
    water heaters, 276–77
    windows, 195
manpower, 74
manufactured logs, 86
manufacturers' rebates, 115–16
manure, burning, 454–55
masonry heaters
    installation of, 442–43
    overview, 440
    wood stoves compared, 440–42
materials for an energy-efficient home
    appliances, 501
    construction materials, 498–501
    flooring, 501
    HVAC system, 501
    insulation, 500–1
    overview, 498
    plumbing, 501
    PV system, installing a, 502–3
    swimming pool pump, 502
    ventilation options, 501
    window blinds, awnings, and sunscreens, 500
measuring the energy-efficiency potential of a lot, 489–92
mechanical filtration
    activated carbon filtration, 250, 252–53
    filters, caring for, 253

The employees of Thorndike Press hope you have enjoyed this Large Print book. All our Thorndike and Wheeler Large Print titles are designed for easy reading, and all our books are made to last. Other Thorndike Press Large Print books are available at your library, through selected bookstores, or directly from us.

For information about titles, please call:

(800) 223-1244

or visit our Web site at:

www.gale.com/thorndike
www.gale.com/wheeler

To share your comments, please write:

Publisher
Thorndike Press
295 Kennedy Memorial Drive
Waterville, ME 04901